WITNESSING AIDS:
WRITING, TESTIMONY, AND THE WORK OF MOURNING

Witnessing AIDS addresses testimonial literature produced in response to the AIDS pandemic, focusing on texts by four individuals: film-maker, painter, activist, and writer Derek Jarman; writer Jamaica Kincaid; anthropologist and media theorist Eric Michaels; and journalist Amy Hoffman.

Sarah Brophy challenges the tendency to treat AIDS testimonial literature as a genre particular to gay men. By examining Kincaid's and Hoffman's memoirs, in conjunction with the diaries of Michaels and Jarman, Brophy expands the territory of mourning beyond one group of people, an exercise that she believes is fundamental to understanding the depth of personal grief and the ways we respond to grief in literature.

Witnessing AIDS demonstrates the extent to which these memoirs and diaries intervene in the creation of cultural memory. Brophy's aim is to develop a framework for reading, one that begins to grasp the significance of our unresolved grief in response to AIDS and its effect upon testimonial writing. By highlighting our profound investment in the mundane intimacies of illness, death, and grief, Brophy resituates a number of critical debates surrounding autobiography, trauma, and memory at new and provocative intersections.

(Cultural Spaces)

SARAH BROPHY is an assistant professor of English at McMaster University.

Witnessing AIDS

Writing, Testimony, and the Work of Mourning

Sarah Brophy

UNIVERSITY OF TORONTO PRESS
Toronto Buffalo London

© University of Toronto Press Incorporated 2004
Toronto Buffalo London
Printed in Canada

ISBN 0-8020-8773-6 (cloth)
ISBN 0-8020-8567-9 (paper)

Printed on acid-free paper

National Library of Canada Cataloguing in Publication

Brophy, Sarah
  Witnessing AIDS : writing, testimony and the work of mourning /
Sarah Brophy.

(Cultural spaces)
Includes bibliographical references and index.
ISBN 0-8020-8773-6 (bound)   ISBN 0-8020-8567-9 (pbk.)

1. Hoffman, Amy. Hospital time.   2. Kincaid, Jamaica. My brother.
3. Michaels, Eric. Unbecoming.   4. Jarman, Derek, 1942–
Modern nature.   5. AIDS (Disease) in literature.   6. Grief in
literature.   7. Gay men in literature.   I. Title.   II. Series.

PN56.M4B76 2004   810.9'356   C2003-904453-X

Grateful acknowledgment is made to the following for permission to
reproduce poetry: from *Modern Nature* by Derek Jarman, used by
permission, Peake Associates; 'Brief Lives' from *Gardening in the
Tropics* by Olive Senior, used by permission, McClelland and Stewart
Ltd., The Canadian Publishers.

University of Toronto Press acknowledges the financial assistance to
its publishing program of the Canada Council for the Arts and the
Ontario Arts Council.

This book has been published with the help of a grant from the Canadian Federation for the Humanities and Social Sciences, through the
Aid to Scholarly Publications Programme, using funds provided by
the Social Sciences and Humanities Research Council of Canada.

University of Toronto Press acknowledges the financial support for its
publishing activities of the Government of Canada through the Book
Publishing Industry Development Program (BPIDP).

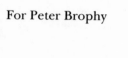

Contents

viii   Contents

Illustrations follow page 134

Acknowledgments

Publication of this book has been supported by grants from the Canadian Federation for the Humanities and Social Sciences, through the Aid to Scholarly Publications Programme, from McMaster University's Arts Research Board, and from the John Thomas Fund for Scholarly Publishing. At earlier stages of research and writing, this project benefited from the support of doctoral and postdoctoral fellowships from the Social Sciences and Humanities Research Council of Canada and from the Harry Lyman Hooker doctoral fellowship. The Edna Elizabeth Ross Reeves Scholarship allowed me to travel to London and Dungeness for my research on Derek Jarman.

Many people contributed to this book in the course of its development. David Clark was an exemplary doctoral supervisor, and I wish to express my gratitude for his challenging criticism of my writing and for his encouragement, generosity, and understanding. Mary O'Connor and Lorraine York provided thoughtful and caring guidance throughout, for which I will always be thankful. I wish to express my appreciation to Ross Chambers and Judith Butler for supporting this work in its transformation from dissertation to book. My editor, Siobhan McMenemy, expertly guided the manuscript through the review and revision processes and has, through her own perceptive commentary on the manuscript, been one of the book's most important shaping influences. The anonymous readers of the manuscript offered suggestions that I found enormously productive in the process of revising. Dilia Narduzzi undertook to prepare the index with her characteristic diligence and thoughtfulness. For listening to or reading my work and asking incisive questions, I am also grateful to Roy Cain, Daniel Coleman, James Gillett, Don Goellnicht, Jasmin Habib, Linda and Michael Hutcheon, David Jarraway, Grace Kehler, Nanette Morton, Susie O'Brien, Zdravko Planinc, Scott Rayter, and Imre Szeman.

An abridged version of Chapter 4 appeared in the March 2002 issue of *PMLA*, and I wish to thank the readers at that journal for their very helpful responses to my work.

To those who agreed to give me permission to reprint images and poetry, my heartfelt thanks for your kind cooperation.

The love and support of my parents, Lorraine and George Brophy, have played an important role in making the completion of this book possible. My grandparents, Dorothy Kelly and Rita and Tom Tobey, I thank for their company and wisdom. Special thanks to Carolyn Finlayson, Neil Kopek, and Jennifer Lee for nurturing me through the writing of this book and other transitions. Peter Walmsley makes my heart sing – and daily life a great pleasure. My last and most pressing debt is to Peter Brophy, uncle and chef extraordinaire, to whom I dedicate this book with much love.

WITNESSING AIDS:
WRITING, TESTIMONY, AND THE WORK OF MOURNING

AIDS Testimonial Writing and Unresolved Grief

Ultimately, the activities and ideas that we organize around the sign AIDS – including the chronicles that we write – have the power to change the fate of the epidemic that, as I write this, in the United States alone has killed more than half a million people and will kill still more. It is in these chronicles that the histories of the AIDS epidemic will be preserved and its lessons offered.

– Paula Treichler, *How to Have Theory in an Epidemic* (329)

AIDS and Cultural Memory

Far from being a phenomenon that we can grasp simply as a set of biomedical facts, the AIDS epidemic is fundamentally cultural, its meanings created through language and visual representation. Over the two decades since it was named and entered public discourse, AIDS has been defined, in scientific and popular interpretations alike, by a series of dichotomies that attempt to reassure a notional 'general public' that there exists a fixed barrier between what is proper to the self and what threatens the self's boundaries.[1] Seemingly natural oppositions between, for example, 'homosexual and heterosexual,' 'active and passive,' 'guilty and innocent,' 'First World and Third World' hold out the prospect of a position of safety and immunity to some, while tending to connect infection with moral corruption, deviance, and doom (Treichler 35). This paradigm has resulted in radically dualistic views of risk groups, sexual identities and practices, and geographical locations. The management of threat through the reiteration of dichotomies appears to offer a reassuring view of the self as effectively barricaded against – and even immune to – groups of people who are imagined as living alien lives, located in other places. At the same time, however, the fantasy of immunity, which is contingent on displacing vulnerability and shifting blame onto others, ultimately serves to increase panic through the very strategies supposed to quiet it: AIDS discourse breathes new life into the binaries that shape it, effectively intensifying anxieties about the twin threats of HIV infection and social difference (35–7).

In light of the powerful meanings that attach themselves to AIDS, the effort to create and to circulate more sophisticated, self-critical, and politically honest stories of the epidemic, accounts that attempt to contest these powerful and entrenched definitions, is a consequential if unpredictable endeavour. One important alternative source of information about the epidemic is to be found in first-hand testimonial accounts of living with infection and illness and confronting the possibility of death. Although links among the resistant strategies of testimonial writing, everyday understandings of the epidemic, and public health policy are certainly far from direct, it can still be allowed that the meanings and narratives circulated under the signs HIV and AIDS play a powerful role in shaping how the epidemic is imagined and that testimonial writing tends to situate itself as intervening in the process of interpreting the significance of HIV and AIDS.[2] By shifting the grounds of our knowledge of the epidemic away from generalizations to emphasize instead the locatedness and immediacy of a first-person point of view, personal chronicles explore the personal and social effects of the culturally constructed meanings of HIV infection and AIDS, while also thoughtfully contesting the recycling of stereotypes and the desire for radical closure that characterizes AIDS discourse.

The major premise of this book is that personal testimonies written in response to HIV and AIDS attempt to intervene in cultural memory by rewriting the story of the body and its locations, thus significantly altering how readers receive and respond to these imaginings and re-imaginings. In the Western media, scenes of threat, depravity, and punishment have been projected through the representation of the HIV-positive body and the body with AIDS. As Simon Watney points out, AIDS is characteristically 'embodied as an exemplary and admonitory drama, relayed between the image of the miraculous authority of clinical medicine and the faces and bodies of individuals who clearly disclose the stigmata of their guilt' ('The Spectacle of AIDS' 78).[3] In the intermingling of fear and fantasy that shapes our shared cultural imaginings of the epidemic, the infected body and the ill body are at once ubiquitous, threatening, irrepressible, and silenced (79).[4] Eve Sedgwick ties the paradoxical status of the body in AIDS discourse to Western culture's 'hygienic imperative' (*Epistemology of the Closet* 42). Emphasizing how 'the terrible accident of the HIV epidemic, and the terrifying societal threats constructed around it,' gave new virulence to the category of 'deviance' ('Gender Criticism' 278), Sedgwick attributes the reinforcement of homophobia in the context of the epidemic to the prevalence in the first place of 'a medicalized dream of the prevention of gay bodies' (*Epistemology of the Closet* 43). The homophobia of AIDS discourse is thus symptomatic of, as much as it is initiated and sustained by, a more encompassing discourse of prohibition and disavowal vis-à-vis sexuality (43).

Stories of HIV infection and AIDS in the mainstream media are invested in managing and containing anxiety. Addressing itself to an imagined 'general public' construed as 'a homogenous entity organized into discrete family units,' AIDS discourse represents the nuclear family as the guarantor of the body's integrity, as the single site of safe sex (Watney, 'The Spectacle of AIDS' 73). Much as it appears to be governed by epidemiological concepts like designated risk groups and vectors of infection, AIDS discourse is also, as Cindy Patton's analysis shows, caught up in a set of anxieties and tropes acquired from tropical medicine, a conceptual pattern that provides maps of disease that construct and arrange it as indigenous to certain terrains and bodies, while marking others, particularly the white, male, heterosexual body, as immune or, if the fiction of immunity cannot be sustained, then as heroically embattled (*Globalizing AIDS* 38). 'Tropical thinking' wants to locate safety here, at home, and disease as occurring 'elsewhere.' Its dualistic vision of social space applies not only to the relation of colony to empire in the original geographical sense, but it extends its conceptual compass into contemporary thinking, providing the tropes by which sexualities and raced bodies are defined as tropics. HIV infection and AIDS are repeatedly displaced from the home-space and the nation-space, dislocated, that is, from civilized space, forgotten, and banished to the floating container of elsewhere (38).[5] Such narratives proliferate because they hold out the consolations of radical closure, imagining familial and geographical space in ways that appear to secure the individual body and the nuclear family against contamination. Remarkably insidious, these stories take a variety of more and less subtle forms. Stories dramatizing the selective, sentimental remembering and re-embrace by mainstream culture of the disenfranchised and the forgotten can, indeed, be interpreted as another, more liberal and tolerant version of closure; they often partake of the conservative position's 'fetishization of life' by replicating an uncritical investment in the nuclear family's procreative potential and protective functions (Singer 29).[6]

Cultural criticism and activism – which are far from homogeneous sets of social practices – have been successful in generating analyses that counter this discourse. As Sedgwick emphasizes,

'It's been one of the great ideological triumphs of AIDS activism that, for a whole series of overlapping communities, any person living with AIDS is now visible, not only as someone dealing with a particular, difficult cluster of pathogens, but equally, as someone who is by that very fact defined as a victim of state violence' ('White Glasses' 261).[7] The explicit aim of many of the various discourses of protest deployed against AIDS is to create disturbance, to fracture complacency about the epidemic. As Linda Singer observes, linking the lessons of AIDS activism to her own experience with breast cancer, 'The tragedy of AIDS has given way to a resistance that does not cast itself within the imaginary of faith, optimism, and hope – it is a resistance cast in the language of *the demand*' (106).

The cultural response to HIV/AIDS continues, too, at an urgent pace, even in what has been too hurriedly labelled the 'second' or 'later' phase of the epidemic. Mapping the cultural productions linked to HIV infection and AIDS in the American context, Marita Sturken, in her recent study *Tangled Memories* (1997), establishes the range of genres that have been engaged for the purpose of representing, and contesting the representations of, AIDS. Among the non-literary genres surveyed by Sturken are memorials, public art, film and video, popular culture, commodities, and activism (1). Confirming this sense of the pervasive, lasting impact of the epidemic on culture, dance critic David Gere, in a 1998 *New York Times* article on new directions in dance in the United States, argues for the profound and continuing impact of the grief inspired by AIDS losses on the 'culture of the arts.' He insists that 'death and grief, mourning and AIDS activism, have, in fact, become so integral to the culture of the arts at the end of the millennium that the stamp of AIDS will surely remain on us long after the epidemic actually comes to an end – assuming it does' (29).[8] If the maps that Sturken and Gere provide are limited to the relatively privileged context of North America, and if they tend to focus on the cultural responses to

AIDS produced by and about gay men, the only caveat that needs to be made is that these commentators may be *underestimating* the impact of HIV/AIDS on the social fabric and its potential impact on culture in the years ahead. As Anne Hunsaker Hawkins points out in *Reconstructing Illness* (1993; repub. 1999), the authorship of AIDS memoirs in the 1990s 'is no longer representative, epidemiologically, of those individuals with HIV/AIDS' in the United States or worldwide (169).[9] HIV infection rates, death rates, and social, economic, and racial discrimination are on the rise in less privileged parts of the world, as well as in less privileged communities (members of ethnic minorities, young gay men, and women in general) within higher-income countries.[10] The AIDS crisis is declared increasingly to be 'over' because of the different ways in which it is rendered in public discourse as being over: 'over' through indifference or inaction, through a refusal to grieve, through its 'Africanization,' which includes the sense of its being 'over' here, in North America. The epidemic's ghosts protest through the voices of their spokespersons against their being exorcized, rendered untroublesome by a public rhetoric of AIDS that would fast-forward public consciousness to a sometime future world, one purified of the scourge and its 'victims,' a world, in other words, purified of grief and of mourning.

The tradition of cultural criticism and activism directs our attention not only towards the apprehension of violence and discrimination, however, but also to questions of subjectivity: to lived experiences of illness and of loss. Thomas Yingling insists in his discussion of AIDS and postmodern identity, writing from his perspective as HIV-positive, that 'we must think of AIDS not only as a public issue of ideology, apparatus, and representation but also *as it is internalized and expressed* by those infected and affected' ('AIDS in America' 303). He argues that we must attend to how HIV/AIDS is internalized and expressed, not because disease is a private matter, nor because individual experience provides unmediated authority and knowledge, but because '"AIDS" as a signifier lodges deep in subliminal zones of memory, loss, and (im)possibility' (303). By attending to subjectivity – to its turns, displacements, aggressions, and possibilities – we might be able to grapple with how the disciplinary and specularizing discourse of AIDS lives its power not just publicly but psychically, that is, in all the ways lives are lived. At the same time, we can begin to explore how the potential for resistance is tied up with 'memory, loss, and (im)possibility,' with the ways in which the signifier 'AIDS' lodges in affective zones that may not be fully available to the calculus of the discourses that define its public meanings, that may linger in reserve, as it were, to be unleashed for other purposes. If AIDS criticism and activism are themselves animated and informed by personal testimony and reflection, then memoirs and diaries explore the existential imperatives articulated by critics in less explicitly theoretical but equally insightful terms. In her memoir *My Brother*, for instance, Jamaica Kincaid wonders at the hold her brother's death has on her emotions, asking, 'Why is it so new, why is this worn-out thing, death, so new, so new?' (193). There are felt personal and affective motivations as well as more immediately political ones for engaging in the project of writing – and of reading – memoirs, diaries, novels, poetry, and plays about HIV/AIDS. Witness accounts in particular have a complicated relationship with the dynamics of narration and spectacle that typify the representation of HIV/AIDS in Western culture at large. They worry about the question of what it means to be 'at odds with AIDS,' to borrow Alexander García Düttmann's phrase, in the midst of a grief that seems new, unfathomable, even unbelievable, in the midst of a grief that may seem to threaten the rending of all sense and, therefore, political opposition.

Testimonial Writing: Questions of Rhetoric, Questions of Ethics

This book addresses testimonial writing – diaries and memoirs – published in response to the AIDS epidemic in the 1990s by writers living in the United States, Australia, and Great Britain. There has been a veritable explosion of testimonial responses to the experience of HIV and AIDS in the past two decades, and their dissemination has intensified rather than waned in the last several years.[11] I focus here on four authors whose work I have found particularly moving, challenging, and provocative: activist, film-maker, painter, and autobiographer Derek Jarman; journalist Amy Hoffman; anthropologist and media theorist Eric Michaels; and fiction writer and essayist Jamaica Kincaid. These writers foreground the dynamics of mourning and memory at play in their diaries and memoirs. They ask themselves and their readers difficult questions about the terms on which memories of the dead are preserved and perpetuated, and they scrutinize how gender, sexuality, geographical location, race, family structure, friendship, and cultural traditions shape the experiences of grief and the practices of remembrance. Confrontational, self-reflexive, and poetic, these testimonial accounts ask for and deserve a more thorough critical engagement with their personal documentation of the AIDS epidemic than currently exists. This study outlines the characteristic features of AIDS memoirs and diaries and develops a critical framework for interpreting the emphasis on unresolved grief in this emerging body of work. I want to begin by establishing the cultural, theoretical, and personal frameworks I believe are essential for their interpretation and by indicating the issues of central concern in my readings of these four key texts.

My study of this not-easily-defined genre has an important precedent in the recent work of Ross Chambers, who refers to AIDS diaries as '"nonnarrative texts" of autobiographical witness,' arguing that

the retrospective orientation of memory, the question: 'What did this life (or these events) mean?' and the need to construct significance through discursive ordering are far less urgent than a need to answer the question: 'How does it feel to be dying of AIDS?' and a desire to make available to others, with some directness, the state of disintegration the experience entails. (*Facing It* 6)

While they do engage with the imperative to register a sense of disintegration, Hoffman's, Michaels's, Kincaid's, and Jarman's texts are at least as centrally concerned with – and troubled about – reflecting on the meaning and significance of the lives they undertake to represent. Speaking of Derek Jarman's journal *Modern Nature,* along with Paul Monette's account in *Borrowed Time,* Derek Duncan claims, in his definition of the relation between AIDS and autobiography, that these two writers 'attempt to form an intelligible structure out of the disarray caused in their lives and identities by AIDS': specifically, they seek to 'invent selves capable of dealing with the syndrome's devastations' (28). And David Jarraway observes that in recent years there has been a 'rhetorical transition' in North American gay AIDS memoirs 'from a debilitating doom to a defiant doubt,' and ultimately to stance of '(de)liberation' or, in other words, to a 'speculative' rhetoric that yields existential insight into the entanglement of love in loss (124–7).[12]

With respect to testimonial writing, what kind of rhetorical approach can convey the experience of living with HIV/AIDS as well as investigate and intervene in its meanings? The decision to write about the personal experience of HIV infection and AIDS is accompanied, as I will explore in my chapters on Michaels's and Jarman's diaries, by an uneasiness about the overwhelming 'common-sense' authority of the myths that have attached themselves to AIDS and about the possibility of being misread. For those who write, like Hoffman and Kincaid, as second-hand rather than first-person witnesses, there lurks disquiet about the danger of misinterpreting and appropriating the experiences of those to whose lives, illnesses, and deaths they bear witness. Writers' awareness of the pitfalls of writing personal narratives about HIV/AIDS suggests the need for a reading strategy that attends to the complex rhetorical and ethical questions about mourning and memorialization inherent in second-hand as well as first-hand witness accounts.[13]

The project of remembering is both essential to AIDS testimonial writing and deeply fraught. The writers I discuss compose – and theorize – their testimonials as a form of 'critical memory' that would pre-empt their easy assimilation by a dynamic of nostalgia or premature declarations of an end to what is now most accurately described as a *pandemic*. Indeed, although the texts I will discuss in detail are all written from positions of relative privilege in the 'First World,' they are far from complacent about that positioning. Keeping in play a sense of the continuing urgency of the AIDS crisis, Jarman, Hoffman, Michaels, and Kincaid have created texts that educate us about the discourses – often homophobic, racist, and otherwise biased or discriminatory – that shape the representation of AIDS. At the same time, they attest in a complex, often tortuous way to the dynamics of love, desire, and friendship that motivate such enquiries and that account, precisely, for their felt specificities.

It is impossible to read these texts straightforwardly for the plot, for the fond evocation of personality, or for spiritual transcendence. On the contrary, they take up and reproduce the shifting dynamics of mourning and memory, blending this with a good deal of polemic, a tendency that often makes them seem like essays as much as life stories and that indicates their rootedness in the AIDS crisis beyond what that crisis means for the memoirists or their subjects. In this sense, AIDS testimonial writing typifies and extends at least two of the principal dilemmas of autobiographical writing in the late twentieth century: specifically, it demonstrates an acute awareness of identity's status as constitutively relational as well as foregrounding testimonial writing's status as a genre of crisis, in which the relationship of witness to listener or reader becomes invested with political as well as psychic or therapeutic significance because, as Dori Laub suggests, it is in the act of being heard by an empathetic listener that testimony enters reality (70–1).

Many critics of autobiography have observed that the practices of life-writing, and the identities it constructs, are inherently relational. Susanna Egan has, for example, persuasively articulated the process of 'exploratory mirroring' that turns autobiographical writing into a dialogue between self and other. According to Egan, dialogic tendencies are particularly evident in autobiographical texts that respond to crisis and loss, such as 'autothanatographies'; this mode of writing struggles to piece together meaning from the fragments of a disorienting experience, and so relies on exchanges with one or more narrative interlocutors, whose varying perspectives can both help to attribute meaning to traumatic events and to underscore the writer's point of view as provisional (7). By elaborating the murky complexity of memory and, in particular, by focusing on the discomfiting physical presence of the medically ill body, the dying body, and the corpse, AIDS testimonial writing seeks, in Jacques Derrida's words, to 'defy all reappropriation,' to position the perspective of subjective experience of AIDS 'beyond mournful memory' (*Memoires for Paul de Man* 38). While Kincaid and Hoffman both write memorials that are ostensibly about lives and deaths other than their own, the experiences of their 'brothers,' they are also preoccupied with reflecting on their own positions as mourners, a situation that in the context of HIV infection and AIDS disrupts the autobiographical impulse to self-restoration through the redemption of a lost or resistant 'other.' Michaels and Jarman struggle, in turn, with fears that they – and their generation – will be forgotten after their deaths or, worse, remembered by others in distorted, self-interested versions.

In their vexation about the interplay of personal and public memory and their anxiety about reception, diaries and memoirs written in response to the AIDS epidemic share several features in common with other contemporary autobiographical forms

that endeavour to testify to experiences of crisis. John Beverley
has identified the origins of subaltern 'resistance literature' in
oral testimony, defining the *testimonio* as a book-length narrative
told by a first-person narrator who recounts a life story or transforming experience, with the intent of winning support for the
struggle and achieving legal reparations (92–4). AIDS memoirs
and diaries possess in common with *testimonios* the sense of writing to a particular occasion or event as well as a degree of
self-conscious political engagement, although they do not seek
tangible reparation, focusing rather on strategies of affective
engagement and re-education. In addition to their affinities with
this explicitly political form of testimony, AIDS memoirs and diaries recognize that the process of transmitting testimony is far
from unmediated: memory always muddies the picture. The
mediated nature of memory has been a major concern, too, of
commentators on other forms of personal testimony. Looking at
personal narratives of witness that incorporate photography, and
focusing in particular on Holocaust memory, Marianne Hirsch
identifies the 'indirect and fragmentary nature of second generation memory' (23). She reads photographs as 'the leftovers, the
fragmentary sources and building blocks, shot through with
holes, of the work of postmemory,' and suggests that post-memory tries to grasp, through a process of piecing together such
fragments, not only 'familial conflict based on gender or generation' but also 'those violent historical forces that have rewritten
family plots in the twentieth century' (23, 35). Moreover, in their
relentless questioning of memory and knowledge and in their
improvisational qualities, AIDS memoirs and diaries can be
thought of as participating in a wider trend towards challenging
the implicit but entrenched boundaries governing what can and
cannot be said by autobiographers. Leigh Gilmore has recently
argued that contemporary memoirs and autobiographical fictions are collectively 'test[ing] the limits of autobiography' (*The
Limits of Autobiography* 3). Shaped by a discourse of propriety, the

conventions of autobiographical discourse tend to screen out histories of trauma and harm. In raising questions about the pressures of omission that inhere in autobiographical conventions, the new generation of autobiographers seeks 'an alternative jurisprudence,' one different from, although not necessarily opposed to, the legal remedies sought by *testimonios* (146). Recent autobiographical writing renegotiates the conventions that have shaped autobiographical representation and, in this way, seeks also to transform 'the relations that underpin how we live' (147). Exemplifying self-conscious struggle with the received conventions for autobiographical writing, and the partial, fragmentary condition of post-memory, AIDS testimonials take part in the collective, ongoing history of the epidemic. Their impetus is profoundly personal, embroiled in a series of interconnected questions about familial, societal, and civic identity and belonging. They position themselves in resistant relation to our commonplace assumptions about HIV infection and AIDS and, indeed, about the very grounds of mourning, memory, representation, and narrative. The collective project of these memoirs and diaries is to intervene in cultural memory, the field of contestation over meaning that, even in the context of shifting epidemiological trends and new pharmaceutical discoveries, remains indelibly affected by AIDS.

Theories of Mourning and Melancholia

In his *New York Times* article, David Gere characterizes art produced in the context of HIV and AIDS as melancholic in its affective and psychological orientation (29). The terms mourning and melancholia have served as crucial touchstones for critics seeking to understand how the AIDS pandemic has obliged artists and writers to address its lived experiences, its social consequences, and its political ramifications as HIV infection and AIDS are imagined, remembered, and forgotten in the shifting terrain of cultural memory. And, indeed, is cultural criticism – my own text included, of course – not also caught up in grief and mourning? Does it not *enact* grief even as it is *about* grief?

For my own part, I find myself asking in what sense was I always preparing myself for my uncle Peter's death from AIDS-related illnesses, always setting up ways to mourn this loss? This is possibly why memories of the weakness of his rage, the little cruelties of his behaviour, his jealousy when I went to visit him and departed too soon are so upsetting. I wonder whether I had selfishly been anticipating something much more spiritually significant, and thereby some consolation. What could it possibly mean to feel disappointed by the manner of someone else's death? In becoming preoccupied with my own memories, needs, and desires, as seems inevitable in recollecting these events, I fear that I risk losing sight of Peter's wonderful and exasperating particularities, his political commitments and determination to argue for them, the loves, enjoyments, and fears he expressed, and the ones he sometimes hid. What may I do with my own grief and regret, or how may I understand it? Will dwelling on it lead inevitably to other recuperative gestures, patterns of denial shaped by the panicked media narrative about the epidemic that has conditioned my frame of vision?

Douglas Crimp has argued in 'Mourning and Militancy' (1989) that melancholic tendencies ought to be deliberately and thoroughly transformed. He focuses on how homophobia and its 'violence of silence and omission' have prevented people from mourning losses to AIDS (9).[14] Like Edmund White, who suggests that humour and melodrama, which he sees as forces of repression and domestication, are best avoided as responses to AIDS (71), Crimp worries that a melancholic response to loss would in effect collaborate in the forgetting of HIV infection and AIDS by acceding to a loss of agency. He fears that 'capitulation' to the incompleteness of the mourning process leaves the individual and the gay community frozen and overwhelmed by grief. Repudiating melancholia as 'moralizing self-abasement' and for its association, in his words, with the 'excoriation of gay culture' (12–13), he advocates for the 'militant' reversal of this condition, arguing that 'because this violence also desecrates the memories of our dead, we rise in anger to vindicate them. For many of us, mourning *becomes* militancy' (9). Citing Crimp's rejection of the melancholia loss might inspire, Gere similarly proposes that 'the gay man transforms melancholia to activism in the crucible of his righteous anger' (29). The suspicions registered here are warranted: untheorized, the leap may indeed still seem too large between the derogatory cliché of the melancholic homosexual, itself derived from the normalizing impulses of Freudian psychoanalytic theory, and the imperatives of activism. But can Crimp's modelling of mourning and melancholia adequately account for the complexities of AIDS memoirs and, in particular, for their varying emphases on unresolved grief, on anger, guilt, despair and self-berating, on the complexities of recording and remembering?

This debate about mourning and melancholia has also been a prominent touchstone in memoirs and personal essays, texts that may themselves be read as 'theoretical' documents. The spectrum of responses is well represented in the 1995 anthology *In the Company of My Solitude*, edited by Marie Howe and Michael Klein, from which I will draw two examples in order to mark out the conflicting positions on this issue before introducing further theoretical paradigms from the writings on mourning of Judith Butler, Walter Benjamin, and Jacques Derrida. Mark Doty, author of the book-length memoir *Heaven's Coast* (1997), which documents his experience as lover, caregiver, and mourner for his partner, Wally, provides one of the anthology's introductory essays (later to become the preface of his memoir), entitled 'Is There a Future?' Here, Doty identifies an obligation to memorialize the dead, asking, 'Is my future, then, remembering you? Inscribing the name, carrying the memory, being remembered as one who remembered?' (8). Emphasizing his conviction that 'Wally is in my body; my body is in this text,' Doty proposes that the future may be filled, and thus restored to us, by awareness of being 'part of this vast interchange of Being' (11). For Doty, fundamentally Romantic in his view of the world, it seems that the natural world's beauty and cyclical permanency offers consolation, as well as assurance that the text of grief will receive a reading consistent with his intentions when the text reaches others' eyes.[15] But a juxtaposed essay by Deborah Salazar, entitled 'The Bad News Is that the Bad News Is Still the Same,' adumbrates quite another point of view. Intimate and confrontational in its tone, Salazar's essay concludes by listing the actions and emotions forced upon the visitor to the sickroom, and by suggesting some of the psychic consequences of this positioning:

You deal with whatever needs to be dealt with then and there. You adjust I.V. tubes so they don't bend, you pass the vomit bucket, you sit in the hospital room and watch endless television, you listen to the medical machinery bleep and whir, and you answer the phone every time it rings and say 'No change.' Even after the death happens, the bad news is that the bad news is still the same. It's only been a few months since David's died ... but I'm still waiting for something to happen, for some wisdom to emerge, for some revelation to shake the world. And I'm still waiting for David to haunt me. Imagine waiting for all these things while waiting for friends to die. You never know who's next. It's like it was all those days in David's hospital room; you expect to learn a kind of saintlike patience, but you never do. You just *are* patient while you're waiting to learn. (17)

While Doty shares with Salazar the impression that there is 'a strange kind of physical permanence' to loss, their essays mark out divergent paths for grief. In Salazar's rendering of the future of remembering, time has not progressed; she still lives in the sickroom. Her friend David's death does not confer an unambiguous authority on her writing. Far from providing a revelation that would 'shake the world,' as Doty's essay suggests it might, Salazar's loss has made her writing subject to the untimely contortions of a strange, unspeakable, and yet inescapable burden: the burden of a body and a testimony, a position of witness into which she corrals her readers, too, as she switches so rapidly between first- and second-person narration. To some degree, she measures herself against the regulatory ideal of wisdom as the necessary destination of grief, as if death can only be revealing, a bringer of wisdom, if a truth is wrung from it, some narrative is produced out of it, some assurance that the death was 'not in vain.' What I begin to learn from Salazar's brave and smart counter-claim based on her life in the context of the sickroom, though, is something rather more oblique and ungrounding: that the security of wisdom never arrives, that the 'world-shaking' that has been witnessed (and, importantly, is being witnessed now in her very words) cannot be economized. While the psychic and cultural expectations of mourning work are such that one either has wisdom or does not, one mourns or is melancholic, for certain resistant grievers, such as the writers I investigate in this study, and such as myself, the narrative of mastery over grief does not match the experience of loss as it is written out.[16]

Is a stance of completed mourning – in Crimp's terms, of loss sublimated entirely into anger – the only sure way of counteracting the representation of the seropositive body or the ill body as stigmatized? Is it even possible? In other words, how may we begin to read a pessimism – and a self-doubt – so acute as Salazar's? Out of a suspicion of grief's absorption of energy, Crimp proposes a slightly reconfigured definition of mourning and melancholia as a way to retrieve a position of strength. In so doing, he aligns his argument with Freud's privileging of completed mourning, specifically with the argument 'that when the work of mourning is completed the ego becomes free and uninhibited again' ('Mourning and Melancholia' 245). But by hinging this position of strength and activism on a relatively narrow definition of what might constitute opposition, he may risk inscribing a normative masculinity for gay men: what is being proposed seems to be a new mournful 'warrior' who must finish with grief before he can take up the torch of political action. Must he also finish then with the erotic attachment that inspires his grief in the first place? As Michael Moon asks us to consider, while Freud's theory of the work of mourning valorizes 'moderation, resolution, and closure in the form of a return to "health" and "normalcy,"' this economizing of grief 'may seem to diminish the process and to foreclose its possible meanings instead of enriching it or making it more accessible to understanding' ('Memorial Rags' 234). The sense that we risk diminishing the 'erotic component of grief and sorrow' is especially strong given that these feelings are already subject, in the context of AIDS, to containment, repression, and denial of their existence and value (235). Moon's point is a suggestive one, not least because the plurality of his reference to the 'urgent needs and feelings' that animate grief indicates that this component of mourning is far from being singular. As my subsequent chapters will explore, what eros might be amid grief is far from obvious, despite what we may be accustomed to assuming, namely, the privileging of the romantic love of a couple, regardless of sexual orientation, as the single, natural, most meaningful model for passionate love and remembrance. And given that memoirs and diaries about the epidemic are embroiled in unresolved emotions (certainly anger, *pace* Crimp, is far from being absolutely clear in its motivations or consequences), what I find myself asking along with Moon is this: Might there be a way of rethinking mourning and melancholia that could allow for a reading of the critical insights that a focus on *unresolved grief* may enable?

Memorializing accounts written from the perspective of a survivor-witness to the events of illness and death are particularly prone to these ambivalences. In *Facing It*, Chambers considers the anxieties that AIDS *diaries* actively cultivate for their potential readers, but without directly addressing how memoirs address their readers (6). The defining feature of diaries, according to Chambers, is the tendency to offer a 'chain of confrontations': readers are made overwhelmingly aware of their position as survivors and are confronted by the text with the accusation of feeling indifferent about and even of benefiting from the author's death (22–3). The cultivation of anxiety is potentially 'therapeutic' for both the author and the reader: it is designed to work as 'a form of preventive medicine, an act of decontamination' (27).[17] This question of the positioning and implication of readers can be productively extended and rethought to take into fuller account how in diaries, but especially in *memoirs,* readers continue to encounter the lurking presence of narrative patterns and images that would encourage reading for other sorts of plots. Even if, as Chambers suggests, AIDS diaries 'do not want the pieties of memorialization' (32), there persists nonetheless a desire for 'discursive ordering' on the part of readers along with cultural context that overwhelmingly facilitates this desire. The temptations of a discourse of redemption are a concern especially in memoirs that are already mediated, written, that is, by a secondary witness, written 'to the memory of' the dead, a situation that makes them provisionally different from the diary or chronicle. Likewise, if in the context of diaries the lasting impact of the witnessing project depends on the reader taking up the role of 'relay' (132), then the reader's dilemma is also multiplied and made more urgent in the context of memorializing texts: considering the ways in which memoirs are already mediated and tentatively ordered, I contend that the most pressing question for the reader may become how *not* to mourn – that is, how not to become caught up in mourning as compensatory, as an aggressive action of normalizing closure, even while there may be no evading the law that commands us to mourn, and to mourn 'well.'[18]

Critical resources I draw on in my thinking about the cultural

significance of grief in AIDS testimonial writing include Judith
Butler's and Jacques Derrida's recent writings on mourning, as
well as Walter Benjamin's suggestive work from earlier in the century on melancholy, allegory, and history. These theoretical
points of reference are far from being simply routinized or fash-
ionable ones. On the contrary, both Butler and Derrida address
the topic of AIDS and grief, and their philosophical speculations
have not yet been discussed at length in connection with specific
examples of testimonial writing. My view is that analysis of AIDS
memoirs can be furthered by connecting it with these philosophical perspectives on melancholia, and that the boundaries of theoretical discussion can be illuminated by turning to testimonial
accounts, which allow us locate the discussion of melancholia
in lived responses to loss. Let me take a few paragraphs here to
indicate the relevance of these theories of mourning and melancholia to my subject.

   In her discussion of AIDS losses, social identity, and grief in
The Psychic Life of Power, Butler outlines how feelings of guilt, fear,
and ambivalence produce an intensified 'desire for triumph'
over those who are socially marginalized on the part of those who
remain invested in protecting a privileged domain of social legitimacy, defined against a domain of excluded and delegitimized
others (26–7). She argues that 'melancholic aggression and the
desire to vanquish ... characteriz[e] the public response to the
death of many of those considered "socially dead," who die from
AIDS: Gay people, prostitutes, drug users, among others' (27).
But she also asks, 'How might we begin to imagine the contingency of that organization [of social life], and performatively
reconfigure the contours of the conditions of life?' (29). Melancholia, writes Butler, involves a grief that we can neither own nor
bring to completion: it 'rifts the subject, marking a limit to what
it can accommodate' (23). In turn, she raises the possibility that
this 'rifting' can, if we commit ourselves to thinking and feeling
against the grain, lead us to ways of grieving loss *other* than those

sanctioned by the law, that would differ from 'its lure of identity' (130). We cannot *not* grieve, she says, but can we grieve 'elsewhere' or 'otherwise' (130)? What is at issue for Butler is the question of how people negotiate between the social conditions of a legible social identity and the persistence of diffuse 'passionate attachments' that do not fit within social norms (6). Can the constraints that structure our 'accommodations' – in particular, our sense of what kinds of lives are liveable and lovable – be thought of as 'open to transformation,' rather than as fixed and immutable (6, 28)? Perhaps in chancing 'the incoherence of identity,' suggests Butler, we can find a possible point of leverage for thinking about melancholia as a 'scene of agency,' if a necessarily ambivalent and inconsistent one, where the outcomes of our negotiations and renegotiations of the conditions of social legitimacy cannot be predicted in advance (149, 15).

Walter Benjamin's formulation of melancholy in *The Origin of German Tragic Drama* posits a view of history as a 'ruined' landscape and allows us to think of melancholic subjectivity in historical and material terms. By interrupting – freezing – the passage of time, death makes visible, according to Benjamin, what we otherwise deny: the agony of existing as a material body, and the transient incompleteness of the world and of our knowledge of it. This theorization of history as fragmentary helps in understanding what insights are made available by the melancholic's incoherent view of the world: 'Whereas in the symbol destruction is idealized and the transfigured face of nature is fleetingly revealed in the light of redemption, in allegory the observer is confronted with the *facies hippocratica* of history as a petrified, primordial landscape' (166). Conceptualized as a ruin of 'amorphous fragments,' or as a 'face' that hovers between life and death, inscrutable and irretrievable, the individual life is rendered a social site available to archaeological investigation (176). We generate multiple interpretations to explain this ruined terrain, but the allegories we produce proliferate endlessly, without cancelling one another, leaving us in a world bereft of secure meaning but newly lucid, somehow, if still aggrieved, about the teeming multiplicity of interpretations that this view of the world in ruins makes possible. AIDS memoirs, as I shall demonstrate, generate a host of allegories of belonging, obligation, and agency, in both familial and civic contexts, and meditate on the significance of material sites of memory, gardens and memorials, which, while they do not furnish a cure for suffering and death, do prevent the erasure of its material presence in our lives and memories. The act of interpreting necessarily if painfully parallels the decay of the material world, the 'collapse of the physical, beautiful, nature': 'allegories are, in the realm of thoughts, what ruins are in the realm of things' (176, 178). But we are always tempted, warns Benjamin, to adopt another response to interpreting ruins: namely, we are lured by an overwhelming desire to redeem this landscape and its contradictory, dizzying allegories, to restore it to propriety and progress under the sign of a master allegory of redemption. Benjamin stresses the necessity of resisting the almost irresistible desire for restoration of our reading and interpreting selves to wholeness through the redemption of the ruined world, which is always other to us, defying our wish to behold in it a consolatory vision. Only unredeemed or fallen nature can convey the fragile transitoriness of material suffering, for only it 'bears the imprint of the progression of history' – and of what history conceived as progress would triumphantly leave behind (176).

The implications of a reconceptualization of melancholia in connection with AIDS diaries and memoirs are further illuminated by Derrida's writings on mourning and memorialization, especially when these materials are read together with his discussion of AIDS in 'The Rhetoric of Drugs.' Although the two problems – AIDS and drugs – that concern him in this interview are certainly linked in their shared association with 'delinquency,' AIDS, Derrida insists, instigates an 'absolutely original and indelible' rupture in our systems of meaning and value (250). This rupture goes to the heart of subjectivity because 'the various forms of this social contagion, its spatial and temporal dimensions, deprive us henceforth of everything that a relation to the other, and first of all desire, could invent to protect the integrity and thus the inalienable identity of anything like a subject' (250). The use of the phrase 'social contagion,' far from referring in any simple way to AIDS, signals 'the epidemic of signification' that has arisen in response to HIV infection and AIDS, out of a panicked set of relations between the disease, homophobia, and biomedical discourse, which intensively recycle 'prior social constructions' of difference and delinquency (Treichler 11, 15). What is at stake according to Derrida, as for Butler, is the 'symbolic organization' of subjectivity ('The Rhetoric of Drugs' 250–1). For although 'this is how it's always been,' 'now, exactly as if it were a painting or a giant movie screen, AIDS provides an available, daily, massive *readability* to that which the canonical discourses we mentioned above had to deny, which in truth they are destined to deny, founded as they are by this very denial' (251). Derrida's comments thus pinpoint the pressure that the AIDS emergency brings to bear on the fictions by which we seek to secure our integrity as subjects and, by implication, the strategies of erasure, exclusion, and redemption by which we articulate and reinforce these ideals; these are conditions of subjectivity that predate AIDS to be sure, but which the epidemic continues to intensify, to particularize in unique ways, and to render problematic. Corroborating Butler, Derrida raises, too, then, what she identifies as the 'political question of the cost of articulating a coherent identity position by producing, excluding, and repudiating a domain of abjected specters that threaten the arbitrarily closed domain of subject positions' (*Psychic Life* 149).

Beginning with *Memoires for Paul de Man* and the essay 'Fors,' and continuing in his further forays into social and political theory in *Specters of Marx*, Derrida has become increasingly concerned with the exorcisms that seem to justify the self-satisfied assumptions of authority and power. Like Benjamin and Butler, he queries the temptation to redeem history. 'This triumph,' he argues, is celebrated by the privileged 'only in order to hide, and first of all from themselves, the fact that [liberal capitalism] has never been so critical, so fragile, threatened, and in certain regards catastrophic, and in sum bereaved' (*Specters of Marx* 68). What we 'hide' from 'ourselves' – in undertaking the work of a 'possible mourning' – becomes slightly more specific than his references to 'the *spirit* of the Marxist critique' might at first glance suggest (68).[19] Is what we hide from ourselves not the cruel correspondence between definitions of 'delinquency' and the economic and cultural 'margins of society'? And is it not these 'margins' that call out most pressingly for justice, against the work of mourning, of forgetting, of selective (and motivated) remembrance? 'Manic, jubilatory, and incantatory,' the impulse of 'triumphant mourning work' is to exorcize troublesome ghosts (52). But HIV infection and AIDS – because they so profoundly fracture the 'canonical discourses,' and because they remind us incessantly of what those discourses seek to 'deny' – ask us to think about something we can tentatively call 'impossible' mourning. In a sense, it is the 'failed' or 'ruined' text of mourning that 'succeeds' in being most faithful to the experience of crisis it records, for 'an aborted interiorization is at the same time a respect for the other as other, a sort of tender rejection, a movement of renunciation which leaves the other alone, outside, over there, in his death, outside of us' (*Memoires* 35). Intimate relations of alterity, when they are not devoured for the purposes of self-restoration, persist to give evidence of passionate attachments to the very objects that would ordinarily constitute the subject's outside. As melancholic texts, which refuse compensation for feelings of loss, AIDS memoirs and diaries make the process of reading and interpretation impossible to bring to a conclusion as well as shattering for our assumptions about how intimate relationships are structured. AIDS testimonial writing demands acknowledgment of the 'domain of abjected specters' that the 'canonical discourses' would have us obsessively, triumphantly deny. It refuses the comforts of any 'guaranteed economics of salvation,' and of any belief that the epidemic occurs elsewhere or that any of us can think of ourselves as immune to its effects (Benjamin, *Origin* 216).

Allegories of Citizenship and Familial Belonging

How do questions of mourning and memorialization inform strategies for sex education and the prevention of HIV transmission? What are the connections between melancholia and postcolonial and racial anxieties in the context of AIDS as the pandemic continues to follow the fault-lines of globalization? And what differences do gender and sexual orientation, strikingly mutable and fraught categories in the context of HIV infection and AIDS, make in the dynamics of grief? Throughout this study, I emphasize the testimonial writers' convictions that cultural memory is at stake in their representations, and I explore the implication of their texts in ongoing, public processes of remembering and forgetting, an entanglement that is complicated by the texts' visceral investments in the mundane intimacies of illness, death, and grief. I have chosen to discuss these texts in individual, in-depth chapters in order to allow for a full play of relevant contexts and intertexts. If my method is more 'immanent' than diagnostic or conclusive, I hope that may be the measure of a commitment to thinking about grief in a way that might oppose making criticism into diagnosis, narrative, autobiography, or obituary. I stage my reading encounters with the autobiographical texts of Jarman, Hoffman, Michaels, and Kincaid as self-theorizing documents situated at the interstices of cultural memory, exploring how their engagement with grief and remembering exposes the limits of current theoretical discourses on mourning in psychoanalytic and postcolonial theory. And although I concentrate on four memoirs as I open up these questions, I also engage with an array of other texts written in response to the epidemic, thus suggesting the broader applicability of my central arguments.

Central to my approach to reading AIDS testimonial literature are the relations among mourning, gender, sexual orientation, and changing concepts of 'family'; the complexities of witness accounts, written about another's illness; the proliferating analogies the texts draw between the rewriting of kinship and the redrawing of other kinds of cultural relationships, including questions of citizenship, public health, sex education, and economic privilege; and the dialogue these testimonials carry on with analogous cultural practices, including memorial sites, gardens, visual media, objects, and rituals. Also, by examining Kincaid's and Hoffman's memoirs in conjunction with diaries by Michaels and Jarman, I challenge the tendency to treat AIDS testimonial literature as a genre particular to gay men, opening up a dialogue among a diverse array of testimonial accounts, one that is important given the changing demographics of the disease in North America as well as worldwide. And I interrogate the common assertion that writing about the pandemic can be categorized in distinct phases of development (so-called 'early' and 'later' responses), modelling instead how the exploration of specific contexts and reading strategies is necessary if we are to engage rather than to deflect these texts' provocations to rethink assumed categories of proper mourning.

CHAPTER ONE

'Flowers, Boys, and Childhood Memories'
Derek Jarman's Pedagogy

Fragments of memory eddy past and are lost in the dark. In the yellowing light half-forgotten papers whirl old headlines up and over dingy suburban houses, past leaders and obituaries, the debris of inaction, into the void. Thought illuminated briefly by lightning.

– Derek Jarman, *Modern Nature* (20)

'Politics in the First Person': Writing HIV-Positive

The evolution of Derek Jarman's garden at Prospect Cottage, planted defiantly on Dungeness's shingle beach, exposed to incessant winds and harsh sunlight, and in full view of a decrepit, looming nuclear power development, is chronicled over the course of several published autobiographical texts.[1] As Jamaica Kincaid observes, speaking of Prospect Cottage in her *New Yorker* gardening column, its collection of 'worn-down objects' and of plants and pebbles indigenous to the local seashore makes it seem 'as if they were the remains of a long-ago shipwreck, just found.' A massively mediated combination of the indigenous and the exotic, of the natural and the refuse of human technology, 'when you see [Jarman's garden] for the first time, it so defies what you expect that this thought will really occur to you: Now,

what is a garden?' ('Sowers and Reapers' 41). *Modern Nature*,
Jarman's chronicle of the years 1989 to 1991, which saw both
the beginnings of the garden and his body's shift from non-
symptomatic to symptomatic HIV, explores most fully of his
writings the complexities of his intertwined testimonial and hor-
ticultural projects. In particular, *Modern Nature* is preoccupied
with the potentially deforming pressures of writing for public
consumption.[2] In the first place, Jarman is cautious about the
consequences of exposing his feelings of loss, and notes his tendency to freeze 'emotions' 'for fear of.filling the world with tears'
(*MN* 54). He seems to fear that he may 'drown' others as well as
himself in his grief and, in so doing, risk not only the exposure
but the sentimentalization of his concerns, a kind of 'over-
watering.' He worries, too, that by editing the journals for publication he has imposed a more cohesive pattern than really
existed, and frequently disclaims whatever orderliness or narrative logic the journal might be interpreted as projecting in favour
of an emphasis on its dreamlike qualities: 'This diary gives the
wrong impression, it's much too focused. I'm emerging from a
strange dream' (275). Referring to his garden, Jarman is at pains
to point out the traumatic difference between the seemingly
cyclical and enduring life of the natural world and the implacably temporal lives of human beings, highlighting that 'behind
the façade my life is at sixes and sevens. I water the roses and
wonder whether I will see them bloom. I plant my herbal garden
as a panacea, read up on all the aches and pains that plants will
cure – and know they are not going to help. The garden as pharmacopoeia has failed' (179). Loosely echoing Robert Burton,
whose *Anatomy of Melancholy* Jarman sought out and read during
this period (170), he conveys his pervasive sense of loss, his feeling that the whole world must be 'mad,' 'that it is melancholy,
dotes' (Burton 39). *Modern Nature*'s documentation of the quotidian is unsettled by the pressure of Jarman's sadness, to the
extent that the natural world becomes viewed as a montage of

desolation, a ruin, in the sense suggested by Walter Benjamin, that defies belief in 'beautiful nature' and its 'spiritualization of the physical,' refusing to be interpreted as a medium for transcending mortality (*Origin* 176, 187). As Jarman admits, 'Everything I perceive makes a song, everything I see saddens the eye. Behind these everyday jottings – the sweetness of a boy's smile. Into my mind comes the picture of a blood red camellia displaced in the February twilight' (*MN* 207).

Prospect Cottage is invested with all of his longings for paradise, and for escape from the burden of his knowledge of his having tested positive for HIV. As Keith Collins summarizes in his preface to the photographic record *Derek Jarman's Garden*, although 'the garden started accidentally' when pieces of driftwood and flint were used improvisationally to stake and protect the plants, 'slowly the garden acquired new meaning – the plants struggling against biting winds and Death Valley sun merged with Derek's struggle with illness' (Preface). In Jarman's account, Prospect Cottage is home also, however, to many 'ill omens,' to a proliferation of signs that seem to corroborate Jarman's fundamental, all-encompassing sadness and that complicate how we may interpret the landscape's allegorical function: it exists as a 'petrified, primordial landscape,' one composed of 'amorphous fragments' that disturb and provoke us but refuse to yield to our attempts to make coherent sense out of them (*Origin* 166, 176).[3] Opening a car door, for example, Jarman finds himself confronted with the image of 'a large grass snake writhing at my feet – it opened its mouth in agony' (*MN* 157). The world is out of sorts, all potential for wisdom and consolation undermined by the casual cruelties of the modern world's machinery, as exemplified in the snake's death: 'We hadn't seen it – the snake of wisdom who brought the knowledge of good and evil, man's best friend, serpent of memory, great figure of eight, lying with its back broken and its mouth open, crying in silence' (157). Earlier in *Modern Nature*, however, Jarman visualizes the HIV virus as a snake in order to emphasize its predatory behaviour and the debilitating consequences for those it seems to target: 'Could I face the dawn cheerfully, paralysed by the virus that circles like a deadly cobra? So many friends dead or dying – since autumn: Terry, Robert, David, Ken, Paul, Howard' (56). The image of the serpent plaguing an Edenic space – he subsequently refers to VD as 'the old serpent' – suggests that any paradise Jarman might attempt to construct is always tainted by the spectre of HIV (63). Whether he identifies with or against the serpent, it symbolizes a life and a generation traumatically interrupted. This feeling that 'all the brightest and best [have been] trampled to death' is an insight that Jarman solidifies by way of an ironic comparison to the losses of the First World War, a comparison suggested by his just-completed film *War Requiem* (1989): 'Surely even the Great War brought no more loss into one life in just twelve months, and all this as we made love not war' (56). Jarman's periodic reiteration of the names of friends who have died – a move he repeats in the film and text of *Blue*, the autobiography *At Your Own Risk*, and the text that accompanies the photographic record of his garden – echoes the paradoxically silent cry of the serpent of wisdom. Attempting to embrace those he has lost, he finds that although he may repeat their names, their persons are somehow not tractable to representation; what characterizes these 'dead friends,' as Jarman's subsequent poem suggests, is the silence of their deaths:

> I walk in this garden
> Holding the hands of dead friends
> Old age came quickly for my frosted generation
> Cold, cold, cold they died so silently
> Did the forgotten generations scream?
> Or go full of resignation
> Quietly protesting innocence
> Cold, cold, cold, they died so silently. (69)

Speaking the names of his friends again later in *Modern Nature* as his losses continue to increase, and as he starts to experience serious illness connected with HIV, Jarman feels himself to be 'wandering aimlessly in this labyrinth of memories,' trapped by the virus's ravenous denuding of the garden's most vital sweets: the vibrant men whom he loved and loves still (169).

To what extent did Jarman turn to autobiography – to the process of writing, elaborately drawn out of the course of several interlocking memoirs, but also to self-narration in painting, film, and garden – as an antidote to the tortuous venom of melancholy? Answering this question involves exploring several interconnected threads in Jarman's thinking: his conception of the politics of autobiographical writing; the problem of reception and contextualization (exemplified in the cultural phenomenon of the AIDS quilt); the challenges and the implications of writing from a perspective that attempts fully to inhabit an HIV-positive body; and the way in which his project redounds on questions of pedagogy and responsibility, in personal, national, and international contexts.

In his biography of Jarman, Tony Peake marks the turn in Jarman's career upon the news that he had tested positive for HIV with the observation that 'starting with *The Last of England*, he would use the time he had left to produce a quantity of films, paintings and books commensurate with the very longest of lives' (385). As Peake further explains, 'The key to his entire campaign was work. He had always worked hard; now he would work even harder, frenetically almost, using work as a means of riding his despair and combating loss' (385). The role of Jarman's copious writings in countering 'despair' and 'loss' is not without its complications, though, given that work's fraught relationship to conventions of biographical and autobiographical writing and reading that would smooth the edges of his identity as a gay man, or even erase it entirely. And, indeed, his writings are much more than straightforwardly autobiographical, but rather may be read as confrontational theoretical reflections on subjectivity, activism, art, and the overlapping representational contracts of testimony, obituary, and elegy – all informed by his perspective as queer and HIV-positive.

Jarman had been evolving for years his strategies for surviving as queer in a straight world, a project that was to him altogether necessary and yet frightening, given the void into which he felt he spoke. His first foray into autobiographical writing came in 1982, when his 'friend Nicholas told [him] to write it "out"' and Jarman was prompted to write his first memoir, *Dancing Ledge* (*AYOR* 27).[4] His subsequent films *Caravaggio* and *Edward II* are concerned to rework history and biography in order to 'out' what history would conceal. Similarly, Jarman's writings about his own life seek to redress 'the terrible dearth of information, the fictionalisation of our experience' by demonstrating that 'the best of it [our experience] is in our lives' (*MN* 56).[5] Deploring the lack of 'gay autobiography,' especially the fact that almost 'no-one had written an autobiography in which they described a sex act,' Jarman determined upon the following remedy:

That seemed to be a good reason to fill in the blank and to start putting in the 'I' rather than the 'they'; and having made the decision about the 'I' to show how things related to me so that I wasn't talking of others – *they* were doing this and *they* were doing that.

It was very important to me to find the 'I': *I* feel this, this happened to *me*, *I* did this. I wanted to read that. My obsession with biography is to find these 'I's. The subtext of my films have been the books, putting myself back into the picture. (*AYOR* 27)

When Jarman states that 'it was very important to me to find the "I"' he is speaking retrospectively, casting his readers back to the context of his own sexual liberation in the late 1960s. For the Jarman of *At Your Own Risk*, 'The problem of so much of the writing about this epidemic is the absence of the author' (5). This state-

ment suggests a certain continuity in Jarman's thinking: somewhat indirectly, he insists here on the increased importance of
celebrating sexual liberation in the face of the panic – renewed
by the pandemic – about the threat posed by 'deviant sexualities'
to a putative general public. In *Dancing Ledge*, however, AIDS
enters the book only in its final chapter, prompting a late foregrounding of the way in which 'sexuality colours my politics,' and
a citation of 'homosexuals'' 'struggle ... to define themselves
against the order of things,' while enduring 'suffering' 'at the
hands of the ideologically "sound"' (241).[6] But, writing from his
perspective as HIV-positive in *Modern Nature* and *At Your Own
Risk*, Jarman is fully enmeshed in this complicated scenario for
the authorship of testimony, and finds that this situation necessitates a reinvention of what he came to call 'politics in the first
person' (*AYOR* 106).

The turn we may mark in Jarman's autobiographical methods
correlates with the way in which the very label 'HIV-positive' subjects individuals as well as 'risk groups' to a certain 'narrative discipline,' a desire to diagnose so-called pathological or delinquent
subpopulations (Nunokawa 313). The contradictory genres to
which Jarman feels he has been consigned by his HIV-positive status (and their potentially paralysing effects) are evoked by the
items he purchases at the stationer's on his way home after
receiving the news that he had tested positive. What he buys subsequent to this much-delayed and resisted appointment are 'a
daybook for 1987 and a scarlet form to write out a will' (*AYOR* 7).
The gesture of purchasing a daybook emphasizes the urgency of
accounting for his life (Crusoe-like, in the manner of a spiritual
autobiography), while the purchase of the 'scarlet form' involves
a projection into the future, to the stopping place of death.
These official forms for accounting for one's life also anticipate
the 'endless questionnaires' to which Jarman finds himself subject while in hospital, suggesting continuity among these various
kinds of surveillance and self-surveillance (*MN* 253). The genres

emphasized here – daybook and will – model the preparation of his legacy along certain predetermined lines, as they emphasize the disposal of time, of property, and of his person. Even in the more elevated genres of life-writing, such as biography (and here Jarman is referring to Genet and Cocteau), 'it is still quite common to read that the uncovering of a Queer life has diminished it'; and the lesson Jarman implicitly spells out for us by recording his purchases is to 'Beware the executors of the estate' (*AYOR* 72).

Situated amid these imperatives and traps, Jarman's life and death can only stand as a political or educational one by engaging with these conditions; to ignore them would have been to court anonymity. Jarman's risky encounter with hostile public discourses courts the possibility that his book and the public persona they assist in creating might be all-too-readily 'diagnosable' as yielding 'symptom[s] of a diseased lifestyle,' one driven towards self-destruction and death (Reinke 17).[7] In other words, to submit one's own experience to the public discourses of HIV/AIDS risks confirming that 'pervasive homophobia' based on 'a deep cultural idea about the lethal character of male homosexuality' (Nunokawa 311). Jarman distils his predicament as follows:

What is certain is that strangers in the street all look on me as 'dead.' I have to underline the fact that I'm OK; but doing this doesn't convince them.

On the other hand it makes me twice as determined to survive, to find a gap in the prison wall that society has created and jump through it. (*MN* 232)

As Eve Sedgwick observes regarding AIDS and the risks of personal testimony, 'It has been characteristic of the discourse around AIDS to be ... tied to a truth imperative whose angle is killingly partial' ('Gender Criticism' 287). By the phrase 'killingly partial,' Sedgwick suggests that the call for personal writings that might reveal 'the truth' is far more consequential than it appears on the surface. One overriding function of the 'truth imperative' is to confirm for the majority culture the fated – and yet somehow transcendent and socially cleansing – quality of HIV-related deaths among risk groups. Testimony is always in danger of being interpreted as providing evidence of what the majority culture always thought it knew anyway: that 'degeneracy' courts a punishing death, and in the process provides catharsis and a renewed feeling of security for everyone else. This sceptical view of the social function of testimony is corroborated by Alexander García Düttmann who, in his analysis of Hervé Guibert's *To the Friend Who Did Not Save My Life*, wonders about the sense in which 'a confession is necessarily an affirmation, no matter how else one behaves towards the thing confessed': he speculates that 'by confessing AIDS,' one may, in fact, 'promote AIDS,' in effect providing evidence to confirm the public myths of the disease (14).

Worried as Jarman was about compromise, he was also concerned that his work reach a wide audience, and so his relation to the autobiographical contract is a fraught one.[8] This conflicted attitude is captured in a series of questions he raises at the beginning of *Modern Nature* as he reflects on the conditions familiar to him from his long career as film-maker and painter that are attendant on going public, on 'confessing':

As the sun rose, thoughts jostling each other like demons, invaded my garden of earthly delight. What purpose had my book? Was I a fugitive from my past? Had I condemned myself to prison here? How could I celebrate my sexuality filled with so much sadness, and frustration for what has been lost? How had my films been damaged? Look at the cash sloshing around my contemporaries. (*MN* 56)

Similar to the searingly self-critical questions raised by Hoffman, Michaels, and Kincaid about the purpose of their testimonials, Jarman's record of these 'jostling,' disruptive thoughts highlights the complexity of what survival would mean for him. Determined to survive by weathering illness and continuing with his work, how may he do so without submitting fully to the forces that damaged his films, the financial imperatives of patronage (whether originating with British government-funded programs or with Hollywood) that might influence his work? Will sadness and frustration lead him to believe in his own 'delinquency'?[9]

Jarman's very queer melancholy pushes the surfeit of emotion associated with unresolved grief into the realm of what Sedgwick calls the 'reparative' ('Paranoid Reading and Reparative Reading' 8 ff.).[10] Sedgwick postulates the 'depressive position' as 'the position from which it is possible in turn to use one's own resources to assemble or "repair" the murderous part-objects into something like a whole – though not, and may I emphasize this, *not like any preexisting whole*.' These positions are furthermore not to be taken as mutually exclusive: on the contrary, Sedgwick argues, 'powerful reparative practices ... infuse self-avowedly paranoid critical projects' and 'paranoid exigencies' 'are often necessary for non-paranoid knowing and utterance' (8). Seen in this context, rather than constituting an external force that he must conquer, or neutralize, Jarman's inconsolability can be thought of as *producing* the very 'gap in the prison wall' through which he may 'jump.' Jarman's self-identification as an HIV-positive survivor of the epidemic opens up the future to unpredictability. His writings blur any easy divide we might be tempted to make between negatives and positives, between survival and doom, certain life and certain death. If there is something like hope here, it exists as provisional, the result of an insistence on re-'assembling' the physical environment, one's own body, and the bodies of others so that they may provide 'nourishment' and 'comfort' (8). As Sedgwick declares, 'Hope, often a fracturing, even a traumatic thing to experience, is among the energies by which the reparatively positioned reader tries to organize the fragments and part-objects she encounters or creates' (24). Jarman's desire 'to become a work of art and to retain some value in death' turns out to yield an outcome more surprising, I am suggesting, than notoriety, condemnation, or disapproval, or even their apparent opposites, fame and adulation (*AYOR* 103). Paralleling Foucault's interpretation of the implications of Greek and Greco-Roman morality, which emphasizes the voluntary adoption of 'style' over and against universal interdictions, Jarman's diary models (as Sedgwick's essay does using a psychoanalytic vocabulary) how the 'arts of existence' enact 'the care of the self': it draws attention to 'those intentional and voluntary actions by which men not only set themselves rules of conduct, but also seek to transform themselves,' 'to make their life into an *oeuvre* that carries certain aesthetic values and meets certain stylistic criteria' (Foucault 30, 10–11).

Modern Nature's productive uncertainty – and the potential of its deployment of the 'arts of existence' – is exemplified in the pattern of antithesis that we find repeated throughout *Modern Nature* regarding the garden's success or failure as a 'pharmacopoeia' (*MN* 179). Despair at the garden's inability to guarantee a cure alternates with an emphasis on its capacity for functioning, nonetheless, as a balm, as a soothing restorative agency, one that speaks to the senses, as Jarman vacillates between 'paranoid' and 'reparative' relations to the space he has shaped for himself. His observation, for example, that the garden has failed to serve as a pharmacopoeia is followed with the contradictory statement, 'Yet there is a thrill in watching the plants spring up that gives me hope' (179). But optimism about the future is quickly displaced by shadows of another, human sort: 'Even so, I find myself unable to record the disaster that has befallen some of my friends, particularly dear Howard, who I miss more than imagination. He wanders into my mind – as he wandered out a stormy night eighteen months ago' (179). We are directed back to an earlier (temporarily forgotten?) conversation, a final conversation in which Howard Brookner's lack of words – the 'long silences and the

slow wounded moaning,' which invokes, again, the spectre of the
snake – means that Jarman cannot 'know whether he understood
a word,' a one-sided conversation that 'left me confused, tearful,
and fearfully sad' (54). In an effort to still these memories, Jarman occasionally invokes a vocabulary of recalcitrance that
would underplay his affective response to being ill: 'I refuse to
believe in my own mortality, or the statistics which hedge the
modern world about like the briar that walled in the sleeping
princess. I have conducted my whole life without fitting in, so
why should I panic now and fit into statistics?' (151). With the
planting of 'twelve wild roses' around the cottage, Jarman renders the image of the 'sleeping princess' walled about by briars
literal, suggesting that escape may shade into an updated form of
imprisonment when the struggle for agency is given up for the
peace of the narcoleptic. The garden at Prospect Cottage embodies a conflicted relation to time and to the process of crafting history, or making a pharmakon.[11] Resisting capitulation to the way
his death seems preordained by the cultural myths of HIV infection and AIDS that correlate the disease with a certain doom, Jarman seeks less to dull the senses than he does to heighten them,
and thereby to distil some nurturance from the world. Still, the
'sticks and stones' and rusted metal out of which he builds his
Eden persist from season to season, despite the sense in which
'all this disappears in the burgeoning spring,' standing as continuing reminders of the world Jarman finds inimical and painful
(37, 109). Likewise, some practice of freedom more tenuous
than escape – some more perilous, and yet less fantastic 'gap' in
the prison wall – constitutes the project of Jarman's autobiographical writings.[12] I wish to seek after its possibilities and its
conditions.[13]

   In *At Your Own Risk*, the more overtly theoretical and polemical
of his two extended written memoirs on living with HIV and
AIDS, Jarman's proleptic intervention in the mourning of his
death occurs by means of a carefully calibrated play with the first-

person pronoun, echoing his early strategy of 'putting in the "I" rather than the "they"' (27).[14] In practice, though, the 'I' is not consistently singular or obvious in its reference to Jarman as an individual. Jarman aligns himself, rather, with his lost friends, casting himself as a spectre in the context of his writing about his own life:

Shall I begin on the day that I was overwhelmed by guilt? – I had survived. So many of my friends caved in under the hate; I have known men to die for love but more to die for hate. As the years passed, I saw in the questioner's eyes the frustrations of coming to terms with life; are you still here? Some were brutally frank: 'When are you going to die?'

Didn't you know I died years ago with David and Terry, Howard, the two Pauls. This is my ghostly presence, my ghostly eye. 'I had AIDS last year,' I said with a smile and they looked at me as if I was treating their tragedy flippantly. 'Oh yes I had AIDS last year. Have you had it?'

'What are you doing next Mr. Jarman?'. What comes after, after, after, that's the problem when you survive. (*AYOR* 9)

As Deborah Esch has observed of this passage, Jarman's play with temporality 'eludes recuperation by a realism that would dictate (in advance and among other things) that "death is only a matter of when"' (134). But if the emphasis is on eluding the apparent inevitability of a certain cultural narrative, then what precisely are Jarman's legacies to us, as we read him now and in the future? Jarman's insistence on the 'ghostliness' of his presence in a passage so emphatically cast in the present tense foregrounds his allegiance with the dead, setting this loyalty against those interlocutors who would possess (and consume) this 'tragedy' in the space created by what they desire: tidily finished deaths. Jarman identifies and plays on what he sees in 'the questioner's eyes,' 'the frustrations of coming to terms with life,' with his persistence in living 'as the years passed.' He offers himself, in response to this inhospitable gaze, not as author, but as *spectre*, as

an untimely, 'ghostly eye' to whose disjointed perspective readers
are demanded, in turn, to submit themselves. Jarman writes, in
other words, as representative of a collective, a generation, and,
furthermore, subjects himself to the collaborative goodwill of
others if his point of view is to be perpetuated, not abruptly
attenuated. Such a linking across 'generations,' as it were, of
authors and readers, acknowledges his privilege as 'survivor' and
witness of others' lives. In the same moment, Jarman risks the
very exposure that he worries about and criticizes: exposure to
the potential for misreading, a possibility borne out of the
impulse to triumph somehow over the dead by appropriating
their voices. This is a necessary exposure to the possibility of misinterpretation, and it goes to the heart of Jarman's 'reparative'
project, suggesting the difficulty – even the unlikeliness – of survival on anything like his own terms, terms corresponding to
'love' rather than to 'hate.' As Judith Butler points out, the very
desire for survival may make one more prone to the exigencies of
power and, therefore, the compromises it would exact (*Psychic
Life* 7). The ghostliness of Jarman's presence in the text works as
a rhetorical strategy that asks readers to think again about how
'the one who holds out the promise of continued existence plays
to the desire to survive,' and about how the conditions of social
legibility shape the form that survival takes, and all too often
mark out a path for grief that would seem to ensure that the dead
will not return.

Rereading the Quilt: Recuperation or Reparation?

Registering so scrupulously in his writings about his own life and
illness the workings of social power on that life and the project of
representing it, Jarman writes in self-conscious anticipation of his
own posthumosity, fretting over the possibility of being misinter-
preted or forgotten. In *The Psychic Life of Power*, Butler discusses
the risks that are run by people who write, speak, or grieve pub-

licly in the context of HIV/AIDS. She worries in particular about 'the melancholic aggression and the desire to vanquish, that characterizes the public response to the death of many of those considered "socially dead," who die from AIDS: Gay people, prostitutes, drug users, among others' (27). Highlighting the dynamic of social abjection that underpins social relations and shapes our psychic lives, where 'social existence' and legitimacy depend on 'social differentiation,' Butler argues that the narrative sentence or plot seems always to be written in the following manner: 'If they are dying or already dead, let us vanquish them again'; and, in a compensatory twist, by way of an 'inversion of that [melancholic] aggression,' the other is in fact 'cast ... as the (unlikely) persecutor of the socially normal and normalized' (27). If, by foregrounding the call to write gay autobiography, Jarman to some degree wants to claim or even to preserve 'the subject as continuous, visible, and located,' offering his own account as an alternative to majority culture's distortions of queer lives, this project cannot be so much a matter of simple substitution, a strategy that, Butler's argument implies, would be destined to be absorbed and neutralized by the majority culture (29). Jarman's writings do not merely contemplate his exclusion from social existence and legitimacy, nor do they only attempt to assuage woundedness with fantasies of escape; rather, they force us to grapple with Butler's central query: Are the norms governing social legitimacy fixed, or can they be thought of as contingent and as open to change? Extending Foucault's emphasis on the purpose of 'philosophical activity' as 'the endeavor to know how and to what extent it might be possible to think differently, instead of legitimating what is already known' (*The Use of Pleasure* 9), Butler asks whether 'existence' can 'nevertheless be risked, death courted or pursued, in order *to expose* and *open to transformation* the hold of social power on the conditions of life's persistence' (*Psychic Life* 28; emphasis added). Jarman's writings seek to bring the civic and pedagogical subject into a more porous, less rigorously defended relation to the 'abject' of the ill body, sex and sexuality, and mortality. His published journals persist in testifying to his attachment to his lost generation and to his commitment to finding sustenance in a hostile world. In this, the journal, like its material analogue, the garden, constitutes an 'inassimilable remainder' that is also a reminder of what we might be in danger of forgetting: by insistently affirming the reality, complexity, and legitimacy of Jarman's life, the diary challenges the process by which 'social power' would deem him marginal, first rendering him 'socially dead,' and then using his actual death as an occasion to complete the process of marginalization and triumphant rewriting (*Psychic Life* 28–9). A ghostly 'eye' or 'I' haunts those who read Jarman's journals, refusing to vanish from our awareness, and, as I have been intimating, this remainder is turned, subtly, to a project of reparation.

My own position as reader of Jarman's texts aligns to a significant extent with the position of a family member, which is itself one of my critical preoccupations in this study. I come to his work as a reader whose personal motivations and concerns are comparable in some ways to those of Amy Hoffman and Jamaica Kincaid, who write as witnesses of others' stories, the stories of their 'siblings.' And I share the feelings of guilt and shame and inadequacy that they experience in response to losses that seem so difficult, almost impossible, to grieve. What I want to pursue here, specifically, is the way in which Derek Jarman's work has become for me much more extraordinarily educational than I had expected upon first picking up *Modern Nature*, how his textual remains have demanded a reading strategy that would force a disarticulation of my own most pressing reading agendas, those 'ongoing' schemes of 'neutralization' that, in Derrida's phrase, 'would attempt to conjure away a danger' (*Specters of Marx* 32). What does this education consist of? How might I write about it without composing a tidying obituary? The question of 'this respect for justice concerning those who *are not there*' is central to 'the politics of memory, of inheritance, and of generations' that I am using to frame my discussion of Jarman (Derrida, *Specters* xix).

In many ways, the cultural practices that have accumulated around the public memorialization of HIV infection and AIDS in North American consumer society ensure that remembering involves the repression of a more complex sense of the realities of the epidemic as it is lived. As Marita Sturken argues in *Tangled Memories*, this potential for systemic 'forgetting' is nowhere more evident than in the practices of memory inscribed in the AIDS quilt, in its various national and more local permutations. If, on the level of an individual panel, naming the dead becomes a synecdoche for 'coming out,' as Sturken suggests, then the process of 'destigmatization' may be arrested in and by that speech act, by the bounds imposed by a certain domesticating context (186–7).[15] Add to that the sense in which 'through the simple act of testifying or confessing to feelings of regret, the speaker achieves a kind of cleansing of guilt,' and perhaps is able to 'assign meaning' by way of 'redemptive transformation' (190), in particular through the staging of a family romance that would restore the integrity of the threatened male body and relocate it within the nuclear family. Gestures of destigmatization seem to work, moreover, with an alarming regularity to mask privilege, 'reiterating' in their hesitancy the 'significant divisions in American society,' namely the inequalities that are brought into relief by the epidemic (209).[16] Jarman, the fabricator of a whole chorus of his own self-memorializations – indeed, his art practice shares with the quilt a commitment to the 'found,' the domestic, and the improvisational – did not hesitate to voice his criticism of the quilt, and his objections reverberate with those raised by Sturken:

When the AIDS quilt came to Edinburgh during the film festival, I attended just out of duty. I could see it was an emotional work, it got the heartstrings. But when the panels were unveiled a truly awful ceremony

took place, in which a group of what looked like refrigerated karate
experts, all dressed in white, turned and chanted some mumbo jumbo –
horrible, quasi-religious, false. I shall haunt anyone who ever makes a
panel for me. (*Derek Jarman's Garden* 91)

The quilt's privileging of emotion creates an opening for two
kinds of responses that bother Jarman. The relation of the viewer
to art becomes one of mere 'duty,' and this dutiful reaction
unfolds in the space of a 'quasi-religious' public ritual, suggesting, furthermore, the mandatory and limited quality of the emotional response that is being elicited; whatever political potential
the quilt might possess is eviscerated by this 'truly awful ceremony.' Extending his suspicions about the commodification of
mourning, in the same passage Jarman insists that Keith Haring's
graffiti art, while it served to 'raise consciousness,' ultimately
'failed to turn tragedy beyond the domestic' (91).[17] Elsewhere
his scepticism extends to the intertwining of the art and fund-
raising worlds – to the sense in which 'dues' are 'paid' by affluent
artists 'in cash not spirit,' and to the suspicion that guilt means
that 'we are all kind to friends who are dying' (*MN* 91).[18] Likewise, speculating on the 'relations of mourning' in 'White
Glasses' in the context of her friendship with Michael Lynch,
Sedgwick points to the quilt's implication in the 'ravenously
denuding' mode of memory that is obituary discourse (265).
Although there is a sense in which the quilt may evoke many
'possible tones,' it can also be read as possessing 'a nostalgic
ideology' that flattens the personal experiences it seeks to represent and, relatedly, as occupying a 'sometimes obstructive niche
in the ecology of gay organizing and self-formation' (265).[19] But
the most unequivocally 'paranoid' reading of the quilt belongs to
Jeff Nunokawa. Nunokawa suggests that the quilt project origi-
nates in 'homophobic reticence,' a pattern of disavowal that he
explains as follows: 'If the majority culture is not inclined to recognize the death of the male homosexual, it is also not inclined

to recognize anything else about him; if the majority culture grants no notice to his death, it also inters him from the start' (319). For him, the media's overwhelming attention to the quilt in its narration of the story of AIDS has its source in this same determination to hide the diversity of sexual practices and identities. These criticisms of the quilt are persuasive; they ring with a certain paranoid truth. Certainly Derek Jarman, who so much values being 'able to explore our problems and celebrate our achievements without being contextualised by Heterosoc' (*AYOR* 79), vehemently (albeit flippantly and somewhat inconsistently) resists the pattern of containment via exorcism that the quilt would seem, according to these analyses, to reinstate.[20]

Is melancholy always contained within the framework of regret and recuperation, or may it also, when its context is shifted ever so slightly, engender a reparative agenda? 'Exorcism,' according to Derrida, may not always be jubilatory, triumphant, manic. With the introduction of another context for reading, one distinct or disjointed from the imperatives of the patriotic ego, it might be possible, as Derrida suggests,

> to exorcize not in order to chase away the ghosts, but this time to grant them the right, if it means making them come back alive, as *revenants* who would no longer be *revenants*, but as other *arrivants* to whom a hospitable memory or promise must offer welcome – without certainty, ever, that they present themselves as such. Not in order to grant them the right in this sense but out of a concern for *justice*. (175)

Under what circumstances may *revenants* – such as Jarman's 'ghostly presence' – return to be 'welcomed' rather than 'chased away' by either denial or domestication? Let me take an example from early activist work vis-à-vis the quilt. In his personal introduction to *In the Shadow of the Epidemic*, Walt Odets describes the experience of viewing quilt panels during the time he spent as a volunteer in 1987 for the Committee for the March on Washington for Lesbian and Gay Rights, an organization that shared space with the Names Project quilt (2). The circumstance of sharing a storefront with the Names Project meant that, as he sat at his desk, Odets found himself confronted with a constant, close-up view of the work of the quilt project; this viewing of the quilt took place out of sync with the timing by which the 'general public' is habituated to viewing public monuments. And Odets's description of this happenstance suggests that the affective impact of the panels exceeds what may be inferred as their originating purpose, when viewed collectively, prior to their installation in a public space. Glimpsed in the process of its making, the quilt is far from being completely explained in terms of a nostalgic ideology. As Odets explains, 'Although the panels are intended to memorialize and celebrate the lives of those who have died, the stacks of unopened boxes, awaiting attention from overworked staff, began to make me think less and less of celebration, and more and more of newly arrived corpses' (3). Significantly, then, Odets views the panels from an estranged view – not in their proposed *national* American context (that is, the Mall in Washington, a state-sanctioned venue for public memorials [Sturken 215]). The panels maintain, somehow, their metonymic relation to the bodies they memorialize; as Odets testifies, 'Each panel, however simple, seemed the story of a full human life, but each had also ended in the awful stranglehold of AIDS' (3). In this unplanned, unforeseen context, the memorializing impulse that motivates the production of panels for the quilt seems to turn against itself, offering life stories and showing how they have been thwarted by a terrible epidemic on a massive scale. If the quilt inevitably flattens the fragments it incorporates, then it does not erase them entirely and leaves open the possibility that the unruly bodies the quilt represents might, through their disruption of place and time, resist their being woven into a national diorama of grief and guilt.

Reflecting on how the quilt foregrounds the labour involved in

its production, Thomas Yingling argues that, whatever the myths
in which it is implicated,

the quilt is in some profound way disturbing (handicraft in an era of
consumer goods, and motivated neither by profit nor beauty; handicraft
where the trace of labor and its social referent remains visible, where
that is indeed what defines its value – an unreifiable practice; labor seeking to intervene in an appalling alienation and both out of love and
anguish encoded on the surface of the object). ('AIDS in America' 307)

Yingling argues that motivated, or at least contextualized, as it
may be by the triumphalist impulses of mourning, 'as an *artifact*
the quilt continues to challenge our understanding, and any cognitive accommodation that is forthcoming remains marked as
radically by difference as by identity' (307). The piecing together
of fabric along with other found fragments to represent a life far
from definitively inters the subjects of its representations. Quilts'
most distinctive characteristics may be, rather, their inclusion and
recontextualization of found objects; their production of decora-
tive, symbolic surfaces; their tactile qualities; and their purpose in
warming, protecting, and comforting the human body. Quilts are
also ephemeral, subject to disintegration over time, since fabric
will fade, rip, untidy itself; so, too, fabric invites the prospect of
mending or alteration. What we are brought to bear witness to in
viewing the quilt is a strange archive, one in which melancholic
incorporation (and its attendant disrespect for boundaries) inter-
mingles with more nostalgic tendencies, and with an idealized
connection across gender, sexuality, and desire, as well as across
familial and national structures. The traces the quilt bears of its
handmade origins are illuminating for my consideration of Derek
Jarman in particular because of the radically found and improvisational qualities of Jarman's own art practice.[21] Quilt-making, as
a local, extemporaneous, and most often *amateur* practice of
storytelling, may be interpreted, as Yingling suggests, as a practice

of survival 'in which experience becomes recognizable through collective frameworks and becomes therefore communicable *as experience* rather than abbreviated or atrophied' (307). This is a practice that may counteract the alienation and destructive fragmentation of a world in which AIDS is constructed as spectacle (307). Indeed, Jarman's favoured techniques as painter, filmmaker, writer, and gardener – collage and collaboration – have an affinity with quilt-making that is obfuscated in the rage he projects onto the nationally celebrated, contextualized AIDS quilt he views in Edinburgh. In describing his autobiographical practices, he notes, for example, his sense of having 'had *to piece together a life* under a great dark cloud of censure and ignorance' (*AYOR* 5; emphasis added). Jarman turned to his art not as a forum for resolving his grudge against 'Heterosoc,' his term for majority culture, but rather as a medium for the production of contexts that would resist his stories being absorbed into the narrative workings of majority culture's guilt complex, that would resist the fetishization that occurs, as Kristeva emphasizes, 'when the activating sorrow' of a work of art 'is repudiated' (*Black Sun* 9). He referred to painting, for example, as his 'lifeline,' even when his continuing to work as a painter required that he depend on the hands – the labour – of others 'to help stretch and prepare the canvases, as well as mix the paint' (Peake 493–4).

At another remove, this conception of the quilt as 'artifact' or handiwork, together with Jarman's practices of 'found art,' allows for a critical rephrasing of the ethical questions that each of these fragmentary cultural productions poses to its interpreters. Presenting himself to us as a 'ruin' – as imbricated in the world of fallen nature and suffering, but also as obscure to our efforts to interpret him – Jarman challenges his readers to adopt a reading practice that tries to resist the compensatory aggressions of mourning. What kinds of reading practices might avoid hurrying interpretation towards the performance of another, more definitive death, but rather would promote the continuation of a conversation with a ghost who persists in the traces of a certain labour? Responses to Jarman's legacy in the months following his death sowed the seeds of a critical practice corresponding to the 'arts of existence' he himself models. Specifically, the reciting of Colin MacCabe's 'official' obituary for Jarman in the context of a special issue of *Critical Quarterly* subtitled 'Critically Queer' displaces the initial reading context with another, more hospitable one; MacCabe's phrasing becomes more personal, as though to reappropriate Jarman back into a queer context: 'it is unbearable,' he writes, 'that *we* have lost Derek' (viii; emphasis added).

Might Jarman's writing inspire a similar response in other readers? Rescued from the status of museum artifact, at least provisionally, by way of their own emphasis on the physicality of loss and sadness, to what future readings are Jarman's texts liberated? Jarman's spectre is an emphatically sensuous one that resists neat correlation with abstractions, whether they are contemptuous or the product of the more subtly exorcizing labels of therapy or prophecy. Fragmented, and often conflicted in the meanings they attach to the memories that are resurfacing, Jarman's writings, especially *Modern Nature*, ask us to do what Deborah Britzman, in her theory of queer pedagogy, describes as 'think[ing] through the structures of textuality,' in order to reflect on what desires and conceptual limits we bring to the text, as well as the places where the text demands that readers engage in reshaping these (93). The forces of melancholy make his autobiography – and, as we shall see, his pedagogical strategies – resistant to being arranged for selective viewing, keeping in view the objects that he accrues in the project of caring for a self, and a generation, over which he agonizes and which he persists in loving (28).

'Through Sick Eyes': Inhabiting a Body with AIDS

Modern Nature, generically best described as a revised diary, balances its record of the quotidian with a pattern of sequential development, as it traces Jarman's transition from defining himself as HIV-positive to inhabiting a body now increasingly prey to multiple opportunistic infections, a body with AIDS (240). Though the emotions are deeply felt and highly personal, Jarman observes that he had always been 'conscious ... of the limitations and loyalties' of the diary 'as I have always been aware that it would be published' (298). Given these inbuilt pressures, the resounding question is 'how much can it [the diary] tell of our dilemma?' (298). At certain moments, he is highly protective about the 'depressed' condition that attends his increasing illness. Fighting flu, for example, in January 1990, Jarman observes that he is 'the most depressed I can remember,' noting that 'the only consolation is I've given it to no-one, just spluttered it into this diary' (218). Far from being held back from public view, Jarman's melancholy becomes the substance of his chronicle of illness; and, indeed, it is the accidental-seeming, 'spluttering' quality of Jarman's journal that makes it succeed in 'telling of our dilemma,' even though in another sense it 'fails' finally to resolve the crisis. Much as Jarman's garden, in incorporating the results of his beachcombing activities in the random section at the back of the garden, while seeking a more formal, controlled, symbolic effect in the front, *Modern Nature* collects and arranges the 'shadowy secrets' that 'congregate like moths' around the generative source of a strange, menacing, and yet illuminating force: his body's vulnerability to illness. At the time of his purchase of Prospect Cottage, Jarman assumed that the property afforded no opportunity to create a garden; it was with much surprise on his part, then, that the garden came into being in such an unlikely place, the 'plants plonked in and left to take their chances in the winds of Dungeness' (*Derek Jarman's Garden* 14). If the 'nuclear industry' represents 'the rot at the core of democracy,' the AIDS pandemic – especially the panic that exposes the prejudices that lurk behind the democratic principles of civil societies – also appears to loom beyond the scale of individual or community agency. Jarman's questions about organizing the community at Dungeness are equally applicable to the AIDS pandemic: 'What can any of us do? And what information do we have?' (*MN* 240).

In *Modern Nature* Jarman takes back the refuse of the social systems that would alternately survey and penalize him, subjecting him, that is, to a certain narrative discipline that would predetermine what it means to inhabit a body with AIDS. Avoiding passivity *and* heroism, Jarman testifies about his illness in a manner that shifts the terms of his own subjection, making room in this account for the circulation of grief, desire, and love. In a situation where, as Julien Smith argues in her discussion of AIDS and ethics, 'the most ordinary capacities of the body, such as the body's ability to retain food, fail,' and where the queer body has accordingly been read as sabotaging its own health, and thus confessing to 'sickness,' Jarman's testimony insists on sustenance (*The Constructed Body* 77). Inviting a comparison, perhaps, with the sea kale of Dungeness, which 'survive in this terrain because they have roots at least twenty feet long,' Jarman's record of his illness identifies, and nurtures, in other words, the sources of his own tenacity in a hostile environment (*Derek Jarman's Garden* 18). Survival is cultivated on a vertical dimension rather than a horizontal, future-oriented one. *Modern Nature* adopts a stance that is, in Derrida's phrase, 'not docile to time,' to a narrative, attempting in this way to resist the narrative drive of exorcism that would repeatedly declare social death in the act of anticipating a literal one (*Specters of Marx* xx). More specifically, Jarman's own identification of three crucial recurring topoi – 'flowers, boys, and childhood memories' – suggest that these are the sources in which he 'can find strength' (*MN* 91). But the journal is far from hinging all its hopes on the retrospective construction of a lost sexual ideal of gay communality. Rather than preoccupying himself with the loss of his body's imagined natural coherence, or the imagined coherent egalitarianism of his generation, Jarman now invests his bodily experiences – excessively – with a wild, wandering, and often inconsistent surge of affect, so that his web of references to 'flowers, boys, and childhood memories' may affirm desire and love in the face of prejudice and doom.[22] And what takes on great importance here is the way in which Jarman's play with shifting levels of immediacy and estrangement transfers his anxiety to his readers; the constantly mutating quality of our relation to his detailing of his illness implicates us in the project of ensuring the continued visibility of his 'sources of strength' in excess of the usual frames for constructing the body with AIDS.

Jarman is wary of 'the idea of the hospital and the socialisation of my death' and, in particular, of the 'institutionalisation of cures,' as in the role of the AIDS quilt in constructing national memory and in the expectations we hinge on science to provide a pharmaceutical cure or vaccine (*AYOR* 99). This circumspection is substantiated through the playing out of Jarman's first-person perspective on the effects of the opportunistic infections to which his body is vulnerable. As Julien Smith emphasizes, 'Illness throws us back upon our bodies, which we can no longer assume will be there for us. The body, so familiar, feels unusual in illness, not quite itself' (77). The chaos that was there all of the time suddenly shows itself, undermining the assumed grounds of a coherent subjectivity. According to Elizabeth Grosz's summary of the implications of Freud's comments on 'Mourning and Melancholia,' since 'mourning is a reclamation of libido from unreciprocated investments which have emptied the ego,' illness tends to the disclosure of the shakiness of this process of reclamation (29). Accordingly, 'when the subject is ill, the ego is unable to sufficiently invest external objects to give them attention' (29). In this state of perpetual irresolution of loss, 'libido is directed towards the subject's own body, appearing to replace an external love object with its own body, or, at least, its pain' (29). In *Modern Nature* Jarman pursues such investment in his own body, though the returns from this project seem to diminish as the body itself does; however, if AIDS may be labelled, as Eric Michaels offers so caustically, 'a kind of cosmic personal reducing plan, where one by one certain functions disappear,' then investment in what remains of the body's functions occurs with unprecedented ferocity (*Unbecoming* 57). Jarman's testimony thus contradicts the media-made narratives that in his view would hasten the deaths of people deemed socially expendable or undesirable; these tendencies are exemplified in what Jarman refers to as the 'starvation diet' for people with HIV who are dependent on the state for financial aid (*MN* 54); they are also evident in the distressed state into which Jarman finds he is forced, so that he goes 'back and forth in the garden, like the boy with anorexia who weighed himself every five minutes' (77).

Small details of daily life register Jarman's indignation, and they often rest without an explicit interpretive frame, leaving them surging with an at first unchannelled intensity of affect. For instance, daily encounters with the mirror, as he prepares his face for others to view, force the marking of time. The dramatic changes in Jarman's appearance take him by surprise: 'The razor bumps across the bones of my face. Even the bones themselves have shrunk. My hands seem half their normal size. My raw stomach aches and aches' (251). The 'amazed' observation that he has 'shrunk' prompts a negation – 'I haven't turned into a little old man' – followed by an admission that 'as I have a bath my bones grind against the enamel, creak ominously' (257). Here his body loses its familiarity, emerging as mechanical and skeletal rather than fleshy, as though taking on a textural similarity to the rough shingle beach of Dungeness. We see the body's transformation not as a wasting away, as a liquefying of the body, but almost as a hardening, a paring down to its more essential elements, a process described with such understatement that we cannot be sure whether to be horrified or not.[23] Still, the components of the personal ritual of shaving are, accordingly, rendered 'topsy turvy,' as Jarman finds that the routine marking of time is

unmoored (257). While he notes that he 'still splosh[es] hand-
fuls of hot water at my face to soften the hairs,' counting 'to 68,'
the significance of the ritual has changed, almost without his
noticing, in a way that reflects Jarman's changed sense of the
relation of his life to narrative time. Now, he finds that he must
alter the words that accompany his actions: 'I used to say to
myself each splosh for a year of life' (257). Crucially, though, Jarman insists that this defamiliarization of the body 'acquaints' him
with it, as though 'for the first time in my life' by the sense in
which he is now compelled to 'explore' it (260). And he correlates his physical 'weakness' with the 'heighten[ing]' of 'every
perception,' noting that the 'snail's pace' at which he is forced to
write makes him attend to the bodily effort that goes into the
recording of his experience (261). By offering these details of his
own body's pushing against the boundaries of the abject and,
specifically, by presenting them in their 'minimal visibility, in
[their] extreme manifestations constituted by pain and melancholia' (Kristeva, *Black Sun* 122), but without installing the 'signifying brand' of 'repugnance, disgust, abjection' (Kristeva, *Powers
of Horror* 11), the diary maintains a sense of Jarman's own body as
an active force, if not an agented one, a newly spectral but still
emphatically sensuous entity that demands recognition of, even
love for, its shifting contours.

Switching, momentarily, to the point of view of the well, mim-
icking, possibly, the vantage point of those who might see themselves as safely distanced from risk groups for HIV infection,
Jarman observes that 'there is a natural impulse to wish those
who reproach our good health with illness quite dead: a great
building burnt to ashes, a painting slashed, a tree fallen, the past
cleared away for the future. Little deaths. All of us feel satisfaction in a dark corner' (*MN* 231). In his commentary on others'
illnesses and death, he contests the inevitability of this impulse to
abject them, as well as the connected assumption that futurity
depends on embracing the healthy to the social exclusion of the

ill. Jarman's account cultivates an oppositional relation to the virus and its social meanings by emphasizing the paradoxical position he occupies: his at once a survivor, a mourner, and himself a 'living' spectre (47). Indeed, Jarman follows up his philosophical rumination about the relation between sickness and health, past and future, with the bare declarative, 'My friend Alan died today' (231). Only two weeks after he records Alan's death, Jarman notes (and this is just one example of how losses tumble quickly one after the other in the journal) that 'Sandy rang at four. Paul died in his sleep last night' (238). Placed in this particular sequence – his summary of the law governing the relation between the 'healthy' and the 'sick' followed without pause by the registering of Alan's death, then the marking of Paul's passing – the relation between the two men, a relation of friendship, is demonstrated as superseding the rules that might otherwise be brought into play to distinguish the living from the dead. Even as he experiences fear and ambivalence about inhabiting a body that is increasingly (and somewhat unpredictably) vulnerable to a host of opportunistic illnesses, Jarman's chronicling in prose and poetry of his friends' deaths during the course of his illness stresses sexual and tactile connectedness with other men, in the past and in the present, not the opposition of his relative 'health.' He speaks both within and outside of his community, annulling the strategy of clearing away the past for the future, insisting, rather, on their necessary interconnection. In this expression of sadness the deaths of others are, remarkably, 'neither dodged nor embellished' (Kristeva, *Black Sun* 122). And this happens despite the fact that the multiple losses he experiences – the fact that 'hardly a day passes without illness invading' – heighten the feeling of being overwhelmed by the disorientation of his experience of the same virus in his own body; the illusion of a 'normal,' 'healthy' life is jarred repeatedly by news of friends' deaths. But the pace of these losses is not mitigated by symbolic interpretation; Jarman records the illnesses and deaths of his friends in simple, even abrupt language that calls us to attend to these events, but not necessarily to explain or interpret them. And in his poetic lamentation he implies that ethical projection into some kind of future that does not merely repeat the 'cold' and 'silent' (because 'untouched') quality of these deaths involves not exorcism but a sustained, melancholic engagement with the past. Readers are exhorted to 'touch fingers' with the past precisely when panic seems most inescapable, when bad news arrives in the middle of the night (*MN* 69–70).

The professional distancing of the hospital staff during Jarman's first hospitalization contrasts sharply with Jarman's self-perceptions of his body and the bodies of others, and enhances his feeling of claustrophobic silencing, as is suggested by his image of being pursued by 'the shadowy black bats of breathlessness' (290). The retorts he offers in response to pleasantries about the weather, for instance, enforce the estrangement produced by his perspective, exposing the bias of the healthy, namely that time will unfold or appear to unfold in its customary way. When 'the doctor worries that the sun will disappear before the weekend, I say not to worry: before his time's up he might wish he could switch it off' (291). How strange this desire seems when it is placed side by side with the threatening interruptions of breath mirrored in Jarman's earlier alliterative prose. This same sadness – diffuse, corrosive, and profoundly estranging of the patterns (of breath, of movement) of which we assume a 'normal' life consists – generates simultaneously a critique of the political and economic inertia that undermines the best intentions and efforts of the staff, whom Jarman in fact frequently praises. *Modern Nature* responds to the 'institutionalisation' of illness and of its cures by insisting on the contradictions inherent in that experience, the overlapping of medical intervention, punishment, and pathologization that the healthy are either incapable of seeing or that they unthinkingly normalize. Released from the hospital, Jarman explodes with rage at a dinner party:

My pills and the euphoria of escaping from the confines of hospital have caused me to create a scene. Michael asks me how I am.

'Fine,' I say, but then launch into the state of the NHS. Where, as my weight drops below 9 stone and I sweat it out, a scan takes three weeks; and Virginia Bottomley, junior health minister, sits sweetly at the foot of the bed saying everything is improving – quite impervious to the serious advice she is being given by everyone who works here. How can such charm have such deaf ears.

I shout this across the restaurant – the diners freeze, counting on their medical insurance: Have they put enough aside for the London Clinic?

As I weaved my way home very unsteadily I felt glad that I had made this scene. The pills loosen you up – no-one raised a voice against me. (282)

Jarman's new, hyper-aware relation to his own body, along with the discipline initiated by the medical regimen, has irrevocably changed his perspective. In particular, his account of the delays in tests and treatment points to the maddening disjunction between the perfection of theory and the delays of practice – would that hospitals were half as efficient and organized as their Foucauldian representation suggests. To be released from the institution is, moreover, not to be absolved from the perspective his confinement has generated. The passage registers a certain lack of control, an outburst of built-up emotion: Jarman describes himself as euphoric, as 'shout[ing]' and then 'weav[ing] my way home very unsteadily.' In a sense he is the ghost at this dinner party, a raging force returned if not from death, then from a liminal experience of near-death. Revisiting Thatcher's junior health minister's attempt to placate him (and the citizenry in 'general') by her mere presence, Jarman juxtaposes her reassurances with the details of his treatment under the auspices of the National Health Service; the comparison is highly unflattering and makes Virginia Bottomley's words sound hollow, as they likely were. Although the positive impact of gestures of compassion on the part of politicians and other public figures is not negligible, from the point of view of the hospital bed a physical presence means very little, next to nothing, when it is fashioned to suit the purposes of producing a made-for-the-media tableau and when charm is a subterfuge masking deafness to the words of those on the frontlines. (One recalls here, too, inevitably, the widely disseminated photographs of Princess Diana shown holding with ungloved hands the hands of PWAs.) It is the quietude, the normality, even, of the violence wreaked by the state on the bodies of the ill, especially bodies with HIV/AIDS, that makes the encounter so disturbing. Jarman's response is an excessive performance that could be dismissed as merely cranky were its acrimony not so precise.

Virginia Bottomley's symbolic efforts at reassuring all that the system is working are presented, furthermore, as paralleling the infuriatingly passive forms of censorship to which Jarman feels he has been subjected during his film-making career. Repeatedly, other people's 'parties' or photo opportunities – held under the dispensation of forgetfulness that prevails in the world of the well – are disrupted by Jarman's sadness, which worries the seams of the linked social violences of censorship, prejudice, and inaction. For instance, during this period of his initial illness, Jarman's attempts to realize the film project *The Garden* (ironically, a story of persecution that retells the passion of Christ, only with a gay couple as his substitutes) ran into serious difficulties: 'Another phone call confirmed that *The Garden* had been pushed aside for the fund-raising cocktail party' (312). Jarman's melancholic perspective extends the analysis, giving it a wider scope: 'I've been the subject of this insidious censorship all my life. What gets funded, what doesn't, what is shown, when and how – it all seems quite ludicrous. Laugh it off, but feel a little sad' (312). As with Bottomley's pretending away governmental inaction, the prejudice Jarman senses he must work against is subtle in the extreme; he is certain of its existence, and yet it cannot 'be proved' (312).

These biases are, however, embodied in Section 28, a law instructing local authorities about how to contain the representation of openly gay cultural production. The legislation reads as follows:

1) A local authority shall not:
   a) Intentionally promote homosexuality or publish material with the intention of promoting homosexuality.
   b) Promote the teaching in any maintained school of the acceptability of homosexuality as a pretended family relationship.
2) Nothing in subsection 1 shall be taken to prohibit the doing of anything for the purpose of treating or preventing the spread of disease.
3) In any proceedings in connection with the application of this section a court shall draw such inferences as to the intention of the local authority as may reasonably be drawn from the evidence before it.
   (Section 28, Local Government Act 1988; qtd in *AYOR* 113)

The implications for culture, and for safe-sex pedagogy, are, as Jarman suggests, enormous. These governmental actions exemplify, perhaps, the 'rot' at the core of democracy, 'the deepening criminality of those who rule over us' (*MN* 54); in fact, Jarman reports his arguing in a television profile that 'Section 28 was an attack on the family,' reversing the supposition that his most important relationships are 'pretended' (75).[24]

Given the psychic consequences wrought by these entrenched – and, in the context of HIV infection and AIDS, panicked – social, medical, legislative, and economic structures, we might well start to feel befuddled as to how a record of such sadness comes to model reparation. Jarman's altered perspective estranges his view of the local environment, and in so doing it evokes as much despair as it does rage: 'Looking at the Ness through sick eyes I notice the burnt-out broom, the foxgloves that have disappeared, the stunted poppies in the bright dry sunlight' (288). Poppies, flower of remembrance, are stationed as

central to Jarman's 'personal mythology' at the beginning of
Modern Nature: 'A flower of cornfield and wasteland,' of unintended beauty, the poppy simultaneously represents 'the staff of
life' (bread) and remembrance of the dead, and is 'bringer of
dreams and sweet forgetfulness' (9). But here poppies are seen
as 'stunted': though they survive, their growth is arrested (8, 23).
As Jarman looks ahead, the future sometimes seems just as bleak
in its predetermination, with only the *number* of attacks on his
body in question: 'How many assaults will my body stand? At what
point will life cease to be bearable?' (304). Glancing back at this
crisis in *At Your Own Risk*, Jarman reflects that at first 'faced with
the prospect of writing about it [AIDS], I faltered; there were too
many stories I wanted to record ... All life became a problem, and
I solved this by shutting my physical self off like a clam. For a
while I could have been a model for the Conservative Family
Association' (83). Most unbearable is the fear of debilitation,
especially the looming spectre of blindness, something Jarman at
first dismisses (self-consciously) as not frightening, 'just aggravat-
ing – so silly to lose your eyes. I can write clearly and in straight
lines across the gloomy page' (307). The decision to take AZT is
set forth, like the decision to be tested for HIV in the first place,
in its full difficulty and uncertainty. Emphasizing the persistence
of the imperative to testify, and expressing frustration with the
numbing repetitiveness of his daily regimen, Jarman lists the pre-
scriptions he takes 'to the pharmacy: AZT, Ritafer, Pyroxidine,
Methamine, Folinic Acid, Triludan, Suylphadiazine, Carbamez-
epine' (313). The catalogue of drugs chimes in with the repetition of another kind of list, the (similarly expanding) list of the
names of friends who have died, and neither of these ritual reci-
tations is capable of guaranteeing a cure or even some kind of
reparation. That such inventories are deeply unsatisfying is corroborated by Jarman's reflection upon reading a biography of
Allen Ginsberg, which he describes disparagingly as 'a laundry
list of drugs and boyfriends,' a move that both recalls the ante-

cedent of gay liberation and prompts Jarman to mark his difference from that time, and from his own implication in it (237).
Despite the sense in which many of his identifications seem – to
follow Kristeva's analysis of borderline states – '"empty," "null,"
"devitalized," "puppet-like,"' Jarman's writing about his body
while he is hospitalized nonetheless highlights the continuity of
his experiences of pain and of desire (*Powers of Horror* 49).
Estrangement from his own body is foregrounded; it is as though
he has been 'snatched' by illness 'into its demon Disney World,
where chairs and tables dance and fight and the room swirls
about. Excruciating pain. Surely someone else is ill in bed with
catheters and drips' (*MN* 314). But his view 'through sick eyes,'
eyes that are variously described as 'itching' and 'drunken,' does
not merely empty out the world and the self (307, 310). That his
perspective on illness implicitly contests this distancing from his
own body, seeking, in fact, to claim it, in all its debilitation, as
capable of pleasure, work, and love, becomes evident in Jarman's
account of his surgery for an infected appendix:

My appendix was chopped out on Saturday, when they were sure it could
not be cured or calmed by antibiotics. I struggled out of the twilight with
a metal zip from top to bottom of my stomach. My traumatised guts,
spilled out on the operating table – so much offal – were now back in a
stomach taut as a balloon. I could not move, but lay for several days
staring ahead like a tin soldier, knocked for six. (314)

With the failure of drugs to effect a remedy, the punitive,
demonic underside of the medical narrative in which he finds
himself comes into clearer view. The surgical approach to dealing with illness, while it is not rejected out of hand, he experiences as immobilizing, objectifying, traumatizing. As the subtle
boundary of the skin is violated by the surgeon's instruments,
Jarman sees his own body as abject, his 'guts' as 'so much offal,' a
description that connotes both refuse and pollution. Subse-

quently, however, Jarman makes a point of reassuming the first-person pronoun: 'Ten days later I pick up a pen, my appetite lost for recording and writing. It's six months since I became ill. I've lost a stone and a half and the razor bumps across my face again' (314). Three gestures are presented as interdependent in these, the final words of the memoir: looking into the mirror, shaving, and picking up a pen. The possibility of assuming once more the work of a cultural producer is connected to a recollection of his body and, in particular, to facing loss of 'appetite' for any of this, and yet determining to enter the fray *again*. Reintroducing the marking of time, and at the same time stalling it in another dimension, Jarman hazards again his vulnerability to the powerful currents inherent in the dependency of subjectivation. The elliptical quality of Jarman's narration is far from being suggestive, then, of reticence, but asks us to read in a manner that disengages normative categories, to acknowledge the remainder that will not be dissolved: the legacy of his loving self-regard in the midst of ravaging illness.

The literally and metaphorically 'sick' body remains susceptible, however, to acts of exclusion and censorship. This vulnerability is especially evident in the recommendation by Jarman's editor that he remove the passages describing cruising on Hampstead Heath from the manuscript that would become *Modern Nature*, on the grounds that they might be read as promoting irresponsible behaviour.[25] Since for Jarman, as for Eric Michaels, 'Gayness remained emergent in social action, so that each night we seek to rediscover that identity by performing those rites of hyperexchange,' a certain 'psychic violence,' as Michaels points out, is inherent in 'the sad fact that I expect never again to engage in those caresses of the body which sustained and defined me for most of my adult life' (*Unbecoming* 58). In *Modern Nature*, the claiming of space – imaginative and 'real' – complements the claiming of an 'I' in the text in a manner that casts back to Jarman's autobiographical impulses prior to the context of AIDS. It is here that the extended passages describing Jarman's cruising on London's Hampstead Heath take on a crucial significance. What they substantiate is the continuing performance of the paradise that is suggested allegorically by Jarman's other gardens in the midst of the present, urban, social world.[26] Stating in exuberantly polemical terms that 'the alfresco fuck is the original fuck,' and that 'sex on the heath is an idyll pre-fall,' Jarman reports:

All the Cains and Abels you could wish for are out on a hot night, the May blossom scents the night air and the bushes glimmer like a phosphorescent counterpane in the indigo sky. Under the great beeches some boys with gypsy faces have lit a fire, which they stoke sending sparks flying, smiling faces flushed with the heat. In the dark for a brief moment age, class, wealth, all the barriers are down. An illusion you say, I know but what a sweet one. (83–4)

The passage is distinctly celebratory. These potential 'Cains and Abels' are restored to a prelapsarian moment, before the original sin and fear of sexuality associated with their heterosexual parents; specifically, they are liberated from the association of fratricide, which is linked in this context to the transmission of the HIV virus. But even as it tries to remake myth, Jarman's first-person testimony of what cruising on the Heath is really like in the context of the epidemic also works to demystify it: 'For those who know,' Jarman insists, 'the place has changed.' While its pleasures remain 'exciting and joyous,' they are marred by the absence of friends (84). Jarman's observations about the Heath emphasize how grassroots activism within the gay community has affected sexual practices, taking aim at the stubborn perception among those who identify as heterosexual that they are by definition not at risk for HIV, an assumption that dangerously clouds more important questions of sexual practices and precautions. In reality, 'Sex these days [on the Heath] is as safe as you'll find it, few risk penetration, it's mostly confined to what my mum would call "horseplay"' (84). Despite the clarity of these explanatory statements, as Jarman establishes by including as an appendix to *At*

Your Own Risk a series of letters originally published in the *Evening Standard*, there was a tendency for the press to interpret his public acknowledgment of visits to the Heath as contradicting efforts at HIV prevention (127).[27] On the contrary, as Jarman emphasizes in *At Your Own Risk*, in the 'early eighties ... there was a confusion in which we acted responsibly. All our energy was spent looking after friends and raising money. It was *we* who provided *you* with the information that may have saved *your* life' (84). In this connection, then, Jarman's memoir attempts to save sexuality by drawing attention to survival strategies generated at the community level: he strategically evokes a reworked vision of paradise as a world in which sex is consensual and explicitly negotiated.[28]

The project of demystification is deeply entwined, still, with the aim of celebrating the range of sexual practices that might be collected provisionally under the term 'queer.' And, as though to flout their editorially controversial inclusion in the text, Jarman's accounts of his experiences are bound together by the recognition of their excessive beauty – the 'sweetness' of the 'May blossom' and the 'indigo' sky – a recognition that refuses the logic of annihilation. Reading Jarman's performance of sexuality in the context of illness, we may note a subtle but remarkable shift in the significance of his melancholy. Jarman's testimony takes on the dimensions of love-melancholy, emphasizing his wrenching but inescapable fascination with the sensuous world. Even in the absence of a medical cure, regard for others and self-love prompt him to reject narratives founded in the protective promise of abjection, moving his outlook from one of despair and withdrawal to one that celebrates the possibility of continued engagement with the world, in work and in love.

Derek Jarman's Pedagogy

With the publication of *Modern Nature*, Jarman began to receive letters from all over the world, making him into a global literary phenomenon (Peake 479–80). And yet *Modern Nature* is emphatically 'local' and introspective in the sense that it is committed to recording daily life; the journals document both the beginnings of Jarman's garden at Prospect Cottage and his body's shift from non-symptomatic to symptomatic HIV. If *Modern Nature* has an educational, therapeutic, or what Sedgwick would call 'reparative' role to play, on a cultural stage vaster than Jarman's own life, then what precisely does it have to offer its diverse readership?[29] But the memoir's message is far from being simply consolatory. The positing of the garden as a pharmacopoeia – as a source of refuge, and of hope for a spiritual if not a bodily cure – is consistently questioned by Jarman. Rather, by opening up the forces of memory, and in particular by connecting his present experience of illness with his childhood and adolescent memories of education, *Modern Nature* pursues a radically *pedagogical* project – in a queerly provocative sense. Jarman's memoir, through its archaeological investigation of Jarman's personal history and its vision of nature in ruins, seeks to educate readers about what happens when moral panic about social hygiene takes the 'sex' out of education and about how we might rethink the education process in the interest of saving lives. As it searches for other models of education from the past, the diary at once partakes of and rewrites pastoral fantasies of the nation. Jarman wants to redeem an England he sees as lost and decayed, but confronts the recognition that his ideal world never existed except in fragments. Accordingly, he finds that he must work out a strategy for survival in light of his recognition of landscape, memory, and history as ruined and incomplete.

Increasingly in the late 1980s and early 1990s Jarman found that as one of 'the few [publicly] identifiable HIV+ men in the world' he was called upon to speak to questions of 'AIDS and civil liberties' outside as well as within the national British context (*MN* 251, *AYOR* 108). And while he reports frustration about trying to talk about 'responsibility when there is no information on

these matters, and none of our political parties will give a lead,'
the urgency of this project increased exponentially once his activism took an international turn (*AYOR* 5). For instance, Jarman's
documentation of his visit to Warsaw in February 1990 suggests
how his role as visiting film-maker was superseded by the need
for an HIV-positive spokesperson to address just-emerging activist
groups. With the recent democratization of the 'Second World,'
or at least its partial integration into the global circuit, the spread
of HIV rages.[30] And in Poland, the combined conditions of a
decayed infrastructure and Catholicism's prohibition against
condoms seemed to Jarman to render the project of taking
action next to impossible. As he reports:

The situation here is so desperate, there is literally no information and
the subject is treated completely negatively. The doctors won't contemplate treating people. One of the floors of a ministry has been invaded
by desperate people who are body positive. There are no syringes and
condoms are old-fashioned and not lubricated. At the moment there has
been no intervention by the government – perhaps they have so many
other problems that AIDS is marginalized. (245)

Should it surprise us that AIDS should be marginalized in the
former Second World when it is so pervasively sidelined in the
First World, while at the same time serving as a wide-screen for
the projection of cultural phobias? Still, Jarman's account is
effective in furthering the connection between illness and new
opportunities for state violence to impress itself upon the bodies
and minds of those labelled 'deviant' or 'delinquent' as against
an imagined 'general public.' In the Polish context, responsibility redounds on Jarman as a representative of the West: 'The only
hope is seen as coming from the West: funding from the World
Health Organization or Dutch gay groups' (245). But respond-
ing to this call has inherent risk as well: Jarman's trip to Poland,
his physical presence there as an advocate for seropositive people

and as a proponent of safer sex, brings him into contact, in an ironic and revealing twist, with a new flu virus (a bug he nicknames 'General Jaruzelski') that results in his hospitalization (*MN* 260). He thus brings home, in a strikingly literal, bodily way, the crisis he witnesses abroad.[31]

In many respects, Jarman displays considerable confidence in his autobiographical writings about what Peake summarizes as Jarman's self-conceived role as 'prophet,' 'spokesman,' 'cultural irritant,' and 'Controversialist' (319–20, 533). But what makes his sadness so persistent is the connection he sees between his losses to AIDS and the losses and exclusion he experienced in his youth. *Modern Nature*'s project is, at least in part, to provide a context for considering the significance of the childhood memories that are being unleashed in the context of illness. My sense is that Jarman's recollection of several scenes of education from his early years become a platform for his more general, wide-reaching criticisms of the failure of traditional, punitive modes of education, and sex education in particular, positively to address human desire and pleasure in the full diversity of the forms they take.

Revisiting what it was like to live under a cultural regime that he could barely even recognize as repressive, Jarman contends in retrospect that he lived his 'adolescence so demoralised [he] became reclusive' (*AYOR* 32). Sustained throughout his autobiographical writings and films are a series of pointed and plaintive criticisms of his experiences in English public schools during the 1950s, criticisms that contradict the response of gratitude that his parents by all accounts expected for the sacrifices they made to pay for his elite education. Jarman tries to bring into focus the damage he feels was inflicted by his education along with the privileges it also afforded him. His critique of his education is encapsulated in the repeated detail of his father 'proudly present[ing] me with a complete set of receipts on my twenty-first' birthday (*MN* 58). As Jarman notes with unmistakable sarcasm, 'Paradise Perverted was intended to set us up for life –

dimly perceived as starting some time after our eighteenth' (59).
With this epithet 'Paradise Perverted,' he deploys the label 'perverse' against the system that would define him as not normal
and as a threat to the category of normality, preparing readers
for his remembering of the system's baroquely interested and
complex strategies for containing sexuality: 'To divert us from
the temptations of the flesh a muddy, muscular "christianity" was
employed – "healthy body, healthy mind"' (59). What are the
consequences of this situation but the continuation of repression
by the subjects of this education themselves, in the form of various cruelties and exclusions? Jarman, like other British film-
makers of his generation such as Terence Davies and Lindsay
Anderson, pinpoints the connection between this prohibitive system and systemic violence among the pupils: 'Smarting under
this tortured system, the boys tortured each other, imposed val-
ueless rules and codes of conduct, obeyed imaginary hierarchies
where accidents of origin and defects of nature were magnified'
(58). Later Jarman poses an emphatic riposte to these assumptions, setting it apart from the flow of the anecdote: 'Could all of
this conceivably be thought "a normal upbringing"?' (58). This
question initiates a process of re-education that highlights the
pathological, even perverse, displacement of sexuality motivating
the public school system's passion for discipline. Gardening and
painting, by contrast, he sought out and nurtured, only a little
knowingly, as markers of his difference from the heterosexual
norm. So, while 'on holiday, he [his father] sailed – I pruned the
apple trees' (192).[32]

Jarman's approach to representing his childhood memories
provides a clue as to how we might re-imagine sex education in
order to salvage sex and education. Turning the tables on the
rhetoric of 'healthy body, healthy mind' is particularly urgent in
the context of HIV/AIDS because of the sense in which, as
Edmund White observes, the epidemic 'repatriates' gay men to
'lonely adolescence,' to 'the time when I was alone with my writ-

ing and I felt weird about being a queer' (69). In her work on queer pedagogy, Deborah Britzman meditates on the classroom as a site where subjectivity and identities are formed, tested, and, potentially at least, creatively reconfigured. I refer to Britzman's important work (which is less well known than it ought to be) because it brings the problems of exorcism and triumphalist mourning to bear on the realm of education and the conceptualization of childhood sexuality. She foregrounds the classroom as a political space, one that is implicated in the social production of normality, and suggests that the central question in re-imagining education is how 'to provoke conditions of learning that might allow for an exploration that unsettles the sediments of what one imagines when one imagines normalcy, what one imagines when one imagines difference' (95).[33] Indeed, even as they are implicated in an overwhelming and problematic nostalgia for a male homosocial world of cultural privilege, Jarman's stories of education also claim a remarkably provocative role, as they ask readers – indeed, demand us – to think differently about difference. The diary effects this demand through the fragmentation and recontextualization produced by the forces of melancholic attachment.

Multiple retellings of certain educational encounters over the course of Jarman's several memoirs - written and visual – suggest their significance in addition to their continuing power to wound.[34] Jarman's technique of recording bits and pieces of stories that amuse or console him, and then glossing them with a contextualizing 'essay' that 'tampers' with the memory in order to release its more unruly side, is well captured in this entry in *Modern Nature* for 23 February 1989. In this anecdote, Jarman recounts the myth of the god Apollo's love for the boy Hyacinth, going on to observe:

We learnt nothing of the love myth of these heroes in a Dorset school in the 1950s – Ovid was off-limits. Instead we marched to the beat of Cae-

sar's interminable *Gallic Wars*. The Latin teacher Mr. Gay (long before
this word had any connotations except joyful abandon) confined himself to *'we undertook a forced march of 80 miles and set up camp.'* – Are you
listening Jarman? ...

> *bellum, bellum, bellum*
> Ancient history was an interminable war. All violence and
>   no sex.
> *bellum, bellum* – No *amo, amas.*

Surfacing in the first section of the memoir (winter/spring 1989)
and then again towards the end of *Modern Nature*, these memories
of Jarman's schooling provide us with a retrospective narrative in
the midst of a fragmented text, but the story is far from nostalgic.
Like the descriptions of the 'demon Disney World' of hospitalization, or the passages documenting (and attempting to demystify)
cruising on Hampstead Heath, we might call the passage 'ethnographic' in that it documents and attempts to tease out the power
relations that structure a certain place, time, and cultural milieu.
The above passage records what the curriculum consisted of and
what it excluded. In particular, Jarman emphasizes the gap
between two accounts of history – a queer account and a military
account – with the suggestion that the former might disrupt the
latter, which would focus exclusively on the expression of violence. Jarman thus suggests that the violence and mystique of military culture, and of imperialist views of the nation, are rooted in
the repression of love between men. Subsequently, the passage is
also reflective, critical, and anxious, moving us (subsequently)
towards recognition of the adolescents' frustration, searching in
desperation through an expurgated copy of a novel, *Lady Chatter-
ley's Lover,* which they've heard is 'dirty' but is in fact edited in a
way that removes precisely what they are curious about. This
scene of education was particularly resonant for Jarman in the
context of Section 28, which, as I mentioned earlier, exhorted
local authorities to block public funding and support for any
material (in the arts and in the classroom) that would 'intention-

ally promote homosexuality' or even suggest its 'acceptability.' In this logic, visibility is equivalent to advertising, the speech act to an act of seduction, and therefore any references to same-sex desire must be narrated in the mode of panic as protection. Although the legislators' attempt to make the point that 'nothing' in this set of regulations 'shall be taken to prohibit the doing of anything for the purpose of treating or preventing the spread of disease,' the logic that conflates 'homosexuality' with 'disease' reveals the homophobia that undergirds the surface posture of 'tolerance.' This legislation – a formal articulation of the kinds of cultural biases I will be discussing apropos several different but overlapping national contexts, American, Antiguan, and Australian, as well as British – served to heighten Jarman's rage against the 'debris' of governmental denial and 'inaction' (20). The ironic juxtapositions of his school memories with these present details highlight the continuation of 1950s-style censorship and misinformation in the present – with television, for example, which will only show Jarman's films late at night and feeds the public with 'loathsome inept youth-orientated arts programme[s] which dro[p] any issue before [they have] picked it up. Devalues everything, all ideas, all values' (82).

The journal entry adds to this account of censorship a description of how sex education proper was dealt with in the schools Jarman attended, emphasizing how the students' curiosity prompted them to read reparatively, for the sustenance they required, figuring out for themselves, too, the unacknowledged motivations of adults. According to Jarman, he and his fellow students were thus able to obtain from the distorted lectures to which they were subjected some of what they needed to know, although no adult had taken on the responsibility 'to teach us, or love us':

Dr. Matthews rummaged in his battered Gladstone bag, pulling out ancient slides as if from a lucky dip at a gymkhana. Silver hair awry, eyes glistening, the dirty old sex educator to the crowned heads of Europe eyed his blushing audience who squirmed with embarrassment as their innermost secrets were revealed to them – huge images of private parts, 20 ft pubescent and pre-pubescent cocks, balls dropping, huge lost sperms wandering into a slide rather than the fallopian.

Sections, diagrams. Our secrets were invaded, as when the doctor grabbed your balls in the first school medical and twizzled them about before letting the elastic of your pants snap back with a sting. 'What,' asked Dr. Matthews 'are little boys made of?' – 'Slugs and snails and puppy dog's tails.' (63)

As Britzman reminds us, when it began to be formally constituted as a component of adolescent education at the beginning of the twentieth century, sex education became '*the* site for working on the bodies of children, adolescents, and teachers' in order to rid them of 'problems,' defined as any failure to conform to an increasingly rigidly defined norm (67). Observe the stinginess of the positions being carved out and assigned in Jarman's story of Dr Matthews: boys are taught self-loathing, and queer kids that their desires are 'problems' (*MN* 63). Jarman's anecdote conveys the violence and voyeurism of this scenario, with its invasion of secrets and its blurring of the scientific and the mythic. At the same time, though, the journal's return to this scene disinters the expurgated knowledge hiding behind the 'glistening eyes' of the 'dirty old sex educator.' In a sense, then, we relearn the story of sex education as *Modern Nature* stages the return of the repressed, pulling to the surface of the text interpretive possibilities that have been excluded from the story of sex education.[35] While the lasciviousness of Dr Matthews is subjected to a parodic (and critical, I think) reiteration, another reading of the educator is also made possible, for Jarman attributes to Dr Matthews a sexuality that exceeds the bounds of the message of utility he preaches – after all, someone is responsible for the fact that the sperm is on the slide, mysteriously astray from its 'proper' receptacle. Jarman, future pioneer of Super-8 film-making, reads the sex educator's use of visuals as home movies, even taking from them perhaps a kind of model. One film-maker and sex educator teaches another who would go on to become a film-maker and a sex re-educator.[36] The spectre of the masturbating boy thus reappears in the person of the authority figure himself, who starts to appear as a kind of revenant. Thus, the Greek pederastic scene – of initiator/initiated – haunts this memory, invoking the spectre of another imagined, idealized school. More generally, though, the point of the anecdote is to foreground how sex and desire circulate even when they are not acknowledged: Would it not be more responsible to address and articulate these desires (however fractured they must remain), rather than thinking we might pretend them away? It is precisely this 'not yet tolerated' approach to sex education, Jarman is implying, that might address difference and desire without invoking a policy of correction (Britzman 68).[37]

Despite the humour of these scenes, there is a 'feeling of trapped unease' (*MN* 21) that follows Jarman from such early experiences, and this feeling now threatens to overwhelm him in the face of the loss of his friends and his own illness. Its source is revealed by his father's injunction against his perceived weakness and tears: 'Don't be such a pansy, Derek' (29). Echoing Dr Matthews's offer to assist 'any boy who felt he had a problem,' Lance Jarman's words wield the adage of a 'muscular, muddy christianity': 'healthy body, healthy mind.' Childhood memories, if they are to serve the function of sustaining rather than sabotaging Jarman, must be recontextualized. Indeed, the juxtaposition of such reconfigured anecdotes with other fragments, the stories of flowers, of herbs, and with medical language, figures prominently among the diary's rhetorical strategies. And it is in this way that painful memories are interrogated from within, reconfigured to form a 'personal mythology' that refuses to settle accounts: 'A personal mythology recurs in my writing, much the same way poppy wreaths have crept into my films. For me this archeology has become obsessive, for the "experts" my sexuality is a confusion. All received information should make us inverts sad. But before I finish I intend to celebrate our corner of Paradise, the part the Lord forgot to mention' (23). Jarman attempts to construct a concept of paradise hospitable to his desires. But his version of pastoral is always accompanied by a sense of the vision's contingency. This mixture of celebration and circumspection is evident, for example, in Jarman's reiteration of his father's words, in the context of a friend's administering of herbal remedies as well as companionship: 'Pink pansies,' he pronounces, 'are good for you' (217). The impertinent recycling of education resounds throughout Jarman's corpus of film and is especially resonant in *The Garden* (1990), the film whose making Jarman documents in *Modern Nature*. The leering schoolmasters in *The Garden*, a restaging of Genesis, with their chorus of rapping canes, parallel the police who torture the male couple and the infernal Santas who taunt and crucify them. Likewise, scenes of punitive, demoralizing education predominate in *Wittgenstein* (1993), where the brilliant philosopher's relation to the world is shown to be so damaged by his own experiences of education that he cannot teach, but only pass on the brutalization he experienced as a child.

A particularly painful and difficult-to-assimilate memory for Jarman involves being discovered in bed with another boy at boarding school:

The idiot who betrayed us was the one who thought that if he masturbated his brains would spurt out. They prized his hands from my tight cock and left us to shiver naked in the cold at the foot of the bed. We were hauled out of our element and left to asphyxiate by the Noes.

'Christ! What are you doing?' 'You'll go blind!'

Then the blows rained down, millennia of frustrated Christian hatred behind the cane. What a terrible God to take on the hurt and then hurt us all! That day a childhood idyll died in the bells and sermons, the threats to tell our parents and derision; and we were shoved into the wilderness they had created, and commanded to punish ourselves for all time. So that at last we would be able to enter their heaven truly dead in spirit. (50–1)

While, in the first example, the adult Jarman voices a series of ironic questions that reconstruct the teenager's hypothetical knowledge, this passage captures a child's inchoate desires and confusion in the face of punishment. Jarman presents the impulse to explore sexuality as integrally connected to the imagination, curiosity, spirit, and desire of children, and so we are drawn into a critical view of the pathologization of children's sexuality. As Sedgwick argues, suggesting that there exists a link between this pathologization of childhood desires and Western culture's homosexual panic, 'the scope of institutions whose programmatic undertaking is to prevent the development of gay people is unimaginably large,' and 'effeminate boys' are particularly vulnerable to this 'war,' perhaps to the extent that they constitute 'the haunting abject of gay thought itself' ('How to Bring Your Kids Up Gay' 161, 157).

The most powerfully uncanny connection lies, again, though, in the way the words of adults resound in the present context, linking childhood losses with present ones: 'Christ! What are you doing? You'll go blind' (51). It is this curse, so full of performative power, that condemns the boys to suffering, not their actions. In the larger context of the memoir, Jarman discovers that he is afflicted with AIDS-related cytomegalovirus, an eye infection leading to blindness; and in 1990 he suffered a significant loss of sight. But his overwhelming determination remains to celebrate 'how happy I am' (168). Spurning the 'neurotic anxiety' that such an incident might instil (that is, the tendency to internalize the normalizing point of view that would lead to self-blame), Jarman's retelling of the anecdote creates an occasion, instead, for anxiety of a more 'existential' kind in order to articulate two linked agendas (Britzman 68). First, VD loses its status as 'the old serpent'; what wrecks the idyll in this recasting of Genesis are the cruel curses of the pedagogues, the amateurs as well as the professionals. Second, the anecdote emphasizes that childhood sexuality be considered as impossible to define in any easy or totalizing way and that memories of desire in childhood are intractable to being evaluated according to an unreflective concept of normality. Resisting the reconstruction of his childhood self as 'innocent,' devoid of sexuality, then, Jarman's retelling quietly preserves the ambiguous eroticism of the event, the way in which the memory survived all of that 'hatred' after all. That he survived the hatred of his school years fuels his determination to survive HIV infection and AIDS with his self-love similarly intact.

These memories of education continue to return, however, over the two-year period covered by *Modern Nature*, suggesting that however much Jarman has been able to disarticulate the system that sought to punish him, they remain unresolved. It is the unpredictability of memory as a force that gives this memoir its dynamism and fuels its critique. The openness of the journals to the complications of memory is crucial to Jarman's offering of his own experiences as a source of information for others, as an ambiguously exemplary personal genealogy of desire, and particularly, in the time of AIDS, as a warning against the dangers of euphemism in sex education. He writes a fragmented, memory-ridden text that actively shapes the reading practices by which his potential audience consumes the stories. Readers of Jarman's autobiographical writings are actively encouraged to resist collaborating in what Sedgwick describes as the 'nightmarish overdeterminations' ('Gender Criticism' 286) that equate HIV and AIDS with death, and with 'diseased' sexuality. Constructed as curious, and acknowledged as anxious, readers of *Modern Nature* become Jarman's students, impertinent scholars of his 'fragments of memory.' We are urged to consider a new future for sex and for education, even though that hope for the future, as Jarman's rage, pain, and doubt insist, exists only as torn and improvisatory.

CHAPTER TWO

Queering the Kaddish
Amy Hoffman's *Hospital Time*
and the Practice of Critical Memory

A white woman wearing white: the ruly ordinariness of this sight makes invisible
the corrosive aggression that white also is: as the blaze of mourning, the opacity of
loss, the opacity loss installs within ourselves and our vision, the unreconciled
and unreconcilably incendiary energies streaming through that subtractive gap,
that ragged scar of meaning, regard, address.

— Eve Kosofsky Sedgwick, 'White Glasses' (255)

Melancholia as Critical Memory

Amy Hoffman divides her memoir *Hospital Time,* which testifies
to her friendship with Mike Riegle, into four sections that appear
to move readers through a linear pattern, from an initial section
entitled *Living with AIDS,* to Mike's decline in *Memphis Stories,* to
his death in *Mike Dies and Is Laid to Rest,* and, finally, to *The After-*
life.[1] But although its narrative architecture corresponds to the
working through of grief, *Hospital Time* is thoughtfully and painfully confused about what it means to write 'to the memory of'
her friend and colleague, Mike Riegle, in the wake of his death.
This confusion is connected to Hoffman's uncertainty about
whether she was a dutiful and loving friend, a scepticism that is,
in turn, linked to her feeling overwhelmed by the extremity of

the devastation of AIDS and the lack of a public register for her grief. Commenting on another friend's certainty about having fulfilled her obligation to Mike, Hoffman registers her own anxiety: 'She and others have no doubt that their presence at his bedside made a difference to him, a great difference – whereas I sat with him too, every day, but I don't know' (124). While written from the perspective of a witness rather than offering a first-hand account, Hoffman's memoir nonetheless shares with Jarman's diary a preoccupation with grief, mourning, and practices of memorialization, as well as a self-critical and wondering attitude towards telling a personal story about living with AIDS.

Hospital Time's characteristic affective register is one of bewilderment, which often veers into self-excoriation by the autobiographical narrator, born out of her feeling that faithful grief would be characterized by clarity. Distinguishing melancholia from the work of mourning, the work that produces closure and reintegrates the individual into the reality principle governing daily life, Freud characterized melancholia as emptying the ego of energy, leaving the individual incapable of functioning in a normal way and full of self-loathing as a result of this incapacity.[2] Certainly this understanding of melancholia resonates with the way Hoffman describes her own position as a caregiver:

I was overwhelmed, it was all too much for me, how could it not have been? I wanted to run away, I wanted it to be over. I'm sorry. I wish, I wish, I wish *every single day* that I had been more genuinely kind, more open and loving and freely generous. Although if it happened again, someone I know having AIDS – and it has, it will – I'd do it again and feel the same, because that's what AIDS does, the fucker. (22; emphasis in original)

Repetition, apology, and a sense of entrapment characterize this passage: Hoffman seems to feel at once victimized and unworthy. As Ross Chambers suggests in his study of early French modernist writing, melancholy manifests itself in narrative as a relentless interrogation of certainty that 'decentres' and 'vaporizes' speaking subjects, banishing them to the 'drift of signifiers' in 'a world given over to change, without beginning or end' (*The Writing of Melancholy* 33, 168). Such disorientation is not exclusive to Hoffman's text, but is shared by other testimonial writing about HIV/AIDS, as I will explore as this study unfolds.

Do the sadness, despair, and confusion of Hoffman's text imply a capitulation to the emotional drainage produced by the lack of an audience for her testimony? And why indulge in a personal memoir, focusing on a particular private experience, especially when language is so demonstrably impoverished, as Hoffman's despairing epithet ('AIDS ... the fucker') implies? If the perspective is one committed to politicizing AIDS, in other words, why not write an account in the manner of an 'epidemiological' narrative, if not in the form of a critical essay?[3] A conversation Hoffman records in *The Afterlife* indicates the emotions as well as the sense of obligation that have motivated her choice to write a memoir about her experience as Mike's friend and caregiver, alerting readers, I want to suggest, to the activist context of Hoffman's writing, a context that, significantly, includes her work (and Mike Riegle's) for the Boston paper *Gay Community News*. In response to her friend Kevin's objection that grief is irrelevant, even a waste of energy, that 'every AIDS funeral should be a massive protest march,' Hoffman queries: '"Protest march against whom?" I said. "To where? It's a virus"' (105). The debate, prompted by their friend Bob's funeral, took place, Hoffman admits, prior to 'the real heyday of ACT-UP, before people began chaining themselves to the FDA and blockading the Brooklyn Bridge during rush hour and fantasizing about secret squads of PWA suicide saboteurs – before that guy dumped his coffin on the White House lawn' (105), and by listing these strategies, she does display a certain respect for them. But Hoffman still objects to the proposition that personal grief must at some point be set aside so that it does not compromise political aims. Instead, she insists on the value of individual experience: 'For a minute, Kevin, can't it just be us? Not hundreds of thousands of AIDS cases worldwide, but just this one person, here in this bed, quietly dying?' (106). These statements, far from being an endorsement of 'quietly dying,' ask for an expansion of the possible range of what it means to be 'at odds with AIDS' (Düttmann), at odds with a virus and with the at once pervasive and elusive, indeed virulent, homophobia of the culture at large.

Hospital Time thus responds to – and interrogates – the mourning versus activism debate articulated by Douglas Crimp and, furthermore, suggests how blurred are the boundaries that supposedly make activism 'critical' and art 'pathetic' or 'pathological' (see Introduction). Indeed, the refusal of recognition for individual deaths may mean that these deaths will never be allowed material specificity but remain, rather, statistics, part of the narrative calculus that characterizes public health discourse and media renditions of the AIDS epidemic, part of 'the overarching, hygienic Western fantasy of a world without any more homosexuals in it,' as Eve Sedgwick startlingly states (*Epistemology of the Closet* 42). As Lee Edelman argues in *Homographesis*, if majority culture reiterates AIDS in terms of 'a linear narrative progressing ineluctably from a determinate beginning to a predetermined end,' then activism may risk corroborating the panic logic of majority culture when it 'defines itself against the "narcissism" and "passivity" that figure the place of gay male sexuality in the Western cultural imaginary' (89, 117).[4] In this context, Hoffman's pleading acknowledgment of 'just this one person, here in this bed' identifies her resistance to making peace with the AIDS deaths she has witnessed. Resistance to making peace is articulated in terms of a determination – indeed, a duty – to set herself to the impossible task of doing justice to the particularity of this man, her friend, at the moment of his illness and dying. Like Sedgwick, though, as she looks at the AIDS quilt and thinks about her relation to Michael Lynch in 'White Glasses,' a vertiginous mixture of feelings and thoughts ripple through Hoffman's mind as she reflects on the project of memorialization: the rush of wanting this justice and knowing that each attempt homogenizes and erases to the precise extent it remembers. Duty and obligation are inextricably bound up with the needs, emotions, doubts of the mourner, creating a double bind for the project of memorializing: the task is at once as unstable as it is imperative. Hoffman's memoir – concerned as much with her own emotions as it is with Mike Riegle or with the larger questions of AIDS and its representations – adumbrates what Sedgwick calls, writing of another friend, Craig Owens, 'this strange, utterly discontinuous space of desire euphemistically named friendship' ('Memorial for Craig Owens' 105).

In light of the way that *Hospital Time* foregrounds activism as perhaps its chief context, and considering how it highlights the entanglement of the duty to mourn faithfully with outrage, disbelief, and a desire for it all to be over, it would surely be a serious misreading to see Hoffman as merely caught in a temporary delusional or self-indulgent state. Recent rereadings of Freud on mourning and melancholia in light of *The Ego and the Id* have shifted the concept of melancholia away from the realm of the pathological to indicate both its status as a founding dynamic of subjectivity and its potential as a kind of critical memory. Modified from its earlier uses in psychoanalysis, the concept of melancholia can provide a precise and critically powerful way of describing this condition of response and of adumbrating the text's somewhat oblique approach to ethics, politics, and representation.[5] *Hospital Time*'s melancholic orientation complicates the politicization of AIDS by insisting that the representation of Mike Riegle, and of those who surrounded him in his life and in his death, remain unresolved and critical, and that our strategies for reading him live up to this rigorous standard of irresolution. Hoffman's memoir foregrounds the melancholic incorporation of the other in the self, but, I want to argue, it does this in a way that is often quite opposed to the consumption or 'devouring' of the other in the mourning process, and opposed, too, to the possibility of relinquishing attachment by bringing grief to a conclusion. 'Since the moment he died,' reflects Hoffman, 'I've taken him with me everywhere' (78). The image is less one of 'devouring' than it is a matter of an unrelinquishable bond, or even of stewardship. In a sense, she takes the role of a custodian, lifting or carrying a child. But if Mike is a burden she struggles to lift, he is a strangely weightless, impossible one, and one she does not elect or choose to carry: he is impossible to refuse lifting, but impossible to lift. Hoffman cannot seem to detach herself from Mike, and she is not speaking of 'his memory' per se but of his unending haunting of her.

As Derrida elaborates over the course of several essays, death produces a contradictory licence for representing and for mourning other people, where the project is at once mandatory, forbidden, and impossible. If mourning, as the working through and normalization of loss, entails the interiorization of an idealized image of the other, and hence a smoothing out and a forgetting, melancholia or 'impossible mourning' designates the impossibility of such closure, insisting instead, as Derrida summarizes, on a 'tendency to accept incomprehension' and to adopt 'those modes of language' that would 'deny the whole rhetoricity of the true' (*Memoires* 31). In his preface to Nicholas Abraham and Maria Torok's study of encryption in *The Wolf Man's Magic Word*, Derrida insists that the 'breakdown' or suspension produced by melancholia is connected to the unlocatable substance of the loss that is being grieved:

The referent is constructed in such a way as never to present itself 'in person,' not even as the object of a theoretical discourse within the traditional norms. The Thing is encrypted. Not *within* the crypt (the Self's safe) but *by* the crypt and *in* the Unconscious. The 'narrated' event, reconstituted by a novelistic, mytho-dramatico-poetic genesis, never appears. ('Fors' xxvi)

Although 'everything' appears to 'remain' '"in me" or "in us," "between us,"' that sense of possession is an illusory one (*Memoires* 33). If the crypt disguises or hides a body (or, to use Hoffman's phrasing, involves 'taking' or 'carrying' a body), thus preserving it, the crypt is (paradoxically) not a location: it is impossible for us to find, let alone read. Because it is structured in the first place by loss and disavowal of loss, this knowledge is not available to reading, or to fully successful exorcism. Encryption occurs beyond our control: it is performed not by the individual as a rational, conscious act but rather '*by* the crypt and *in* the Unconscious' ('Fors' xxvi). As Butler suggests of Abraham and Torok's theory, confirming these implications, 'incorporation is not only a failure to name or avow the loss, but erodes the conditions of metaphorical signification itself' (*Gender Trouble* 68). Hoffman's statement that she takes Mike with her everywhere camps out on the border of figurative language and cold enumeration, a seemingly literalized but actually cryptic not-quite-metaphor that is at once fanciful and truthful, an index of her 'incomprehension.' In the final section of *Hospital Time*, which is entitled *The Afterlife*, and should, according to the model of mourning as working through, provide resolution, the puzzlement over the way memory encrypts the dead is only augmented. All she can profess to 'believe in' is 'memory,' the belief that 'you carry the person within you, and thus he lives, as part of you and yours' (104). Yet she meditates, too, on her frustrations with the unreliability and opacity of memory, with its 'cold substance,' its 'pits, faults, abysses, volcanoes,' its inability to make the dead 'present' and fully readable, all of which make this sense of 'holding' the dead so that they 'live' problematic: If Mike lives, then where is he? And why does he not speak? (91, 104).[6]

In this connection, we may move productively through psychoanalysis towards an ethical, political, and rhetorical examination of the intonation of Hoffman's AIDS memoir. By what force is the impulse to idealize the lost other held in suspension? Melancholic attachment to the grieved object prompts the rejection of the compensatory options offered by the symbolic; in the refusal of compensation, the loss itself is perhaps refused, reversing the disavowal of love upon which the concept of mourning as completed grief depends. For instance, the repeated refusal of catharsis is a telling index of the way in which mourning confronts its own impossibility in *Hospital Time*. Hoffman's memories of the reality of Mike's pain, dementia, and humiliation prevent her from releasing herself from the suspicion that she did not really help him, did not really do anything to alleviate his suffering. Recalling the task of doing Mike's laundry on one of the occasions when he is afflicted with diarrhea, Hoffman notes how 'I berated myself alternately for being too fastidious and for not protecting myself with latex gloves' (54). As Urvashi Vaid emphasizes in her foreword to *Hospital Time*, the 'shit-stained' (xiv), painful reality of his body's decline is never put peaceably aside, but is carried around, oddly lovingly, by the witness. Refusing to relinquish its burden, and taking on all of its heaviness, leakiness, even opacity, *Hospital Time* mobilizes what William Haver calls in his book about social relations in the time of AIDS 'the primordially *erotic* historico-socio-*politicality* of the body' against 'the (entirely fantasmatic) clean and proper body politic' (*The Body of This Death* 7). While the lack of clarity in this relation may seem to contradict activism's imperative to action, consideration of how these passionate attachments are lived by survivors may be one of the conditions of a more fundamental kind of opposition to AIDS. If, as Haver argues, the fantasy of the 'clean and proper body politic' 'is maintained only in the processes of the exclusion of an expendable social surplus comprised of people and peoples of color, sex workers, IV drug users, and queers' (7), then it may be precisely this stigmatized and excluded 'social surplus' that calls to be addressed. And if memory encrypts what is lost in death, it also preserves the lost other and our libidinal attachment to it, although the conditions for the survival of love seem to be confusion and anxiety.

By speaking to a particular situation – Amy Hoffman's relationship with Mike Riegle – *Hospital Time* attests to the overwhelming force of grief and to the ethical and political considerations it compels when it remains unresolved and unresolvable. These considerations have, in turn, a bearing on the mode of storytelling in which the memoir engages. Initially known to one another socially and as colleagues, Hoffman and Mike were not close friends until the time of his illness, when, to her surprise, she made a commitment to participate in his care. In the intensity of Hoffman's immediate witnessing of Mike's illness there emerges an unsolicited, uncontainable intimacy. Questions of responsibility now abound: Hoffman is reluctant to usurp Mike's prerogative to author his own story, and yet in his absence she is compelled, at the same time, to create some kind of public record. This task of representation is especially urgent, and especially problematic, in the context of the 'socially-produced' trauma of AIDS (Crimp, qtd in Caruth and Keenan 541), for, because of the stigmatization of both AIDS and homosexuality, the epidemic generates, as Thomas Keenan explains, 'a double trauma': 'On the one hand there's a cataclysmic event, which produces symptoms and calls for testimony, and then it happens again, when the value of the witness in the testimony is denied, and there's no one to hear the account, no one to attend or respond – not simply to the event, but to its witness as well' (Keenan, qtd in Caruth and Keenan 541). *Hospital Time*'s peculiar playing of rhetoric against structure stages a melancholic politics of recontextualization. Furthermore, it self-consciously raises a number of provocative questions about the ethical and political dimensions of its status as a *gendered* text of grief.

Recollecting Mike

As a memoir preoccupied with recording the experience of witnessing another's death as well as with memorializing the dead,
Hospital Time responds to several conflicting but equally strong
imperatives: the imperative to allow Mike's life and death scope
for meaning and recognition, and the imperative not to foreclose meaning, or to play into discourses that would homogenize,
even when the survivor's desire for such closure is most pressing
and finally irresistible. Addressing these paradoxical demands,
Hoffman adopts, through her memoir's melancholic obsessive-
ness about the status of her love for Mike, through her willingness to engage what she refers to as the 'messy' details of Mike's
life, death, and afterlife (91), a mode of critical memory that
contests her own and others' potential complacency about what
it means to remember him. Through its hesitancy about such retrospective reconstruction, *Hospital Time* balances between the
tendency to assume that Mike – or at least his memory – has
become the narrator's possession and the tendency to 'abort' or
'renounce' such 'interiorizations,' with the necessity for what
Derrida calls 'tender rejection' of the other moving to the foreground, even as Hoffman recognizes the way in which Mike
maintains *his* hold on *her* (35). In *Hospital Time,* potential
responses to Mike's death unfold along multiple trajectories:
we are confronted with Hoffman's memories of Mike, Mike's
hypothesized posthumous responses to Hoffman, and the readings of both of them by other friends in their circle. At the same
time, we are also regularly reminded of the larger context of the
memoir as a public text to be read by strangers. Readers are thus
also drawn into *Hospital Time*'s vertiginous social and self-
questioning. So situated, anger, guilt, and self-berating fuel the
practice of critical memory and yield criticism of the pattern of
containment that has characterized mainstream American culture's response to AIDS.

Throughout the memoir, and especially towards the end, Hoffman speaks against the impulse to beautify, and thereby to sanctify Mike's death, to distil from the relation a too easy wisdom. The fourth and final section of the memoir, *The Afterlife*, far from putting Mike to rest, and far from assuming that Hoffman's memoir can fully account for his life and death as it moves towards a conclusion, registers his continuing presence as an elusive force, as a textual remainder similar in its disruptive, confounding effects to that of Jarman's evocation of his 'ghostly presence' or 'ghostly eye' (*AYOR* 9). The memoir's preface on the topic of 'hospital time' prepares us from the beginning for the irresolution of the final sections. Waiting for Mike to die, Hoffman finds that time suddenly fails, is suspended: 'Nothing's happening – or maybe it's that everything is happening, or is about to' (3). With this recognition, her perspective changes, as she entertains the possibility that this experience of 'Eternity' is 'the real thing,' and 'your vigor, your life outside,' is by contrast 'an affront' (5); more than that, it comes to seem 'utterly frivolous, the world and its stupid time' (5). Writing, moreover, in the second person in this section, addressing the reader as 'you,' Hoffman interpellates readers of *Hospital Time* into this dislocated point of view.

In addition, the memoir's conspicuously conventional linear structure is foregrounded through the use of subtitles only to be undermined by the fragmented and repetitious nature of Hoffman's recollections. This deliberate contradiction advertizes the memoirist's inconsolability, while at the same time demonstrating the pressure that exists to achieve proper mourning. The first two sections of the book focus largely on giving voice to these disjunctions. Mike desires agency, and this desire manifests itself in his attempts to escape his local environment, to be on the move and so, perhaps, to escape his illness. But travel does not provide him with respite – in fact, it only exacerbates his and Hoffman's suffering. On holiday in Provincetown, plans for a relaxing day at the beach fall apart because 'we had forgotten that he was sick' (37), and later, in Memphis, when Mike collapses changing planes en route to visit a friend in Austin, we see the illusion of normalcy finally crack open: Mike and Hoffman are both '*hospital/ized*' (as his companion she is given a place to stay in the hospital), and they now 'wait' for death 'like the damned' (45, 50; emphasis in original). Forgetting Mike's illness has not really happened, of course, only the pretence of forgetting; this repression itself is a strange, destabilizing disavowal in a text that so complicates the distinction between recollection and forgetting.

Even more, perhaps, than with Jarman's representation of the hospital in *Modern Nature*, Mike's and Hoffman's experience of hospitalization makes visible the ways in which they are subjected to and by institutional discourses of disease and illness, a situation that makes it difficult to maintain a stance of ironical opposition. If a prison imprisons, a hospital 'hospitalizes,' producing not only medical treatments but a certain inflection of subjectivity – a more palpably subjected subject, one less capable of articulating an attitude of resistance (as Jarman believes he is capable of sustaining) to the hospital's denuding narrative of its own beneficent helpfulness. Hoffman observes that 'the bed is narrow, the patient bristling with needles, electrodes, and other ICU accoutrements that must not be displaced' (4), making this body perhaps not unlike a butterfly collector's specimen pinned awkwardly and subjected to the possessive gazing of an enquiring expert. This vulnerable body is prone to being misread. Doctors in suburban Memphis, perceived by its inhabitants to be far away from the major urban epicentres of the AIDS epidemic in the United States, mistakenly diagnose Mike with pneumonia. Although Memphis will certainly have had its share of cases, public panic produces such profound denial that the doctors here offer 'the only diagnosis they know that goes with AIDS: PCP [pneumonia], that's the ticket. Never mind that the bronchoscopy came up clean' (49).

If the hospital effects a kind of capture, reproducing the subject under a rubric of containment, *Hospital Time* refuses to 'col-
lect' Mike even as it is committed to recording his life and death,
resists setting up an idealized image of him. But this refusal
always involves a complicated linking of avowal and disavowal.
While Hoffman has (perhaps despite her intentions) 'become
known as a Mike specialist, a Mike collector' among her friends
(145), labels that suggest her 'ownership' of Mike's memory, as
well as the almost entire absorption of her existence in this
project, her attitude towards the enterprise of remembering
Mike by writing about him remains ambivalent. She claims, on
the one hand, to love Mike more faithfully and accurately than
anyone else and melancholically laments, on the other, that both
she and Mike are unworthy of love, even despicable.

This ambivalence corrodes the memoir's putative linear structure, returning us consistently and emphatically to the sense that
Mike continues to live an unsettled, incomplete, almost mechanical 'life' within Hoffman's memory. Throughout the memoir, the
progress towards completed grief that is suggested by the linear
structure is interrupted by a series of ironic episodes, organized
under titles that create briefly the expectation that the about-to-
be-narrated event will affirm the work of mourning, but that ultimately return us to a corporeal reality that estranges ordinary life
along with any consolatory gestures. Take, for example, the subsection from Part 3 entitled 'Mike Dies Peacefully' (77). Hoffman parodies in this title the comforting assertion offered by
Mike's friend Rob: 'Mike died peacefully, Amy, I want you to
know that' (77). Hoffman strenuously rejects this reconstruction
of his death: 'Peacefully. If you want to believe that, go ahead'
(77). Previously, anticipating the event, Hoffman presents us with
another perspective on Mike's death, a more horrific one, one
that Rob's placating comment attempts to erase. Hoffman
emphasizes the way in which death was 'manifestly before our
eyes' already, observing how Mike's body looks no different after

his death than it did during the four days before he died – 'His
skin yellow, his face a skull, his eyes rolled back into his head'
(69). And when Hoffman's partner, Roberta, asks the nurse how
Mike can still have diarrhea, they learn that his body is consum-
ing 'the lining of his stomach' (69). Hoffman groups the doctors'
attempts to placate her together with Rob's: 'No hope. Nothing
to be done. We can make him comfortable' (79). And, similarly,
she objects to 'their irrepressible confidence, the optimism of
their power. (Would they, too, describe Mike's death as "peaceful"? Maybe "comfortable"?),' remarking upon the posture she
herself occupies in these conversations: she somehow herself
adopts the position of 'invalid' as she sits passively listening to the
doctors (78–9). Hoffman's contestation of Rob's reconstruction
and the doctors' interpretation directs us back to a less thoroughly edited account. The memoir thus pursues a persistent
pattern of denying comfort, and this refusal of appeasement
undermines the coherence of the witness's subjectivity, such that
she feels possessed and deadened by the task of grieving. To say
that 'in the end, Mike left me twisting in the wind' takes on a
wide-reaching resonance: it is not only that his lack of direction
made it difficult for Hoffman to make legal decisions, but that
her very involvement with him has taken over her sense of self,
seeming to divest her of 'ordinary' involvement in the world,
leaving her without peace and even 'dead,' which is the implication of the grim trope she uses to describe herself (16). The
address that would preserve the dead redounds upon the one
who addresses, so that, absorbed in her grief, the witness
becomes an object in her own narrative, a passive, weighty, vulnerable body. In addition to grieving the loss of Mike, she also
mourns her own lost self-coherence and rational self-control.

This condition of obligation also complicates Hoffman's attitude towards the memorial service, when Mike's friends meet to
scatter his ashes in the Fenway, an urban park where he often
cruised for men. There is embarrassed confusion among the

group about how to approach the task. Hoffman, who has brought the ashes with her, 'invited the others to follow me, but there was a moment of hesitation. The *goyim* didn't want to get near the box' (87). The word *goyim* is used disparagingly here to mark the friends' distance from religious ritual, their confidence (which is also Hoffman's confidence or hope in some senses) that they can make up a personalized ritual that will do justice to Mike. Secularism masks reluctance to come into proximity with Mike's corpse: the friends are generally primed with consolatory fictions that articulate and limit their proximity to the reality of the corpse. The friends may also be considered as stagey aspects of Hoffman's own consolatory fantasies, but safely distanced by being identified with others – so that Hoffman may better 'possess' her friend by dispossessing others, rendering them as unworthy of the right to mourn him. Witness Rob's comment, mentioned earlier, or Jacoby's confidence that the teddy bear she placed in Mike's room 'eased his pain' (125), though everyone knows that he 'famously despised possessions' (140). Hoffman responds to the friends' reluctance to approach the ashes by referring to Jewish tradition for an alternative precedent, noting how 'the mourners have to dig until the grave is filled, and it's a dirty job' and how it is customary to 'wash our hands before reentering a home after a funeral anyway' (87). I will return to the significance of Hoffman's reference to religious tradition in the final section of this chapter, where I deal with her references to the Hebrew prayer for the dead, but for now I would like to underline the contrast between the recognition that they have just been forced to make and the eagerness of the mourners to seize upon a symbol that promises to compensate for this recognition. Indeed, upon the completion of the ritual scattering of the ashes, one of the friends, Loie, alerts the attention of the others to the appearance of a great blue heron 'making his way among the reeds and the ashes' (87), crying out that the bird 'is Mike's spirit! It is his totem!' (87). For Hoffman, however, this conclusion is not quite possible. Although she tests out points of comparison (like Mike, the bird is 'lean, long-legged, deep-voiced'), she rejects Loie's interpretation, acknowledging that 'I wish more than anything I believed that. The Great Blue Heron' (87). If Mike continues to be present in the world, it is only in the ruined and yet stubbornly persistent form of the ashes that cling to her hands, 'the heavy, heavy ashes' that remind Hoffman, with a cruel incongruity, of 'Michael's emaciated body' (86).

Hospital Time resists, with a remarkably precise negation, the consolatory vision of the natural world that Mark Doty articulates in his memoir *Heaven's Coast*, seeing it instead, as Jarman, too, finds he must, despite his desire for solace from nature, as fragmented and incomplete.[7] More loosely organized, on the surface, than Hoffman's text, *Heaven's Coast* works eventually towards an affirming conclusion, in which the spirit of Doty's lover, Wally, is implied to linger, benevolently, in a rich spiritual place. Doty remarks apropos burying Wally that 'I understand, differently, the longing of Antigone to bury her brother properly. Something shifts, with the body where it belongs' (283). Doty works with an understanding of non-human nature as symbolic, as an enclosure, a safe haven for the self (though this is not the only possible meaning of the claim that Antigone makes in relation to the body of Polyneices). In Hoffman's text, by contrast with Doty's, the ashes are cast to the wind and water, and 'The Thing' – the connection to the dead or lost other that we refuse to lose – is 'encrypted.' We are thus not released from grieving with this act but rather immersed in an opaque, misery-laden language, a mode of storytelling that can only barely be labelled narration. Just as Hoffman charts her own abandonment of the clamshell she had thought to use as a scoop for the necessity of having to use her bare hands, even as she asserts that Mike would have liked her turning towards 'something natural, from the Sea,' so too her account of the memorial service puts into crisis the possibility of symbolic resolution (86).

Turning to the fourth and final section, *The Afterlife*, I suggest that the 'after' (the 'future' for which mourning ostensibly clears the way) in which *Hospital Time* is interested is something quite different than what we might have expected – Mike is a cryptic, disruptive presence in the unconscious of the witness rather than a messenger from beyond the grave. He returns to Hoffman in puzzling glimpses: he is present as a ghost, a force that disrupts the temporal connections between present, future, and past and compromises the boundaries that would define the individual psyche's inside against its outside. When, for example, 'the snapshot of Mike that I've propped up on the bookcase' impresses her with its lifelike quality, making it 'hard to believe the picture is not of a person who resides in this world,' the image returns to her in the context of a dream:

He visits me later in my dream, wearing the same shorts and tee shirt he's wearing in the picture.

'Touch me,' he says, sitting down next to me, knowing I think he is a ghost.

I reach out to his thigh, and his thigh is real – I feel the hair, the flesh, and the bone – and my hand does not pass through it as through a mist. He is not dead. He has proven it to me. (134)

While this apparition may be read as a conventionally elegiac disavowal of death, the ultimate effect of Mike's return is to restore us to 'hospital time,' to that disorienting netherworld: he is neither alive nor dead. At issue in the dream is her fidelity to him: the two of them were once united against uncomprehending strangers, and now she fears she has betrayed him by allowing herself to be drawn back into her waking life and by feeling guilty that she feels relieved. But their estrangement is far from complete, as the dream suggests. Mike continues to claim her attention and commitment, to the extent that he seems to live an independent existence within Hoffman's unconscious, confronting her with evidence of his solidity, his physicality, which she has struggled hard to recognize has become ash and been dispersed by her own hands. To be haunted by the sensation of Mike's physical presence is to be reminded of his otherness, his resistance to her desires, even now that he is, in a sense, her possession or invention, for he exists as *her* memory of him. His undeniable death unsettles what Hoffman thinks about life and death, bringing her to the sorrowful recognition that perhaps it is not she who possesses or dreams him, but rather the dream of Mike that, more accurately, possesses her.

The most powerful instance of the political effect of this refusal of compensation for grief occurs in the second last chapter of *The Afterlife*, the chapter devoted to 'Mike's Dick,' the part of his anatomy that remains to this point all but occluded for his lesbian friends. At a subsequent memorial gathering, Hoffman learns from a former lover of Mike's that Mike 'had a bent dick,' a detail, Larry notes, that is only possible to recollect for those who had seen him aroused (145). Just as Mike demands, in the context of her dream, for Hoffman to touch him and to recognize him as real, this story offers a fragmentary glimpse of Mike's erotic body that demands a place in her account, despite the fact that it is conveyed to her at second hand, or that she allows into the text only as displaced. Hoffman's focus on this detail, and her placement of the story towards the end of her narrative, in a tantalizing substitution for a summary of the significance of Mike's life, constitutes an embrace, across gender and desire, of that which might violate the boundaries of the 'clean and proper body' of mourning, the body implied in Hoffman's rendering of Rob's comment about Mike's 'peaceful' death. Indeed, as Douglas Crimp explains, there is a need to make gay sexuality differently visible – on something like its own terms – in the context of the epidemic. Reflecting on stories about AIDS in the media, Crimp observes that he has not

seen a story in the mainstream media during the entire ten years of this
epidemic that deals with the anxieties of gay men generally, regarding
for example what this epidemic has done to our experience of our sexuality. This is how one of the worst aspects of homophobia shows itself, in
the suggestion that homosexuality is a simple choice, because it's
assumed that we could all now make the choice not to be homosexual.
(qtd in Caruth and Keenan 546)

Especially in 'Mike's Dick,' with the section's extreme self-
consciousness about Hoffman's role as the potential censor of
Mike's life, *Hospital Time* is very aware of its responsibility to avoid
the widespread 'fatal nostalgia' for the clean, properly, and heterosexually bounded body, a nostalgia that would erase same-sex
desire in the first instance (Haver, *The Body of This Death* 8). Hoffman attests to the difficulty she encounters in writing about
Mike's body, given the incomplete status of her experience and
memories of it; but she also affirms its erotism, even in the midst
of its 'decomposition': 'As I write I create him, and he's mine all
mine, all his deeds and effects. I think of his body. I flash on it
decomposing horribly in its coffin, the busy dick, however it was
made, bent or straight, long gone' (145).

Yet Mike remains a disturbing presence, one that seems to
have, by its own peculiar force, insinuated itself into Hoffman's
psychic and narrative space: 'He is ashes but his body persists in
memory: weary, wicked, wandering. Bent and delicious. I don't
give him any peace, dragging him around like this' (146). The
tone is self-berating, as though Hoffman is irritated with her
inability to relinquish Mike and wonders if this continuing
attachment on her part might be an unwelcome interference.
These are certainly two possible ways of reading the phrase 'dragging him around like this.' But given her earlier criticism of the
tendency to impose peace, the statement would be more accurately read as an affirmation of her uneasy melancholic incorpo-

ration of Mike. Her melancholic attachment to Mike preserves him, but without masking the relation, and without purporting to understand it either: it allows for traces of the decomposing body and the bent and delicious body, but not for reconstructed memories of the peaceful body.[8] Working across sex and gender identifications, then, Hoffman's memoir gestures towards her investment of libidinal energy in Mike's person. And, indeed, can we not describe her bond to him as having all the intensity of a love affair, with its jealousies, resentments, fascinations, infatuations? *Hospital Time* thus participates in what Michael Moon describes, in the context of HIV and AIDS, as 'the project of restoring the "scandal" of sexuality, specifically gay male sexuality, to the mourning process' ('Memorial Rags' 235). Considering grief as continuous with libidinal energy (rather than as opposed by definition to the erotic), we might consider memorialization working as 'a re-memberment that has repositioned itself among the remnants, the remainders, and reminders that do not go away' (239).

   Mike's unpleasantness is preserved, too, for while Mike's body is eroticized on the one hand, on the other Hoffman's text is given over to remembering his disregard for his own body, most specifically in the third to last section in *The Afterlife*, the section on 'Mike's Eating.' She recalls, 'He had the mental attitude of a bulemic, if not the behavior, despising food, yet craving it, needing it of course, yet despising his body's pleasure.' Contradicting his denial of the body, he consistently exhibited a greedy opportunism (141). Thus, although Hoffman asserts the accuracy of her memory, claiming that 'from the very beginning I saw him, Michael, in all his Michaelness, and I never lost sight of that no matter what, and I think that is love' (143), in practice her text demonstrates a much more complex sense of what it means to love her friend and to preserve his unique specificity. She represents Mike with obsessively detailed particularity, showing him to be gloriously varied, even inconsistent, impossible to summarize.

He remains present in traces, in glimpses: as gay community activist, prison rights advocate, linguist, friend, lover, a witty, bitchy, sloppy, opinionated, brilliant, hypocritical, demanding, radical fairy man.

Significantly, the focus on 'just this one person' does not simply replace the many, but creates room for specificity while also constituting a gesture in the direction of the even greater multiplicity of the collective. If Hoffman is in a sense the keeper of a set of memories about Mike, her narrative also necessarily, under a traumatic compulsion, extends its embrace beyond his person. In 'Influences from Beyond the Grave,' we are acquainted with Bobby, whose illness (ironically) was the occasion for Hoffman's meeting Roberta, her partner. Like the image she carries with her of of 'Mike's dick,' Bobby's visitation overwhelms with its wicked excess: 'And suddenly, Bobby, big as life, is beaming down at the two of us from a fluffy pink cloud in Paradise. Little wings flutter at his shoulders, and he's wearing only a celestial jockstrap that glistens whiter than white' (99). This 'vision' provides a glimpse of Bobby's body as he might well have fantasized it, a vision of vigour that prefaces and so competes with what we then read about his illness, when his neuropathy 'annihilat[ed] even the simplest comforts – a blanket, a cup of tea' (102). Possibly, Hoffman fantasizes, 'they've restored his health. Not only has he gotten a tan up there, but his muscles are seriously pumped, his hair as brown and glossy as it was in his Florida youth, his eyes as clear and blue as the heavens' (99). Similarly, in 'Walta's Birthday,' we learn the story of Michael Bronski and his partner Walta, of Walta's inability as his illness progressed to read the poems he had once composed, and of Bronski's feelings of bewilderment upon Walta's death: 'He's no longer living the life he loves, although he used to. He's so lonely. There's no cure' (136–8). Though there may be hope for a pharmaceutical cure, there is no cure for the grief that AIDS has already caused: What do we mean then when we talk of a cure for the disease? Does that

hopeful grasping inadvertently erase or censor those who have
already died and the trauma to those who love them?

Hoffman's introduction to *The Afterlife*, 'Calling the Names,'
reinforces that the scope of her grief extends beyond Mike, that
the text refers as much to the collective as to the individual. Here
Hoffman comments, in a kind of voice-over, on what it means for
a witness to ritualize loss by uttering the names of the dead.
Speaking the names of the dead reveals the impact on those who
remain alive: '*The accretion of names reveals an image: a glimpsed
freeze-frame of our lives hollowed out by loss*' (91). Suggesting that she
encounters AIDS as a traumatic experience, an interruption of
everyday life that produces 'lives hollowed out by loss,' Hoffman
wonders: 'Why did I do that [repeat the names]? What can it
mean to these strangers around me to hear these syllables?
They'll never know the whole story' (91). There is an accumula-
tion, however, of a social presence: 'But as the calling of the
names continues, it becomes a kind of theater or living work of
art – a tableau vivant, perhaps' (91). Though she can imagine
others asking, 'Must we not make peace, must we not move on?,'
there continues to be a sense that she is obliged on a visceral
level to the 'ghosts' of the men she has lost: 'But my teeth are
chattering, my body humming, I can't stop feeling the reverbera-
tions ...' (91).

Melancholy is recirculated, reread, as revealing the intense
love born of their intimacy, and the libidinal energy that motivates the resistance to 'working through' and relinquishing loss:
perhaps libidinal energy even elaborates loss. But the possibility
that her account will submerge Mike beneath her own desire for
a certain image of him (which is one way of grappling with how
much of Hoffman we get in this memoir), burying his story, is an
outcome of which Hoffman is evidently wary, for as she notes
towards the end of the book, Mike might well object to her 'dragging him around like this' (146). And yet, on another level, Hoffman has no choice but to write about Mike; she does not choose

to 'drag him around like this.' The phrasing suggests the collapse of her ability to construct meaning in language: Like this? Like what? Indeed, there is another way to interpret the statement, for the full context reads: 'I don't give him any peace, dragging him around like this' (146). Throughout the memoir the desire for peace is seen as threatening to impose the placating gloss of memorial reconstruction, and 'dragging' him with her as she charts her own affective responses to his illness and death means that our intepretations neither of Mike nor of Hoffman ever settle into a comfortable, coherent whole. Only this amorphous, restless activity can approximate the traumatic experience, or the complexity of their erotic and emotional lives. Restlessness and incomprehension may be read as indexes of a tendency towards critical memory, towards the refusal to disavow loss. As Mike's variable motto suggests, there is (ironically, painfully, but fittingly) 'No rest for the weary' and 'No rest for the wicked' (146).

A Contemporary Antigone? Gender, Caregiving, and the Reinvention of Mourning

> I would not urge you now; nor if you wanted
> to act would I be glad to have you with me.
> Be as you choose to be; but for myself
> I myself will bury him. It will be good
> to die, so doing. I shall lie by his side,
> loving him as he loved me; I shall be
> a criminal – but a religious one.
> The time in which we must please those that are dead
> is longer than I must please those of this world.
>
> – Sophocles, *Antigone* (ll. 79–87)

What are the ethical and political implications of Hoffman's obsession with grieving Mike Riegle's death, given the acknowledged gender polarities of the scenario?[9] The critical debate about Sophocles' Antigone as a figure for the question of the social significance of women's grief can help to put into critical focus the unsteady mix of rebellion, duty, and equivocation that permeates Hoffman's memoir. When Antigone rejects Ismene's too belated, regretful offer to join her in publicly commemorating the death of their brother Polyneices, she pinpoints the cost of holding on to the dead, in the context of grieving a death deemed by the state powers to be ungrievable: one risks becoming a 'criminal.' At the same time, though, Antigone's speech expresses absolute conviction that this is the correct path for a loyal sister: 'The time in which we must please those that are dead / is longer than I must please those of this world' (ll. 86–7). We may read Hoffman as one of a long line of women in literature who have been given, left, or who take on the task of burying the dead, beginning with Antigone. But where Antigone (and this is perhaps the source of Mark Doty's identification with her in *Heaven's Coast*) is unequivocal about the supremacy of 'God's ordinances, unwritten and secure' (l. 499) that compels her loyalty to her dead brother over the law of the state, Amy Hoffman, although committed to mourning Mike Riegle, appears relatively undecided and, at first glance, decidedly unheroic.

Antigone can be read as proto-feminist for its focus on the young woman's defiance of Creon's tyranny and misogyny, but it has also been interpreted as confirming the patriarchal gendering of mourning, even as it models a kind of rebellion against authority.[10] If we follow Hegel's influential references to the play in *The Phenomenology of Spirit*, the sister's duty to grieve her brother's death forms the very substance and purpose of familial relations. The '*Family*' constitutes the '*natural* ethical community,' and its '(unconscious) role is to preserve,' through its various practices and rituals, the 'elemental individuality' of the male individual from 'the desires of unconscious organic agencies and by abstract elements' (468, 472). Luce Irigaray has criticized this

reading, pointing out how women are themselves negated by the
duty assigned to them in Hegel's ethical vision, for if women's
'inherent duty is to ensure *burial for the dead,* thus changing a natural phenomenon into a spiritual act,' then 'we see that it is the
task of womankind, guardian of the blood tie, to gather man into
his final figuration, beyond the turmoil of his contingent life and
the scattered moments of his Being there' (cited in Jacobs, 'Dusting Antigone' 898; *Speculum* 266–7). Sisterly devotion to the male
dead is, according to this interpretation, a form of false consciousness that naturalizes female self-immolation in the service
of patriarchal norms, and for the purpose of maintaining the
boundaries that contain the abject, symbolically insulating the
patriarchal body politic from forces that threaten disintegration.
When mourning men is framed as women's duty, we find not
only the consumption – and disfiguring – of the other, but the
female self also consumes itself in the work of mourning in order
to refigure the other in a way that underwrites patriarchal
interests.[11]

But as a figure uniting questions of ethics, the feminine, and
mourning, the significance of Antigone may be rethought in the
context of *Hospital Time.* Read together, these two texts provide
another way of thinking about women and grief: unresolved grief
can suggest the existence of an obligation that exceeds the
bounds of 'feminine' duty, of a gender identity that would affirm
conventional roles. Like Amy Hoffman, Antigone faces everywhere evidence of a male body's disintegrative corporeality. And
it may not be so clear, as Carol Jacobs has argued of the play, that
Antigone's words and actions do function to 'guard' the 'blood
tie' by preserving her brother's body from contingency: 'She who
would bury Polyneices and give him meaning and form also
produces or rather has already produced the dispersal of that
form-giving, as mother of the dust, as carrion feeding bird, as
prefiguration of intelligibility gone awry' (910). Indeed, Butler

has recently suggested, in an extension of her discussion of
mourning from *The Psychic Life of Power*, that Antigone's dilemma
can be read as 'an allegory for the crisis of kinship,' namely, the
question of 'which social arrangements can be recognized as
legitimate love, and which human losses can be explicitly grieved
as real and consequential' (*Antigone's Claim* 24). Although she is
'difficult for anyone to romanticize or to consult as an example,'
Antigone's 'refusal to obey any law that refuses public recognition of her loss,' and the deadly consequences of her refusal,
'prefigures the situation that those with publicly ungrievable
losses – from AIDS for instance – know too well' (23–4). The
extravagance of Antigone's commitment to her dead brother
presents an unresolved relation of obligation to the other that is
subtly at odds with any 'final figuration' of him. Despite the surface conventionality of the scenario, there percolates beneath
that level of meaning a certain inadvertent or ironic pressure (of
identification replacing difference) that counters 'the manhood
of the community' (Hegel 496), something that Thomas Yingling
has referred to in the context of AIDS as the 'national body,' the
imaginary relation to the body that treats 'the refusal of disease
[as] essential to nationhood' ('Wittgenstein's Tumor' 24).[12] Both
the foregrounding of the sister-brother bond (in him the woman
finds 'a man on a level with herself' [Hegel 497]) and Antigone's
status with respect to state authority as a 'manly and verbally defiant figure' work indirectly to level gender hierarchies and to
expose the contingency of kinship forms (Butler, *Antigone's Claim*
9, 21). In an 'unrevealing rite of unintelligible frenzy' such as
Antigone's (Jacobs 910) – in a text of grief produced under the
auspices of obligation to the other's *experience* (rather than what
he is supposed to represent as a national masculine symbolic
body) – neither the male other nor the female self is consumed;
indeed, it is implied that neither one existed as such in the way
this description presumes. This insight opens up the possibility of
inventing forms of 'radical kinship' based on 'consensual affilia-

tion' and 'the social organization of need,' although it does not resolve the question of whether they will be socially recognized (Butler, *Antigone's Claim* 74).

Hoffman's own 'unrevealing rite of unintelligible frenzy' – *Hospital Time* – likewise disarticulates the very process of mourning that it invokes; it is at once 'criminal' and 'religious.' But her melancholic attachment to the particular, the material, and the bodily is less obliquely present than is Antigone's, and its effect is a political one: to radically restructure social identities and relationships. Motivated to record her grief for a man to whom she is – by conventional definitions – neither sister, mother, lover, wife, doctor, or nurse (23), Hoffman's text presents, first of all, a created or chosen (but certainly in no sense pretended) sense of community – an ethical community to be sure, but a departure from, or a complication of, the natural ethical community that Hegel models on the nuclear family. The implications of *Hospital Time*'s rendering of community, friendship, and family are at least twofold: as she negates the privileging of the nuclear heterosexual family, Hoffman claims status and recognition for her bond with Mike. As such, *Hospital Time* constitutes a remarkable exception to the overwhelming replication, as Katie Hogan has demonstrated with reference to a host of visual and literary texts about AIDS, of the ideal of women as self-sacrificing caregivers (5).[13] To be more specific, *Hospital Time* is written against the grain of what Thomas Couser identifies as the genre of 'relational AIDS memoirs' (114). Frequently without acknowledging their own privilege, and without considering their own potential vulnerability to the AIDS epidemic, 'as "family narratives" these books quite literally represent the family's "terms": they tend to encode or enact family values that are sometimes at odds with those of the member being reassimilated' (115). Through sisterly narratives in particular, and as Jamaica Kincaid struggles to question in writing about her brother, 'the nuclear family quite literally reclaims and relocates the body of its errant member'

(121).[14] Considering how it displaces the potential reclaiming of
a gay body by a heterosexually normative nuclear family, the family of 'origin,' Hoffman's text is more akin to AIDS elegies by gay
men than it is to 'sororal narratives,' for AIDS elegies, as Melissa
F. Zeiger notes, 'rarely participat[e] in traditional elegy's consumption and silencing of women' (113).[15] And women are cast
in a much different light 'when released from their roles as cau-
tionary markers of sexual difference or threat': they come into
view as 'partners in activism' and as caregivers, but in a context
where 'this is not a degraded women's job but work embraced by
men in a way that recasts the gendered division of nursing labor'
(116). What Hoffman's text stages, however, is not the nexus of
elegy and epithalamium that Zeiger emphasizes is characteristic
of AIDS elegies by men, but something rather more nebulous,
and more troublesome for the heterosexual categories that furnish our prevalent definitions of intimacy: this is a text not of
marriage or sexual union, but of friendship, of queer alliances.

Like Sedgwick, who in her essay 'Tales of the Avunculate' wonders about 'how to *stop* redeeming the family,' I find myself confronted here by a lack in vocabulary. To call Hoffman's relation
to Mike 'sororal' is perhaps to diminish it, peremptorily to cir-
cumscribe it within the kind of 'natural' or 'Oedipal' circuit that
Irigaray, Jacobs, and Butler are attempting to pry open in their
analysis of Antigone. As Sedgwick argues, 'the worst danger
about "family"' is 'how much the word, the name, the *signifier*
family is already installed so unbudgeably at the center of a cultural value system – so much so that a rearrangement or reassign-
ment of its *signifieds* need have no effect whatever on its
rhetorical or ideological effects' (72). The entrenched opposition of the terms 'family' and 'friendship' makes what we call
friendship seem less important, or registers it – as Sedgwick indicates – only in the most hopelessly euphemistic terms. Paralleling
Sedgwick's identification 'as a gay man' ('White Glasses' 256),
Hoffman's citation of the anonymous note Mike received calling

him a 'male lesbian' gives us a snippet of a name for what Mike is to her by indicating the queer slant of this relation across the sex-gender system. By calling Hoffman and Mike's relation a queer alliance, though this is perhaps also too vague, I am attempting to signal the need for a third term, while not assuming that I've found one that is sufficient.

What can we make, given this context, of the repeated, equivocal disavowals of love that characterize *Hospital Time*? I suggest that they encapsulate – with a queerly negative energy – a struggle with a key ethical and political problematic in the representation of AIDS losses: as Butler puts it, 'the uncertainty with which homosexual love and loss is regarded,' the uncertainty that deprives us, in the context of AIDS, of 'finding a public occasion and language in which to grieve this seemingly endless number of deaths' (*Psychic Life* 138; cf. *Antigone's Claim* 24). While, according to Freud, it is in melancholia that 'by taking flight into the ego, love escapes extinction' (257), such love, as Butler argues, is judged for failing to 'measure' up to 'the ideal of social rectitude defined over and against homosexuality' (*Pyschic Life* 141), and the result is 'self-beratement' [*sic*] (140). Butler's description here may make the situation sound inescapable, but the overall effect of Hoffman's melancholic testimony, I would argue, is to open up, through its very *repetitions* of self-criticism, a textual space in which it becomes newly possible to conceptualize her friendship with Mike as 'a love and loss worthy and capable of being grieved and thus worthy and capable of having been lived' (138). As Butler stresses in her discussion of Antigone, kinship is not 'simply a principle for action' but involves 'performative repetition,' and the 'aberrant repetition of norms' can work to expand what forms of kinship are considered real, liveable, and intelligible (*Antigone's Claim* 58, 70). Recalling how she hated feeding Mike the food he vainly hoped would cure him, the 'food of his delusion' (97), Hoffman reaches a moment of crisis and finally cries over Mike: 'I cry because I miss him, because I loved him, because I feel so mean, because his death was so terrible, hard, and early, because I didn't treat him tenderly' (97). The repetition of self-berating, rather than remaining a matter of self-judgment, becomes a refusal of compensation for forced loss, and for the socially produced trauma that compounds her multiple losses to AIDS, a refusal to relinquish sorrow that in turn foregrounds the strength of Amy Hoffman's bond to Mike Riegle. In fact, Hoffman rereads her own harsh questions about whether she loved Mike and whether she fulfilled her obligation to him – rereads, that is, her own melancholy – as an indication of their deep, mutual implication in one another's lives. As she explains when her mother questions why Hoffman has become so involved (and expresses her concern that her daughter is giving to an outsider energy that should be reserved for 'real' family): 'I did it for him because he was my family' (109).

By naming her relation to Mike 'family,' Hoffman is, moreover, implying that the intimate bonds we label family or friendship might mean more, or differently, than the dominant cultural codes assume. Relations based on acknowledged identification replace instrumental relations that hold identification at bay, on the constitutive outside of the self. This shift is highlighted in Hoffman's comments on the too late but nonetheless 'majest[ic]' and 'righteous' entrance on the scene of Mike's straight brother, Chuck, at the time of the funeral: 'The healthy brother, he turns up with his man-of-the-family authority draped about him like a red scarf and we kowtow to him like deformed trolls living under a bridge to one who walks in the light' (112). Hoffman's treatment of Chuck's appearance exemplifies her suspicion of the sympathy those outside her circle of friends attempt to express. The red scarf, replaced, in the context of a dream, around Chuck's neck, perhaps as a kind of AIDS-awareness red ribbon writ large, points up the hypocrisy of his statement that he had decided to come to the memorial service because 'he wanted to understand his brother's life and why he had become so alienated from the rest of the family' (111). Chuck's presumption that Mike was an outsider, a prodigal who can now easily (and should now easily) be redeemed by his 'family' is reversed in Hoffman's recitation of this scene, which follows quickly upon Hoffman's claiming of Mike as a member of *her* family. The memoir thus registers the disavowals of love that Mike's family of origin has perpetuated during his life and seeks to solidify now that he is dead, precisely so that they won't have to understand, so that they can seal themselves off from the rich realities of his life.

Likewise, the hospital director in Memphis who offers to take home Mike's laundry is viewed with the same resentment for her conformity to the normal appearances of adulthood. In her prim business suit, 'she looked so much more like an adult than I ever would' (54), and Hoffman is irritated by the woman's attempt to appropriate out of sympathy the role of caregiver, a role that she would possess exclusively even as she worries about the possibility that her involvement in Mike's life and death also constitutes itself a sanctimonious, self-interested interference. With these interspersed statements targeting the socially recognized posture of adulthood as just that, a posture or performance, Hoffman implies a critique of the crude Freudian interpretation of lesbians as improperly adjusted women, who have not moved beyond the childhood clitoral stage of sexual development. And it is this division of maturity and immaturity that plays a crucial role in the designation of lesbians and gays as somehow deficient in their achievement of responsible adulthood, a habit of thought so insidious, Hoffman is implying, that it forces her to regard herself and her community as 'deformed' and 'troll-like.' The reality that undergirds Hoffman's parodic commentary on Mike's 'real' family is her experience that 'with AIDS, nine times out of ten it's the fake family who cleans up the shit' (112). The attachment that is expressed to such memories of physical intimacy – to the visceral memory, for example, of being the one 'who cleans up the shit' – fuels a claim to occupying the relation of greatest proximity, of an imaginative and practical kinship, as opposed to the fakery, in this instance, of the birth family's delayed, and highly circumspect, embrace. Strikingly, it is the very 'immature' melancholic emotions generating the narrative voice of *Hospital Time* that make it possible to interrogate the ways in which grief is subject to the editorial interference of prior cultural assumptions.[16]

In addition to confronting these exemplars of responsibility – Mike's brother and the Memphis hospital director – by insisting on the reality and meaningfulness of her bond with Mike in the face of their culturally sanctioned authority, Hoffman responds in provocative ways both to the literature of AIDS and to her inheritance, as a Jewish lesbian, of a certain set of traditional texts and practices that address her central concerns. Her literary and religious references further develop her rewriting of conceptions of friendship, family, and grief. These exploratory allusions constitute successful failures in Derrida's sense, for while they register her discontent, ambivalence, and confusion, at the same time they unleash plural possibilities of interpretation and identification.

Narrating in her own words the scene of Prior Walter's hospitalization in Tony Kushner's *Angels in America*, Hoffman performs in the space of a few sentences the approach she herself takes to representing Mike's death, namely the 'cold enumeration' (Derrida, *Memoires* 31) of details together with the registering of her own emotions, here a sense of familiarity combined with terror and bafflement:

A man is dying of AIDS. They roll an IV pole and a hospital bed onto the stage. He strips, and his body is emaciated. His legs have that AIDS look – no calf muscles, no buttocks. I wonder, Can they do that with makeup? Has the actor starved himself in a Stanislavskian frenzy? Is he really dying? He stretches his hand around to his behind and pulls it away covered with blood. He screams, and I do too. (114–15)

The terror inspired by this scene prompts, in turn, a highly personalized interpretation of the play: 'I've sat by the beds of Bob, of Tim, of Mike, of Walta, as they've chattered and writhed, and I've wondered. Flaming angels' (114). Given this context, the response of Roberta's brother-in-law, who casually dismisses the play with the words 'God, was that corny,' irritates Hoffman, prompting her to clarify once again her impatience with outsiders: 'I don't want these people to talk to me anymore. I'm too damn busy' (115).

By referring to the literature of the AIDS epidemic, and by foregrounding the range of responses to it, Hoffman seeks recognition for the specificity and the magnitude of her losses and angrily draws attention to the difference between those who have been affected by HIV and AIDS and those who come to the cultural representations of the epidemic as outsiders, as consumers of images of a disease to which they have not borne personal witness. But *Hospital Time*'s references to *Angels in America* also situate Hoffman's grief, terror, and sense of alienation in the context of religious tradition, specifically the structures for grieving offered by her Jewish inheritance. Consider Hoffman's concluding essay, which is entitled 'Kaddish,' but in which she refuses to recite the prayer to which she alludes, the traditional Jewish prayer for the dead, a prayer, as Hoffman notes, 'of reconciliation ... of acceptance' (149): 'But I won't. I won't. Accept this suffering, this order that encompasses it, this karma, this harmony of the spheres' (149).[17] By linking the kaddish to 'karma' and 'the harmony of the spheres' in the process of rejecting it, she insinuates that religious tradition is no more true or helpful or relevant to Mike's early and difficult death than are the concepts proffered by the cultural raiding that passes for religious faith in the New Age marketing of spirituality. Certainly, in the resistance it expresses towards too easy consolations, Hoffman's melancholic rejection of ritual stalls us when we are on the verge of embracing traditional scripts for mourning, and the kaddish does indeed model a highly conventionalized working through of grief, especially through its marking of time as the ritual declines from a weekly to a monthly to an annual observance.[18]

Hoffman's rejection of the kaddish at the end of *Hospital Time* marks her distance from Kushner's emphasis on reconciliation in *Angels in America*. In *Part 2: Perestroika*, Belize, the play's representative outsider, attempts to convince the sceptical Louis that Roy Cohn, powerful, mean, hypocritical, and homophobic, ought to be forgiven for his offences: 'He was a terrible person. He died a hard death. So maybe ... A queen can forgive her vanquished foe. It isn't easy, it doesn't count if it's easy, it doesn't count if it's easy, it's the hardest thing' (2:3:122). Belize argues, 'Forgiveness ... is maybe where love and justice finally meet. Peace, at least. Isn't that what the Kaddish asks for?,' and the scene concludes with the ghost of Ethel Rosenberg leading Louis through the prayer, so as to perform the reintegration of a secular Jew, by the ministrations of those more oppressed, more persecuted than he, into the restorative language of ritual (122). If Ethel Rosenberg can forgive the man who was responsible for her death, then Louis is asked to acquiesce in the role of son and to reconcile with the diabolical father-figure, Cohn, by ritualizing his death. *Hospital Time*, on the contrary, emphatically rejects any such resolution through reference to a higher order of justice: 'You won't catch me saying a kaddish over anyone's remains. It's not for me to join in praise of the Named One, Who in His Wisdom named for us AIDS' (149).[19]

But rather than implying a mere rejection of the tradition's relevance, this negation of the kaddish may also be emphasizing the necessity both of reinventing inherited forms for grieving and of demanding social recognition for one's grief. Hoffman's invoca-

tion of the kaddish suggests, through the text's implication in the
very prayer that it denies, that mourning rituals, such as the one
that is familiar to her from the Hebrew tradition, might be or
might become in the context of her losses to AIDS an index of
her inconsolability and a medium for the reworking of 'family'
and of what are considered legitimate losses and loves, rather
than a mechanism of quietude, acceptance, or reconciliation. In
'Six Things I Have Inherited,' Hoffman enumerates the bequests
she has received during her life, including 'Bob's grandfather's
novel and Mike's father's (pathetic) life insurance,' noting the
ironic twists this process has taken, specifically 'how, as one's gay
family supersedes one's birth family, the gay family, that is, me,
becomes the keeper of the birth family's legacy' (131). Hoffman
raises the question here of what it means to be next of kin, a critique that complements her appropriation of the kaddish for
grieving Mike. Since the kaddish is traditionally said by a male
child for a parent, reciting it implies the relation of next of kin
and is an enactment of the continuity of generations. So, while
she is dismayed, on the one hand, by the recognition that the
'two redneck old men' from whom she inherited 'would have
been outraged to know that their male progeny had made me,' 'a
middle-class, second generation Jewish lesbian from New Jersey,'
'their heir,' she also relishes, on the other, this reversal of expectations (131). Locating the places in cultural rituals where they
might be subject to a non-compliant reiteration, one that differs
from the 'original context or intention by which [the] utterance
is animated' in the slightest but most ground-shifting of ways,
Hoffman calls attention to, and claims as central to her definition of love, her role as Mike's next of kin (Butler, *Excitable Speech*
14; cf. *Antigone's Claim* 58). Even to propose in this oblique way
that it would be fitting for her to say the kaddish for a friend, a
member of her queer family, is for her to further disrupt the normative chain of relations, to 'produce' 'effects' that 'exceed
those by which it was intended' (*Excitable Speech* 14).

Meditating on these questions of kinship, sexual orientation, and grief in the context of breast cancer, Sandra Butler notes how, at her lover Barbara Rosenblum's funeral, 'as the rabbi completed the service by leading the mourners in the *Kaddish*, the prayer for the dead,' the prayer instigates the cries of Barbara's mother, 'the sound of a shriek, sustained for a heartbeat and becoming a wail,' an outburst that almost overrides the measured tones of the prayer: 'The sound was a barrier, a shield to stop the inexorable process of this prayer, this ending' (*Cancer in Two Voices* 171). In Sandra Butler's words, Barbara's mother 'remembers how to mourn, how to make the sound we have all forgotten and needed to hear. She is a woman who is not muted and well-behaved in her grief as we have learned to be' (172). Illuminating the competing impulses that motivate *Hospital Time*'s denial of the kaddish, Butler and Rosenblum's *Cancer in Two Voices* suggests that this prayer, the kaddish, may be considered less as a script than as an occasion for the enactment of a sorrow, a text that reminds us of 'the necessity to leave space for the sound of the one who unexpectedly survives again' (172). Moreover, what appears as the balancing of claims – between Barbara's role as 'her first-born, my love' – is also an assertion of equity, that Butler's grief for her partner may be compared in its intensity to a mother's grief for the loss of a daughter (172). And Butler concludes her commentary on the memorial service, as Amy Hoffman does, not with an affirmation of peace, but with an insistence on the way in which such a loss demands 'gnashing of teeth. Crashes of thunder. Bolts of lightning' and a celebration of the refusal to be 'muted and well-behaved' in grief (172).[20] This tradition has something to teach us or model for us about grief in the context of epidemic: with these ambivalent recyclings of the kaddish, a sense of cultural continuity, if it is not restored, perhaps becomes more thinkable.

Hoffman accomplishes more, then, through her disavowal of the kaddish than the rejection of sacred ritual: somewhat circuitously, she queers this inherited text (just as in a less specific way she revises the tradition of *Antigone*), opening it up to multiple possibilities for unleashing 'the unreconciled and unreconcilably incendiary energies streaming through that subtractive gap' of unresolved grief (Sedgwick, 'White Glasses' 255). While a focus on what Zeiger calls 'an embrace of the domestic and the improvisatory' is surely a component of Hoffman's practice, then, her melancholic attachment to Mike prompts her to interrogate, and stubbornly to reverse, received cultural texts (124). Replacing the kaddish, and at the same time drawing its energy from this text, *Hospital Time* transforms our sense of the collective cultural form grief may take. Positioning itself against, for example, Hoffman's mother, who asks where Mike's real family is as though she is worried that her daughter will use up her energy for caregiving and for mourning on a stranger (109–11), the text insists, out of its melancholy, on achieving recognition for her bond to Mike. At the same time, and despite the imposition of a framework that would move us through grief in an orderly progression, *Hospital Time* bears witness not just to Mike's illness and death, but to a situation that is exceptionally complex: to the ways in which Mike continues to claim her quite beyond her own choice and intentions, to the ways in which he haunts her efforts to make sense of (and to be freed from) the heavy burden of their unlikely intimacy. *Hospital Time*'s practice of critical memory unfurls a grief that cannot be predicted or controlled or finally worked through, and raises the ethical problems inherent in second-person witnessing of the AIDS epidemic. This project in turn redounds on the questions of duty and responsibility inherent in all of our speaking, writing, and thinking about HIV and AIDS.

The investigation of family in Hoffman's text contrasts with the approach taken by Rebecca Brown in her fictionalized memoir *The Gifts of the Body* (1994), which is also written from the perspective of a lesbian caring for people living with AIDS, primarily men. Brown's final chapter in this series of interlinked, fictional-

ized (but autobiographically based) stories, 'The Gift of Mourning,' compels us to step back with the caregiver from a dying
woman to leave her children to mourn over her body; indeed,
this is the conclusion of the entire book: 'We left them with the
body and they mourned' (9). *The Gifts of the Body* emphasizes the
physical details of labour, death, and grief in a way that counters
the corrosive 'moral etiology' of the body that has so consistently
attached itself to HIV and AIDS (Watney, 'The Spectacle of AIDS'
73), evoking through its rhetoric of restraint a strong sense that
an ill, dying, or dead body should by no means be viewed as just
so much raw material for anyone else's representation. Far from
artless, what one reviewer has called Brown's 'casually vernacular
language' is a vital component of her project (Steinberg 85), for
it calls attention to details that might otherwise seem mundane;
for example, in 'The Gift of Sweat' Rick's sweat when he attempts
to surprise the narrator by preparing breakfast for her (just as he
used to do for his lover) signals to her 'how long it took to get
down the street, how early he had to go to get the best [cinna-
mon rolls]' (9). This bodily fluid, sweat, becomes a sign of the
passionate connection that Rick and the narrator express for one
another through labour, a relation of bodily 'flow' that works
across gendered oppositions and casts labour in the context of
caregiving as passionate, mutual, ethical (Grosz, *Volatile Bodies*
198). However, Brown's conclusion makes a potentially confus-
ing detour from these purposes. Her ending risks re-installing
the nuclear family at the centre, and the end, of the story, as
though this were its narrative destination in the first place. While
the narrative voice is still with the caregiver whom we follow out
of the room, there is a sense of difficulty, loss, and shame that
comes with the pressure to adopt a professional reticence when
the family takes bodily and spiritual possession of a person to
whom the narrator has also become attached, has come to love;
giving the gift of mourning to others seems to require that she
school herself to quietude.

Hoffman's approach, her wild, self-focused, annihilating, and unresolved grief, aligns more closely with the perspective of Sedgwick's 'White Glasses,' the evocative text I cited as my introductory epigraph, than it does with Brown's fictionalized account. 'White Glasses' gives voice to intense and contradictory feelings of loss and, in so doing, identifies the difficulty of bringing the melancholic subjectivity of second-person AIDS testimonial writing into critical focus. Sedgwick reflects on her attachment to her friend Michael Lynch, meditating on the way she has adopted certain elements of his style, particularly his 'cool' white plastic glasses, and observing that the symbolic resonances of 'a white woman wearing white' (purity, sentiment, grief) can make it seem like the position could never be anything more than a capitulation, an instance of 'ruly ordinariness' (255). But although we might read the wearing of white as a banal citation of femininity, just as we might read Antigone's frenzy as a routinized gesture that supports masculine rule rather than contesting it, still there remains 'the corrosive aggression that white also is' (255). The lingering incorporation of an object associated with the lost, or about to be lost, other forms a 'ragged scar' – as Sedgwick says – a bodily marking that tells the genealogy of intimate friendship, with its legacy of 'unreconciled and unreconcilably incendiary energies.' In the face of anticipated loss, the memory of such fusion is painful but also replete with an investment of passionate energy, which responds to the unquenchable demand to sustain relations of 'meaning, regard, address' (255). The relation between the two bodies in this queer friendship is not regulated by sexual difference and, with the suspension of this framing, may be bound to transform itself to something powerful but unrecognizable. Looking towards a future of accumulated resistance to the disciplinary discourses that currently shape gender, sexuality, and experiences of illness, Sedgwick refuses to predict what it will look like, but points out that at the very least the future will not follow the script laid out

for the extinction of collective witnessing of the epidemic: 'I rel-
ish knowing that enough of us will be here to demonstrate that
the answer can hardly be what anyone will have expected' (266).
Amy Hoffman, in the midst of her grief, sees the intensity of her
loss as evidence of the reality and the preciousness of the bond
she shares with Mike, and is somewhat hopeful about how the
new forms of intimacy that the AIDS epidemic have forced her
and others to invent might positively shape the future.

At the same time, however, as it looks towards a new future for
friendship, or queer alliances, *Hospital Time* also worries about
the temptation to hurry towards the comforts of narrative closure. The piece entitled 'Obituary' presents, as we might expect,
a narrative of significant life events, furnishing, for example, the
information that 'Mike was an avid linguist,' that 'over the years,
Mike carried on correspondence with hundreds of prisoners,
many of whom came to regard him as a close friend,' or that
'Mike brought to everything he did – whether it was sex, gardening, singing choral music, reading, or star-gazing – a sophisticated and original mind, a curious imagination, and a deeply
rooted integrity' (81–2). In obituary discourse, the other's life
seems to speak – to produce, effortlessly, the summary of an
identity, and to match up a life to grander patterns and commu-
nally agreed-upon virtues. But when we read Hoffman's newspa-
per obituary for Mike in the context of her more fragmented
reflections on his life, the recognition of the way this discourse
measures out his life in the past tense, making almost exclusive
use of intransitive constructions, is unavoidable – we have been
accustomed to seeing him in her memoir as much less consistent,
much less pleasant, much less socially productive, on the whole
much less tidy. In fact, then, the effect of 'tidiness' is achieved, as
Chambers points out, 'at the price of burying that person [the
dead] with past-tense verbs and in the form of narrative closure'
(*Facing It* 130–1), and we can detect, moreover, a certain 'substi-
tut[ion] for "their" message the concerns ... of the survivors'

(132). Sedgwick similarly emphasizes that the effect of 'the obituary imperative,' because it is so 'implacably inclusive,' is to produce a vocabulary and a syntax that is 'ravenously denuding, homogenizing, relentlessly anthropomorphizing and yet relentlessly disorienting' ('White Glasses' 265). Surely there is a palpable gulf between the measured, objective tones of Hoffman's interpellated obituary for Mike and the headiness of 'dragging him around,' though each mode of memorialization is in its own way disorienting. As Hoffman summarizes midway through the memoir, imagining his disapproval of her representation, just as he tended to voice his disapproval of any choice that privileged the personal over the political, the act of writing about Mike – the act of memorializing him – extends the paradox that is their relationship: 'He put his life in my hands, and yet he mistrusted even a straightforward statement of fact' (78). She is fairly certain that 'he wouldn't like this writing I am doing about him' (78). The purpose of the passage, then, is metafictional: rather than furnishing an overarching interpretation, 'Obituary' draws our attention to the kinds of denuding discourses that are available to the memoirist, or, rather, to the way in which discourses of maturity, cleanliness, and health threaten to engulf the narrative willy-nilly, quite apart from any authorial intentions.

Amy Hoffman's text tries to be responsible both to her own experiences and to Mike Riegle's, granting each experience its own limited, partial authority in the text. While she professes that 'I wanted nothing to do with a memorial service. My philosophy was that when Mike died my responsibility ended' (85), the wound remains open, the burden prescribed, for Hoffman is tied to Mike in an non-negotiable, physical sense, symbolized by the legal relationship he entrusts her with during his illness and her guardianship, subsequently, of his memory: 'But in ashes begin more responsibilities' (85). Torn apart from within about the project of memorializing, Hoffman foregrounds writerly and readerly responsibility, considers the perils of speaking for the

dead, and struggles to resist the gender polarities of obituary discourse. *Hospital Time*'s affective intensity is, then, if not quite
intelligible, then not quite unintelligible either, and the reality of
Hoffman's emotions as they are represented in her written
account nonetheless undeniable and forceful.

CHAPTER THREE

Resisting Redemption
Strategies of Defamiliarization in
Eric Michaels's *Unbecoming*

*The problem is not that gay men with HIV and AIDS are invisible, marginal, and
excluded from citizenship. Rather that they are rendered visible in ways that make
the experience of the disease a particularly agonizing one.*

– Robert Ariss, *Against Death* (10)

The Practice of Autoethnography in the Time of AIDS

The published volume *Unbecoming* (1990) represents the AIDS
diaries composed and revised from September 1987 to August
1988 by Eric Michaels, an American citizen who worked in Australia as an anthropologist under the auspices of the Institute for
Aboriginal Studies and Griffith University, studying what he provocatively labelled 'the Aboriginal invention of television.' The
mandate of his anthropological studies was to 'assess the impact
of television on remote Aboriginal communities' by examining
particular communities 'before and after' its introduction.[1] As
Jay Ruby observes, Michaels departed from his initial assignment
to document the reception of television by the Warlpiri at Yuendumu, choosing to adopt instead an interventionist model, one
that would facilitate some degree of agency for community members (226–7). Working with Michaels, the Warlpiri people began

not merely to watch mainstream television broadcasts, but also to produce videos, to disseminate their productions to other communities, and to create a media association to advocate for their interests as producers.

In the year before his AIDS-related death in 1988, Eric Michaels was just beginning to achieve a measure of public recognition on the basis of his contribution to media studies. The complex contingencies of having his research recognized as he starts to become seriously ill are not lost on him as he records this strange turn of events in his diary. 'The oddness' of 'the experience of being so objectified (recorded, reviewed, evaluated, published)' in academic circles is both highlighted and ultimately surpassed by the weirdness of the prospect of being objectified by the institutions that manage him as a person with AIDS (*Unbecoming* 97). The feeling is more than one of oddness, though. As he contemplates achieving celebrity as a publicly visible person with AIDS, Michaels confronts the question of how he might strategically resist the 'lurid tabloid mythologies about "great potential nipped in the bud"' or 'AIDS: the tragedy of what he could have been' and overcome the difficulty of even contemplating resistance in a media environment so saturated with pre-given meanings (97).

Michaels's dilemma about how to represent his illness resonates with that of the Warlpiri and other Aboriginal groups confronting the question of how to represent their culture in the age of mass communications technology. In both instances, there exists an imperative to counter the silencing and flattening effects of mainstream network television with resistant cultural practices, although oppositional strategies are far from being obvious or straightforward. Certainly, mainstream network television's paradigm for representing and interpreting the AIDS epidemic could have seemed in 1988 (and as it still does much of the time) almost impossible to disrupt. Polished and conventionalized, mixing fear-mongering with reassurance, television melodramas tend to atomize and depoliticize the health crisis. As Paula Treichler has documented, while 'internationally, television is the single most important source of information about AIDS and HIV,' network TV has failed to live up to its pedagogical potential, consistently preferring to narrate the 'AIDS story' as 'always something that happens to individuals ... that is not socially produced and does not demand social action or policy' (182). Sentimentalization is the banal surface of the potential for selective vision that lurks in mass media representations of HIV/ AIDS and, more particularly, in the way that viewers are solicited to respond to representations of the disease. Treichler identifies in televised narratives a drive to contain 'AIDS' and 'homosexuality' manifested in a tendency to 'offe[r] viewers the family's perspectives, trea[t] homosexuality as a central and legitimate problem for the straight characters, mak[e] little reference to AIDS as a national health-care crisis, and rende[r] the rage and political mobilization of activist groups invisible, indeed, incomprehensible' (180–1).[2] For Michaels, who unceasingly theorizes his testimonial project, 'At least one reason for publishing this journal is to counter the sentimentalized narratives that seem to be all that San Francisco has been able to produce about this sequence; and to reconfirm first principles' (*Unbecoming* 97). But, while writing and publishing a written diary that confounds the 'sense' of generic codes may also be seen as a strategy for intervening in AIDS discourse, the conventions established by television's melodramatic narratives are so influential that one contradicts or resists their logic at the risk of rendering one's personal account culturally unintelligible.

Michaels compares his diary unfavourably to his own compulsive viewing of a television drama: 'Why can't I accomplish the same damn effect [as the series] with this bloody journal? I read through most of it last night: the textual moves I made ..., the juxtapositions of time and place, etc., and the effect isn't riveting at all. (Hence, they have been removed.)' (34). His rhetorical devices for binding the text together seem to have failed him; they cannot make sense out of his experiences. Part of the problem is that 'present circumstances,' which limit his mobility, 'offer no ... possibilities for active narrative devices.' Similarly, a second strategy of 'moving around in time' – in effect making the diary 'a kind of time machine, which, while always returning to my present terminal illness,' would extend its reach to 'a more general autobiographical range' – is subsumed by the temptation of 'explicit reflexivity' (19). He worries nonetheless that

I leave nothing generic for the reader to hang on to. Worse, my own posthumous editorial voice keeps resurrecting from a cheaply ironized gallows (as I'm doing now) to confound utterly the cacophony of voices I employ throughout. Hoping the effect will be art is even more arrogant than hoping the effect will be sense. (34)

Anxious about the posthumous fate of his writings, Michaels rereads his journal entries, identifying, even as he mock-laments, his diary's excessive defiance of the 'familiar' (and 'familiarizing') of the genre of the family melodrama, which characteristically attempts to impose radical closure on threats to the social, economic, and sexual arrangements that the family embodies and represents as natural, even as it expresses extreme dissatisfaction with these structures. And yet Michaels also recognizes that he must engage to some extent with the terms of melodrama, and risk being read as melodramatic, if he is to represent effectively and movingly for a diverse audience the material specificities of his life and of his illness and to convey his melancholic refusal of the practices of remembrance and mourning that would redeem him and his death. As my readings of Derek Jarman's diary and Amy Hoffman's memoir have established, it is characteristic of AIDS testimonial writing (whether written in the first-person or remembered at second hand) for the semblance of rationality and the forward push of narrative progress to falter, if not to collapse entirely, under the weight of grief, doubt, and passion. For better or for worse, it seems that melodrama's theatricality and its rhetoric of moral polarization offer the most powerful model available in the context of the epidemic for rendering private lives memorable and meaningful to others (Brooks 59).[3]

Read as a melodramatic gesture that at once claims diary-writing as a heroic endeavour and mocks its pretensions, the phrase 'first principles' draws attention to Michaels's life and death as enacting an ethical drama. The elements of this drama are several. Certainly the phrase refers Michaels's readers to his affirmation of a gay male counter-culture, and his particular generational amalgam of 'marxist/zen/hippy' (*Unbecoming* 13). He laments that the counter-culture's communitarian values are being compromised by consumerism in the 1980s: just as hippy culture suffered a devolution to 'New Age' under the pressure of its market-driven sponsors, so too 'the young'uns at the nouveau preppy discos are taught to believe they are mainstream American consumers, no different from any other upwards socially mobile business major,' and are sold 'the image of the gay capitalist ... along with Nautilus, EST [home security systems], and Coors Beer' (128).[4] But I suspect that the 'first principles' also encompasses the broader issue of Michaels's critical troubling of methodology in the context of anthropology, and his searching application of this argument to the narration of his illness and death.[5]

Grappling with Michaels's professional background as ethnographer – and his self-reflexive questioning of disciplinary assumptions and practices – is crucial to understanding his approach to writing about the experience of living with and dying from AIDS. Throughout his essays and occasional pieces, as in his diary, Michaels interrogates the discourses that oppose civilization to savagery. He argues strenuously against the imposition of Western assumptions about aesthetic value, kinship norms, and political organization onto Aboriginal peoples, and sought to identify ways for people who had been positioned, in the wake of contact with European explorers and settlers, as 'objects' of ethnography to wrest some influence (if not control) over how they are represented. By seizing the visual as well as the literary technologies of colonization for their own purposes, Aboriginal peoples could, Michaels argued, based on his work with the Warlpiri, strategically engage with the colonizers' assumptions and refute their status as authoritative. Self-reflexivity thus formed an indispensable feature of his practice, as exemplified in his determined questioning in his commentary on the Warlpiri of the aesthetic privileging of originality, a concept which, he insisted, stood in the way of understanding Warlpiri cultural work on its own terms: namely, as more interested in the '*practices* of cultural reproduction' than in pursuing the logic of novelty required to make 'art' readable as such for Western observers ('For a Cultural Future' 119).[6]

In the diary, Michaels connects the themes of cultural resistance and survival that he explored in his academic work with his own medical situation in the mid-1980s. He draws on his work in anthropology to analyse not only medical discourse and practices but, moreover, to lay bare the customs, rituals, and myths that shape the lived meanings of illness and death in Western culture. Michaels turns a self-reflexive ethnographic eye on himself, his network of friends, colleagues, and family, and the media and institutions that shape his experience of HIV/AIDS. As HIV-positive anthropologist Robert Ariss, writing about gay-identifying men with HIV/AIDS in Sydney from 1988 to 1991, explains in the introduction to his study, anthropology's 'history of interest in questions of health, illness, healing, and death' lends it to the project of 'weld[ing] local experiences of illness to broader social, economic, political and cultural contexts,' making studies informed by anthropology a crucial component of a 'counter-discourse' about AIDS 'to that of biomedicine' – and to biomedicine's history of pathologizing homosexuality (5–

6, 18–22). In turn, 'anthropology requires that the ethnographer simultaneously immerse him- or herself in the life of a community under study while ceaselessly problematizing that experience' (*Against Death* 3).[7] In precisely this spirit of struggling to critique an experience in which he is also totally immersed, Michaels attempts to bring into focus the logic by which AIDS is domesticated – and some of its more discomfiting implications for the 'general public' avoided or contained – as well as the diary's rhetorical strategies for defamiliarizing this logic. These strategies involve the dual meanings embedded in the term 'defamiliarization.' *Unbecoming* pits a strategy of estrangement against the naturalized links between illness, degeneracy, and social exclusion and against the desire to assimilate illness and death to a set of reassuring fictions. Just as important, it attempts to confound, as Hoffman also attempts in *Hospital Time* – but from her position as an extra-familial mourner and witness-narrator – the privileges and the powers of redemption accorded to the familial.

Let me preface my exploration of *Unbecoming*'s interventions in AIDS discourse by first outlining, with reference to Michaels's own theorizing of the relation between autobiography and ethnography, the possibility that the diaries can usefully be construed as an exercise in autoethnography, that is to say, as a self-reflexive act of writing back to the cultural centre so as to resist cultural forms, assumptions, and hierarchies of value that are experienced as oppressive and dehumanizing (Pratt, *Imperial Eyes* 7).[8] While Michaels does not explicitly label his writing as autoethnographic, the commentaries he offers on other autobiographers' practices lead me to think that this term is indeed appropriate to describe his approach. He records a search for models, encouraged by his friend and editor Paul Foss; however, none of the authors he reads, ranging from Joe Orton to Anais Nin, provides a workable or, to his eye, intellectually honest example for writing his experience.[9] Almost simultaneously, Michaels also put into publication a pointed critique of the role of autobiographical narrative in contemporary debates about 'Aboriginality' and the representation of ethnic identities, and this essay is germane to my point here. In 'Para-Ethnography' (1988), Michaels attacks the assumptions and reading practices he observes in the reception of Bruce Chatwin's *Songlines* and Sally Morgan's *My Place*. These texts, he observes, combine the modes of life-writing and ethnography in their attempts to negotiate between Aboriginal and white settler identities and thereby to arrive at some kind of ameliorating compromise of perspectives. Michaels, who tangles intrepidly with the ethical questions that arise in the project of studying media production and reception among the Warlpiri, spares no criticism for texts he sees as breezing past the necessity of questioning ethnographic practice and, in this sense, as epitomizing the central 'issues within current anthropological discourse and theory' (175).[10] Noting first the tension between Western understandings of the self's autonomy and Aboriginal conceptions of collective identity, Michaels contests the grounds of the popularity of *Songlines* and *My Place* in the context of efforts to define an Australian national identity as the country prepared to celebrate in 1988 the bicentenary of its colonization by Europeans:

Yet perhaps it is precisely the ability of [these narratives] to mediate philosophically and objectively incompatible positions to produce a satisfying narrative construction that is the source of their popularity. The masked contradictions of each authorial persona seem central to accomplishing this. The issues of traditionalism and change become much more accessible, indeed manageable, on these pages than anywhere else. (175)

He argues that such narratives should be considered as 'para-ethnography,' a term that would mark the interested (and mostly hidden) borrowings they make from other primary documents in cultural fieldwork. Despite the exaggeration, his critique of these two popular memoirs effectively foregrounds the difficulty of evading ethnography's historical pedigree as a discourse of domestication in the service of imperialism, whose 'territorial and visual forms,' as Pratt points out, 'are those of the modern state' (*Imperial Eyes* 64). In the cases of Chatwin and Morgan, Michaels argues that if their memoirs were acknowledged as texts situated at a remove from fieldwork, and as textual accounts of the self organized or at least influenced by the narrative trajectory of triumphant individualism, such 'para-ethnographies' would perhaps be less easily or blandly recruited as authoritative representations (as Chatwin's text was when it was offered as testimonial evidence in land-claims trials).[11] Television narratives produced and distributed by major networks can be regarded similarly: as para-ethnographies (and perhaps para-pedagogies) that recycle 'common-sense' knowledge, and that are at risk of abusing their powerful cultural influence.

Michaels's approach to writing about his own life and death is as much a hybrid as that adopted by Morgan's and Chatwin's memoirs, partaking of an ethnographic mode without comprising an ethnographic study per se: *Unbecoming* places its observations within a loosely chronological framework, investigating how the meanings of HIV infection and AIDS are constructed through social custom and symbol and how these meanings shape the everyday experience of illness, constructing an ad hoc and highly personalized medical anthropology. But far from striving to 'mediate philosophically and objectively incompatible positions,' Michaels's diary elaborates contradiction: it pushes its rhetoric into the realm of melodramatic hyperbole and draws attention to the vocabulary it draws from cultural theory as well as to its frequent self-reflexive moments. The definition of auto-ethnography proposed by Françoise Lionnet develops in further detail the possibility of an oppositional deployment of ethnography in autobiographical texts. Lionnet glosses the concept as gesturing to 'the defining of one's subjective ethnicity as mediated through language, history, and ethnographical analysis; in short, ... the book [here, Zora Neale Hurston's *Dust Tracks on a Road*] amounts to a kind of "figural anthropology of the self"' (99). The crucial point to be gleaned from Lionnet's discussion is that when life-writing is approached as the composition of a 'self-portrait' rather than as a linear, chronological, 'realist' transcription of events and characters, then this kind of project aligns itself in a critical relation to ethnography, the writing of culture based on first-hand experience, as is the case with Hurston, who, like Michaels, engaged in extensive anthropological fieldwork.[12]

Lionnet conceptualizes self-portraiture as a self-reflexive activity that parallels and overlaps with the writing of culture; she extends this argument in an existential direction, calling it 'a process of collecting and gathering, of assembling images and metaphors to portray a figural self, always already caught in entropy and in permanent danger of returning to "dust," of becoming again "part and parcel" of the universe' (115). I introduce this formulation to suggest that Michaels composes a self-portrait that reflexively situates the 'self' culturally, creating a testimonial document that is 'related to practices that inform a mode of life while dynamically shaping reality,' and one that is hence organized according to rhetorical topoi. But self-portraits are also written in awareness of imminent disintegration and posthumous misinterpretation, and these are sources of apprehension and danger that Michaels was aware of facing in painfully literal terms. Autoethnographic strategies are nonetheless strategically powerful resources for social analysis and criticism, for, as a consequence of autoethnography's provisional qualities and its self-consciousness about the construction of meaning, readers are positioned as active participants in creating the text's meanings. Yet, where Zora Neale Hurston's self-portrait, for example, becomes celebratory in its interweaving of cultural traditions to create a multidimensional sense of self-in-community, constructing the historical (and yet not simply nostalgic) context that is necessary for building such connections, Michaels's personal ethnographic practice only becomes more anguished, its tropological patterns trailing off into a series of ellipses. In his immediate confrontation with illness and death, Michaels encounters 'trouble with "I-ness" at every moment and writing is no cure for that at all' (*Unbecoming* 6).

The contradictory recognition of both writing's failure and its necessity – a melancholic view of the impossibility of stabilizing meaning – constitutes the grounds of Michaels's intervention in the cultural construction of the 'truth' about the AIDS epidemic. In effect, he offers a series of vignettes that play the individual experience of illness against the recuperative tendencies of AIDS discourse. Motivated on the one hand by impulses towards the surveillance and management of the infected body, AIDS discourse seeks a more subtle form of containment when it attempts to generalize the disease's 'human' face. Shuttling between two forms of visibility – the drive to designate risk groups, and the rhetoric of a universal human condition – AIDS discourse tends to displace the material specificity of lives lived in particular cultural contexts, an erasure of subjective experience that renders the body tractable to biomedical authority and amenable to familial recuperation, which threaten to return the person living with HIV infection or AIDS, or lost to AIDS, to the docility of the closet. Michaels – though his efforts are more diffuse than those of organized activists, who often target specific policy and treatment issues – can be thought of having improvised in *Unbecoming* a self-conscious confrontation with cultural constructions of AIDS from the point of view of personal experience of those constructions. (Michaels wrote the diaries before the establishment of ACT UP in Australia in 1990, almost three years after its founding in the United States, and before the availability of AZT in Australia [Ariss 171, 184].) Regarding himself as a 'hypertypical' example of his generation, Michaels embarks on a reflexive ethnographic investigation of his self as a social site (*Unbecoming* 7).

He approaches his body as a ruin for excavation, an artifact that makes legible in glimpses a legacy of culturally and historically determined damage. Michaels thus writes an autoethnography that works against redemption, an oppositional account of the self-in-culture in the context of AIDS.[13] He provocatively draws an extended analogy between his position as a person living with AIDS and the discourses by which the 'civilized' is opposed to the 'savage,' suggesting that the diseased body and the racialized body are constructed by overlapping linguistic and visual technologies for civilization or domestication. Emphasizing the connections and analogies between the diseased body and the body defined as racially or culturally other, Michaels represents himself metaphorically as colonized by the discourse of AIDS. This textual strategy may seem excessive and self-indulgent, or it may with some justification be read as a white male anthropologist's arrogant conflation of disparate historical struggles; however, if taken not as equation or appropriation but rather as analogy, it yields a powerfully estranging, analytical view of illness, sexuality, and culture. The prominent place Michaels's account gives to its self-reflexive autoethnographic awareness emphasizes that mourning and melancholia constitute phenomena at once psychic and cultural, and that our cultural patterns for grieving are structured by the abjection of stigmatized bodies, in which are conflated the categories of disease, death, deviance, and foreignness. In turn, *Unbecoming* questions the logic of the family melodrama and the role performed by the idea of the nuclear family in mediating the abject status of the HIV-positive body and the body with AIDS in relation to the body politic. Finally, the photographic portrait of Michaels that prefaces *Unbecoming* moves the question of abjection into the sphere of visual representations of HIV infection and AIDS, bringing home, in a visceral and unmistakable way, the entanglement of our picturings of the epidemic in broader ethical dramas of embodiment, racialization, identity, and cultural survival.

Melancholia and Theories of Abjection

Focusing on his bodily experience, Michaels analyses the systems of signification that constitute the meanings of HIV infection and AIDS, in effect offering an ethnographic analysis of the material, spatial, and temporal dimensions of his bodily and psychic predicament. In the opening pages of *Unbecoming*, the appearance of Kaposi's sarcoma lesions on his skin promises, at first, the relief of narrative certainty:

I watched these spots on my legs announce themselves over a period of weeks, taking them as some sort of morphemes, arising out of the strange uncertainties of the past few years to declare, finally, a scenario. As if these quite harmless-looking cancers might, when strung together, form sentences which would give a narrative trajectory, a plot outline, at last to a disease and a scenario that had been all too vague. (3)

The narrator is positioned simultaneously as observer *and* participant in this scenario, and his theorizing about the symbolic structures and narratives that shape his experience are tied inextricably to the problems of affect and self-identity. On the one hand innocuous and 'harmless-looking,' the lesions seem, on the other hand, to constitute 'morphemes' – linguistic units or signs – that, read together, as they appear over time, offer a narrative, the closure of a 'diagnosis' with AIDS by way of 'those little circlets of morbidity' (13, 79). However, although Michaels begins to articulate a distinction between past (uncertainty and vagueness) and present (clarity), 'the strange uncertainties of the past few years' remain, ultimately, the same 'strange uncertainties' of the present (3). The passage continues by adding the wry observation: 'But, of course, this relief proves always a false and premature dispensation' (3). While 'cultural anxiety and dread' seem to entail, as Thomas Yingling argues, that the 'literality' of AIDS 'must also be continually addressed in strenuous, referential nar-

ratives of victimization, punishment, resistance, and healing,'
Michaels's account stages a different relation to this material sign
('AIDS in America' 293). His becoming symptomatic in fact complicates rather than simplifies his relation to his body and to
other people, because it imposes visibility, leaving him with no
choice but to make his illness public: 'Perhaps the oddest thing
about AIDS is that it takes so very long; one is required to live
through all its stages, at each point confronted with insane, probably pathological choices. This week, it's who to tell, and how'
(*Unbecoming* 3). Without clearly defined choices as to the course
of his life's narrative, where or how can Michaels exercise any
agency with respect to how he is interpreted and treated? *Unbecoming* draws attention to the various kinds of dissonance that are
created in his social milieu as his body begins to exhibit visible
signs of illness, including the temptation to accept, even to
desire, the finality of a fatal disease as releasing him from the dis-
tress of temporal uncertainty.

As is exemplified by these introductory paragraphs, Michaels
appears to prefer a strategy of 'coldly enumerating' his losses, as
though he might resist sentimentality by adopting the purer
faithfulness of objective documentation (Derrida, *Memoires* 31).
And yet the voice Michaels records here, confused and deeply
ironic, may also be read as passionately angry, raising the question of the importance of affect in the diaries. He often occupies
a melancholic register that resembles that of Amy Hoffman:

I can't sleep and I can't do anything but. I wake up repeatedly in the
middle of the night with the horrors. I don't even want to call anybody. I
have no interest in working and I haven't even been pursuing my immigration business responsibly. My physician seems to have deserted me.
My conviction that the world I perceive corresponds to anybody else's is
slipping. Maybe I died in November and this is some awful postmortem
fantasy I inhabit now. (*Unbecoming* 80)

Derek Jarman's garden at Prospect Cottage, Dungeness, Kent, domi-
nated by the view of the Dungeness nuclear station. The garden's ac-
cumulation of local plants and its arrangement of found objects may
be read as an allegory of persistence and survival in the face of HIV
infection.

Prospect Cottage (front view), Dungeness, Kent. The contrast between the formal arrangement of the front garden and the randomness of the rear garden emphasizes the dialectic of control and decay in Jarman's Prospect Cottage, as well as in his other literary and visual self-representations.

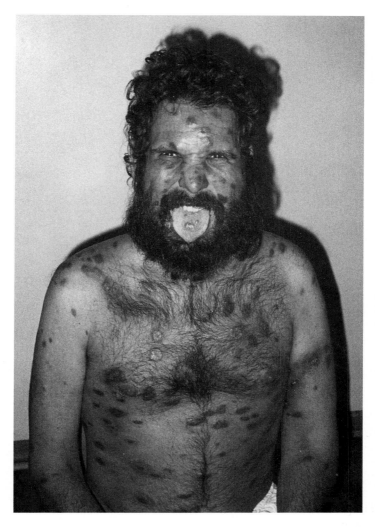

Eric Michaels, Brisbane, Australia, 1988. This startling photograph
appears as the frontispiece to the published version of Michaels's
diary. Multiple interpretations of this image are discussed in Chapter 3, 'Resisting Redemption: Strategies of Defamiliarization in
Eric Michaels's *Unbecoming*.'

This panel, one of four by the gay group Sisters of Perpetual Indulgence, completes an image of the sun and exemplifies the tactility, irreverence, and excessiveness of the quilt's individual panels. Such qualities work against the quilt's being interpreted entirely in the context of disavowal and guilt.

The 1996 display of the AIDS Memorial Quilt in Washington, DC. On display in a national context, the quilt may be read as domesticating and flattening the individual lives and collective identities it represents.

Prospect Cottage (rear view), Dungeness, Kent.

The portrait of Eric Michaels echoes and aims to contest the composition of turn-of-the-century European and settler representations of Aboriginal people, such as this painting, entitled *Head of an Aborigine,* by Girolamo Nerli (born Italy 1860, arrived Australia 1885, died Italy 1926. Oil on cardboard. 25.6 × 18.2 cm. Purchased 1957. National Gallery of Victoria, Melbourne, Australia).

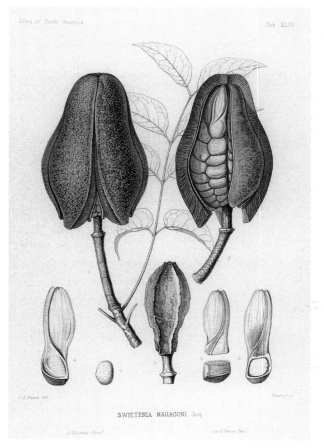

The fruit of the mahogany tree, from *The Silva of North America: A Description of the Trees Which Grow Naturally in North America Exclusive of Mexico*. Jamaica Kincaid's *My Brother* is preoccupied with plant imagery. Kincaid refers to the mahogany fruit as a metaphor for her brother's life, in an attempt to render it beautiful and meaningful to her, but ultimately the image is more resonant as a way of describing the complexity of her own memories.

Despite Michaels's impassioned rejection of 'psychologism' ('I had rather a gutful of psychologizing in my youth,' he complains) in favour of 'culturalogical explanation' ('the individual is a social/cultural collaborative construct, not an atomistic product of individual will'), it remains possible, and is in fact crucial, to look at these two modes of 'explanation' together (6). Michaels's statement that his 'encounter' as a student 'with culturalogical explanation was a revelation, a discovery *embraced longingly'* betrays the sense that affect informs his commitment to cultural analysis, and implicitly blurs the distinction between psychology and cultural theory (6; emphasis added). In the face of his claims to the contrary, the theories and practices of psychology and ethnography often work corroboratively in Michaels's diaries, for, despite his tendency to think of them as opposites, they raise, in fact, many of the same questions (How are knowledge, subjectivity, and cultural formations constituted and legitimated?) and are preoccupied with shared themes (such as trauma, myth, ritual, the body, mourning). With their impassioned, melodramatic rhetoric (often edging into invective), Michaels's diary delineates the interlinking, mutually constitutive relation between the psychic and the cultural in ways that complement and complicate current theoretical understandings of abjection and, in turn, the relation of abjection to mourning and melancholia.[14]

What strains against the 'plot outline' in the opening paragraphs of *Unbecoming* – the narrative certainty that Michaels almost begins to desire here – is the very 'body' that produces the cancers that seems to launch the narrative trajectory towards disintegration and death. Derrida's writings on mourning and AIDS, like Butler's, seem to privilege the linguistic and discursive as opposed to the material dimensions of the question, and might be criticized for appearing to elide the differing material, historical specificities of bodies and, in a sense, to downplay the

passions that most concern them. As William Haver stresses in
The Body of This Death, 'AIDS discourse has by and large sustained
a fatal nostalgia for the clean and proper body, which is also a no
less fatal nostalgia for the clean and proper body politic' (8).
While the 'erotic body' may be an 'unimaginable figure' for cultural theorizing about HIV and AIDS, it remains a crucial consideration precisely because it constitutes 'a thought ... of the limit,'
a thought of what has been delegitimated in imaginings (historical and contemporary) of the social body (xi). I want to suggest
that the conflict in *Unbecoming* between the inclination to search
for narrative dispensation and a persistent (but ambivalent)
return to questions of embodiment – and of the hypervisibility
and vulnerability of the symptomatic body – necessitates considering another theoretical axis regarding melancholia: What do
we mean exactly by the phenomenon of bodily abjection? What
are its poetics? And how does a determination to confront abjection shape Michaels's autoethnographic document of AIDS?

The term 'abjection' requires a little more elaboration given its
importance to my reading of *Unbecoming*. According to Julia
Kristeva's analysis of how bodies are defined and how they function symbolically in Western culture, 'the body must bear no trace
of its debt to nature: it must be clean and proper in order to be
fully symbolic' (*Powers of Horror* 101). Bodily integrity is defined
through and against the corporeal fluidity associated with an
array of excluded, and potentially polluting, others (1–3). Anything or anyone that appears to threaten the self's boundaries
is by definition (and for definition's sake) rejected, jettisoned,
abjected from the self and from cultural recognizability (2–4, 69).
Identities depend, in other words, for their social meanings on
the construction of a 'constitutive outside,' a realm of discredited
others who, as rejected exemplars of what the culture abomi-
nates, in effect work to define the self's boundaries, marking the
self as the opposite or negation of all that is not valued or privileged (Butler, *Bodies That Matter* 20). Given this broader cultural

context, the tendency to render HIV infection and AIDS-related illnesses as abject is certainly far from arbitrary. HIV makes the body prone to a host of opportunistic infections, as well as to the ravages of medications and the press of institutional power – all conditions that contradict the fictions of bodily integrity. As Kristeva points out, skin is a crucial element in defining symbolic boundaries: while, in its intact state, skin emphasizes 'biological and psychic individuation,' *broken* skin is rendered as a figure for 'intermixing, erasing of differences, threat to identity' (*Powers of Horror* 101). With HIV infection and AIDS-related illnesses – as in Michaels's account of looking at the lesions that appear on his body and in the focus on leprosy in Kristeva's analysis – 'it is as if the skin, a fragile container, no longer guaranteed the integrity of one's "own and clean self" but, scraped or transparent, invisible or taut, gave way before the dejection of its contents' (53). Neither, however, should the virus or its various effects be considered exclusively to embody the abject, but rather should be considered as a particularly intense expression of a wider cultural problematic. Warning against our taking the abject as an essential category, Kristeva refers to abjection as a narrative process serving to 'safeguard' civilization: it is 'not lack of cleanliness or health that causes abjection but what disturbs identity, system, order. What does not respect borders, positions, rules' (4). Aligned materially (and socially) with 'waste, blood, decay, bodily fluids and infection,' with what threatens to 'pollute' bodily boundaries and ultimately the integrity of 'individual and social order,' HIV infection and AIDS throws these symbolic boundaries into chaos,[15] provoking the panicked reiteration of bodily boundaries (and the abjection of what appears to threaten them) in the public discourses of AIDS (Zivi 39–40).[16]

Writing cannot cure the body, but can it intervene to challenge the abject position that the body with AIDS is assigned in our shared cultural imaginings of the disease? Echoing Michaels's lament that writing fails to furnish a cure, and Derrida's complaint that as a mourner he loses the capacity for storytelling (*Memoires* 3), Kristeva suggests in her analysis of depression that there is nonetheless a content in the incoherent language of 'melancholy people': they are 'Messengers of Thanatos,' not in the sense of being driven towards death, but rather in the sense of being unwilling 'witnesses/accomplices of the signifier's flimsiness, the living being's precariousness' (*Black Sun* 20). Characterized by an excess of affect, melancholia loosens the subject from the constraints of inhibition and deprives her or him of the capacity to look at the world in symbolically coherent terms, thus undermining, through its failure to 'respect borders, positions, rules,' the hold of the law of abjection (*Powers of Horror* 4). Kristeva's account of depression contributes a description of melancholic language that is particularly useful for reading Michaels's representation of his symptomatic body. The melancholic refusal of compensation for loss results in the cruel undoing of what Michaels refers to as the 'dispensation' afforded by narrative. Kristeva sees melancholic speech as 'the exercise of an impossible mourning, the setting up of a fundamental sadness and an artificial, unbelievable language, cut out of the painful background that is not accessible to any signifier and that intonation alone, intermittently, succeeds in inflecting' (43). Unable to articulate a coherent narrative of the borderline state in which he or she is immersed, the melancholic subject preserves attachment to – and ambivalent love for – bodies that exceed the boundaries of the 'clean and proper.' Through her negotiation between the *inability* to mourn (conceived of as pathological deficiency, an illness or disease of the subject) and the *unwillingness* to mourn (conceived of as dissent or resistance), Kristeva emphasizes the profoundly unsettling effects of melancholic speech for narration as well as the ambivalent agency that resides in melancholic attachment.[17] Exemplifying melancholic awareness of 'the living being's precariousness,' Eric Michaels testifies to the material fragility of his body as he becomes increasingly ill and struggles against his vulnerability to punitive social definitions and to the more subtle pressures of redemption and normalization. Incapable of forming a narrative about his experience, Michaels determines nonetheless to record the luminous, disconnected details of the history of a catastrophic bodily experience and to influence how his account will be interpreted by others, refusing to allow us recourse to the law of abjection. Abandoning readers in a defiantly unbeautiful landscape, one resistant to redemption but always vulnerable to it, *Unbecoming* points out the pattern of disavowals by which the body with AIDS is rendered abject, positioned outside and as a threat to the imaginary 'clean and proper' social bodies, not only of the self, but also by extension those of the nation and the family. In the process of revealing these patterns, it also seeks to destabilize them.

Interrogating Boundaries: Hospital, Nation, and Family in Australia

In *Unbecoming*, the preservation of a melancholic attachment to the culturally taboo is staged as resisting – and potentially counteracting – the 'process of labelling, a struggle with institutional forms, a possible Foucauldian horror show' experienced by the symptomatic HIV-positive person (4–5), that is, a nightmarish resurgence of the conflation in biomedical discourse of disease, mental illness, and homosexuality (Ariss 18–22). *Unbecoming* actively dedicates itself to unworking these fictions, offering a cogent critique of the violence of a mourning that would, through the logic of familiarization, redeem Michaels's prodigality. While Ariss suggests that 'being HIV-positive is a process of self-reconstruction, of becoming. Of realizing oneself in a cultural environment of constantly shifting constructions of illness,' Michaels, rather than directly countering the definitional power of institutions by reconstructing his identity, could be said to disarticulate his identity, to elaborate the decay of his body's bound-

aries, and to draw attention to the symbolic threat his body poses
to the literal and imagined boundaries of national and familial
bodies (55–6). Echoing ethnography's impulse to redeem the
'savage' from anachronism and cultural extinction to modernity,
AIDS discourse, especially its televisual narrative version, is prone
to 'an almost utopian narrative of elegiac fatefulness in which
aesthetic universality redeems individual suffering' (Treichler
105). In analysing the disarticulation of identity and bodily experience, *Unbecoming* intervenes in the naturalization in AIDS discourse of the hierarchy of observer and observed, European and
native, normal and deviant, redeemer and redeemed. There are
three intersecting sites where the logic of abjection is shown to
be at work on medically ill bodies: the hospital, the nation, and
the family, three of the most important and identifiable institutional locations of AIDS discourse. Michaels explores his body's
increased subjection to the matrices of power and knowledge in
the context of each of these sites, and identifies their collective,
mutually reinforcing designs for fending off the abject, the
excluded 'other' to which these systems remain vulnerable
despite their efforts to guarantee stable boundaries. In particular, his structural analysis of space and social custom emphasizes
kinship's role as the intermediary institution that would repair
the rupture in the social body threatened by the body with AIDS,
restoring it to propriety and, symbolically at least, relieving the
state of the obligation to address the epidemic.

According to Michaels – and his propensity for self-conscious
cultural analysis becomes sharply evident here – the hospital is
'one of those superbly rich sites of contradiction, sort of a Foucauldian holy ground' (14). 'Barbaric' definitions of disease and
contamination are 'inflicted' bodily, through the alarming proliferation of prophylaxes: the multiplication of 'rubber gloves, face
masks, goggles, and an inventory of tropes,' suggesting to
Michaels that 'medical practice' does not 'deal so much with the
disease ... but more evidently ... with sin and retribution' (5).

Medical knowledge is analysed as culturally constructed, with specific attention here to the circulation of the belief that HIV is so infectious that no number of prophylactic barriers would suffice to protect an HIV-negative health care worker (and the discourse in 1987–8 tended to assume that all health care workers would necessarily fall into this category) against potential infection.[18]

As an account of the subjective experience of illness, *Unbecoming* not only documents and critically analyses the gaps, contradictions, and inconsistences of medical language and institutional practices of medicine. Like Jarman and Hoffman, Michaels mobilizes the estranging perspective of a first-person point of view of the hospital environment, but in this case the angle of vision is one informed more explicitly by postmodern cultural theory, and the result is a perspective on hospitalization that draws out how both scientific and popular medical discourse tends to conceptualize AIDS in the terms of tropical medicine, desiring to see the epidemic as proper to a space that is 'elsewhere' and as affecting bodies that are in the first place vulnerable, deficient, and in need of containment (Patton, *Globalizing AIDS* 38). While from one side of the Royal Brisbane Hospital patients look at the building's power generator, from the other they see a view of 'the entry drive to an oddly pleasant colonial house and a niche of tropical plantings' (*Unbecoming* 5). The view of the generator suggests the hospital's role in 'generating' or producing the illnesses and dysfunctions it endeavours to treat (but which it also needs to see perpetuated in order to provide its *raison d'être*), a threatening implication that peeks out only occasionally from behind its cheerful public façade (5). At the same time, it is no accident that this description emphasizes the 'colonial house' and its garden, a carefully composed display of tropical vegetation. Far from offering a soothing and restful vista, an escape into a pastoral nature, these details raise, in an oblique and compressed fashion, the historical colonial definition of tropical nature as threatening and diseased, as a pathogenic landscape. As Alan Bewell points out, in

European medical geography of the nineteenth century 'sexuality, disease, race, and tropical environments are mapped onto
each other,' constituting the tropics as a site of contagion that
threatens the health of the British imperial body (24, 28). Metonymically speaking, the house and its garden – and their investment in curing a nature perceived as inherently diseased –
represent the late-twentieth-century hospital's occluded historical connection to the project of colonization. This project is, significantly, figured in domestic terms: European colonial domestic
architecture coexists with tropical nature represented by the garden, but the house and its occupants (whether historical or symbolic, the heirs of this structure's imaginary) have put nature on
the defensive, forcing it to remain within its designated niche. At
the same time, Michaels critically aligns the category of a 'pathological' and 'pathogenic' sexuality with the abject status of tropical nature in the neo-European cultural imaginary. He notes the
absurdity of his being placed in the hospital's infectious diseases
ward: despite the historical, metaphorical associations that align
sexually transmitted diseases with tropical nature, construing
them collectively as 'infectious,' 'AIDS is not an infectious disease: darling, if I had to tell you what I went through to get this,
your hair would curl pink! But we are terribly susceptible to disease' (*Unbecoming* 18). Highlighting this technical misconception
and its dangerous implications for him, Michaels parodies the
fear of infection, half-seriously, half-satirically representing HIV
as a distinction for his outstanding efforts in sexual experimenta-
tion, the knowledge of which, if shared, would be too much for
the unenlightened reader to withstand, would mark him or her as
irrecoverably 'pink': What, he teasingly asks, lies at the root of the
misconstruction of AIDS as infectious but the fear of some other
associated sexual and tropical contamination? Michaels thus plays
on what Patton terms the 'melodramatic narrative sensibility' of
tropical thinking itself: he situates himself as the 'problematic
mobile body' who is also the 'monster inside the domestic space,'

and thus as one who inspires an extreme emotional reaction in others by making it difficult for us to believe in our own immunity or in our ability to return to a safe haven (*Globalizing AIDS* 37, 62, 36).

'Between these two sides' of the hospital, that is, the two views from the windows of the rooms occupied by patients, representing two connected scenes of power (institutional and colonial), the hospital space itself exists as a netherworld where the oppositions of health and illness, purity and contamination require constant reiteration if any distinctions are to be maintained. Describing the 'long, crooked corridor' that links the various rooms of the hospital, Michaels observes it as being 'littered with wheeled stainless-steel objects, holding or conveying a bewildering assortment of wrapped things, wrapped to protect their sterility, or used, tainted things, wrapped to prevent contamination' (*Unbecoming* 14). These objects lose, for the moment, any specificity. Michaels concentrates instead on the symbolic system that constitutes the meanings of objects in what could be described as the medical contact zone. In this alienated, frozen landscape, the logic that defines the danger of medical instruments and materials becomes readable: objects are rendered as either contaminated or contaminating (or potentially so) in the bizarre logic of wrapping, the imposition of artificial skins, as it were, which would delineate boundaries on the paranoid basis of a possible tainting. Behind this obsession with prophylaxis and sterilization, there lurks a desire for protection or containment that exceeds reason, an obsession that echoes the colonial preoccupation with regulating hygiene and diet in colonial environments (Bewell 19, 149–60). (Noting this criticism is not necessarily to discount the ethical importance of 'universal precautions' in medical practice, but on the contrary to highlight how panic about contamination might lead to unnecessary precautions motivated by the symbolic reassurance they seem to furnish while at the same time ratcheting up fear.) The irrational energy expended on this effort to contain contamination has the ironic consequence, Michaels suggests, of making the corridor appear as though it has been strewn carelessly with what might as well be waste or garbage, rather than being a place where instruments and materials are arranged with careful precision for the purposes of healing.

Such patterns of attempted containment are more than merely symbolic; implicated in relations of power, they arrange the material, spatial, and psychic spaces where the individual, subjective experience of illness is lived. Because 'the hospital is the place one goes – or is sent – when something is wrong with one's body,' writes Linda Singer, corroborating Ariss's point, which I have taken as this chapter's epigraph, about the problem posed by medical visibility, 'the threat of hospitalization is the threat of not being all right and not being all right in a way that is all too socially visible' (Singer 100). Michaels interrogates that scenario, suggesting that the view from his hospital room in fact offers a panoramic historical and political perspective on 'not being all right':

A person lying in my bed merely looking around the room and out the window can see great distances, to parliamentary debates on condoms and morals, to histories of Australian asylums, etiquettes, hierarchies, and colonialism. But what most has me flat on my back here is a discourse of 'Tidiness.' (*Unbecoming* 14–15)

Historical links between categories of morality, madness, deviance, class, and colonialism have not disappeared in the late twentieth century, but linger on in the public debate regarding safer sex education and differing definitions of morality in the context of the epidemic (conservative reticence about sanctioning sexual activity by talking about it versus activists' assertion that safer sex practices must be publicly promoted). Michaels's immobilization, far from presenting a limitation to cultural analysis, offers him a chance to draw connections between apparently disconnected spheres. As a space where reticence, fear, and tidiness are concentrated, the hospital room yields, through the process of excavation and analysis to which Michaels subjects it, a far-reaching historical and ethnographic view of contemporary illness. Observed from the vantage point of a hospital bed, the 'endless rounds of cleaning, cleaning, cleaning' become apparent to Michaels as 'probably ... more ritual than rational – that the cleaners were instilling tidiness, not fighting disease.' According to his analysis, 'tidiness,' like the cult of 'fitness,' 'is a process which, while avowedly in the service of cleanliness and health, in fact is only interested in obscuring all traces of history, of process, of past users, of the conditions of manufacture (the high high gloss).' Due to its 'association with health and cleanliness,' tidiness 'is considered an appropriate discourse to inflict on the diseased, the aging, the putrefying.' Ritual tidiness pays no heed to the perspective of the ill: never mind that 'if you're actually the one sick and on your back,' 'you barely see' the floors and that 'what you do see is the ceiling, paint cracked, peeling and falling into the water jar, ceiling fan blades edged in dirt and encrusted with insects,' the point is that these polished floors are impressive and reassuring from the point of view of the 'well' (17).

As Ross Chambers has persuasively argued, *Unbecoming* dedicates itself to a project of irritation in 'its ambition to function as the permanent thorn in the side of Tidy Town and the continuing "Foucauldian horror show"' of illness, with the photographic portrait of Michaels, shirtless, tongue extended, and marked by cancerous lesions, standing as 'a critical counterimage that refuses to be tidied away or otherwise to disappear' (*Facing It* 108). Michaels's refusal of tidiness can be read, according to the theoretical terms I have been working with, as a challenge to the logic of abjection. His analysis of the hospital as a cultural site bears out Kristeva's observation that 'filth is not a quality in itself, but it applies only to what relates to a *boundary* and, more particularly, represents the object jettisoned out of that boundary, its

other side, a margin' (*Powers of Horror* 69). And he testifies to the
painful consequences of this logic for those who find themselves
'jettisoned,' cast beyond the borders of an imagined social body.
Already vulnerable to suffering – 'right now, neither of my
immune systems is worth shit' – Michaels finds himself having to
'share facilities, bathroom, and unsealed rooms with some of the
most exotic illnesses in the tropical world,' infectious diseases to
which his compromised immune system makes him extremely
vulnerable (*Unbecoming* 18). 'The floors may glow, but often as
not, the communal toilet is filthy,' and so he is 'terrified to go out
of [his] room into this tidy world' (18). The obscuring of visible
dirt attempts the forgetting of 'all natural (and finally historical)
processes,' that is, the presence of death and disintegration in
life, while at the same time ignoring how people living with compromised immune systems are affected by their surroundings,
and even subconsciously hastening death in the interests of forgetting this fragility (15). The purposes of critically reading this
pattern of abjecting 'natural' bodily processes are to unearth hidden 'historical' structures of power and domination as well as to
question the state of cleanliness and propriety that the performance of tidiness seeks symbolically to establish.

Exclusion took on a literal, legal dimension for Michaels: as an
American expatriate, without family in Australia, he was vulnerable to the bureaucracy's calculation of the costs of his remaining
in the country, which he represents, in a moment of theatrical
but nonetheless real extremity, as linked to his 'being an American, a foreigner, an Other, and subject to whatever anybody
thinks about that' (108). I want to expand upon Chambers's
emphasis on Michaels's critique of the discourse of tidiness by
arguing that 'anxiety' about the state's power to 'toss' him out
'(where? into the gutter? the sea?) at any moment' is a constant
concern in the diaries, and that his ambiguous position points up
how the abjection of AIDS is expressed in immigration policy
(23). Unable to work, Michaels was ultimately denied an exten-

sion of his residency in Australia, where, officials demurred, he
threatened to become a burden on the state's budget, while continuing to pose a threat to the health of the citizenry (114–15).[19]
In the state's logic, he is imagined as at once so gravely ill as to
require a host of expensive high-tech treatments and as still sexually active, posing a significant threat to others, a contradictory
attribution of passivity and agency that seems particularly cruel
in light of 'the sad fact that I expect never again to engage in
those caresses of the body which sustained and defined me for
most of my adult life' (58).

In the hyperbolic tone he favours as a vehicle for expressing
rage and indignation, Michaels attributes pathogenic, even geno-
cidal powers to the state policy itself, and to his friends' attempts
to explain this policy to him, playing on the valences of the word
'sick' (illness and disgust): 'That's what made me sick in the first
place: these endless dissertations on why, because I reject nationalism, and the nuclear family (for my own practice at least), I
have no rights, no rights at all ... and I may die in a way in which
I, but maybe only I, believe has elements of murder' (24–5). Too
ill, however, to travel, Michaels died in Brisbane while under a
deportation order, a virtual nonentity. While he presents himself
as the victim of the state, he also hints that his death may be seen
as an instance of 'stage-managing my own posthumosity,' a performative approach that points up his intransigence in staying in
his adopted country, despite its determination that he is not wel-
come, does not belong (103). With respect to the application of
immigration laws, *Unbecoming* offers itself as what Leigh Gilmore
calls a 'limit-case,' an autobiographical document that 'exam-
ine[s] the relations among people that exist in the presence of
trauma, and attempt[s] to historicize the relations from which
trauma has emerged in order to conceive of a self who can differ
from the identity trauma imposes' (*The Limits of Autobiography*
146). The 'limit-case,' especially, I would add, when it is construed ethnographically, 'produces an alternative jurisprudence

within which to understand kinship, violence, and self-representation,' with the self standing as 'a metaphor for the citizen,' or, to adapt Gilmore's comparison to the context of Michaels's situation, a 'non-citizen' whom the state sees as an unwelcome vagabond (despite his contribution to its intellectual and cultural life) (12). The mutually reinforcing definitions of nation and family are highlighted in the personal grounds given by the bureaucrats for his deportation: 'Dr. Michaels' treatment is available in his home country; that there are organisations set up to coordinate and provide assistance to AIDS sufferers, such as the National AIDS Network in Washington; and that all of Dr. Michaels' family are resident there' (*Unbecoming* 114–15). Australian federal government AIDS policy of 1989 formally named 'risk groups' (including surgery patients, prisoners, and sex workers) to be subject to mandatory HIV testing, and ordered the testing for HIV of all applicants for permanent residency status (and the universal refusal of applications from HIV-positive people) (Ariss 42–4). The category of citizenship may be extended, however, through the institution of the family. In other words, the family mediates the compassionate zone that can provisionally extend the category of citizenship to extend rights to non-nationals, providing the state the reassurance that the 'burdens' of contact and care will be shouldered voluntarily, privately. As Michaels sums up, 'Compassion is restricted to pair bonds' (*Unbecoming* 24). His bad etiquette in dying while in his adopted home rather than his native land points up the arbitrariness and painfulness of these distinctions, or what we might call the state's inhospitableness (103).

Michaels examines his relationships with his support network of friends in Brisbane and Sydney and reflects on the pressure he feels to reconnect in the context of his illness with his family of birth: through these specific examples he moves the discussion of kinship from a critique of how normative definitions of family mediate citizenship to a provocative rethinking of kinship's meanings and implications in the context of his illness and approaching death. The immigration department's letter is, in fact, one among many letters Michaels received during 1987–8, and the problems of exclusion, containment, and redemption are also readable in these personal communications, which can be viewed, to some extent, as versions in microcosm of the state's document: that is, as conventionalized documents that attempt to shore up the meanings of illness and symbolically to defuse its threatening aspects. Musing on his encounters with the strange genres of letters, visits, phone calls, and flower arrangements, the formalized varieties of personal communication that his hospital-ization seems to call forth, Michaels undertakes to analyse them from a depersonalized point of view, asking what is at stake in this resurgence of stylized behaviour in the context of illness. As in his analysis of the hospital, Michaels removes these genres from their immediate, personal contexts, focusing instead on how they work to constitute the meaning of his illness. The gifts and com-munications he receives are often disproportionate to his percep-tion of the level of intimacy he has with the individual sender: 'shows of support' contradict the relatively 'reserved conduct' that has previously governed many of these relationships (28). Letters, visits, and other gestures of support and reconnection, although they are in some sense crucial 'to maintaining resis-tance to the institutional discourses of the public hospital system so as to retain some dignity, assurance and self-definition,' he also reads as complexly motivated, often aggressive, and in any case far from uniformly benign in their effects (95): 'They're wonderful and they're scary; wonderful in what they say, scary in that they seem to represent some kind of genre/ritual – a little like looking up from your bed and discovering a priest giving final rites' (53). All in all, as Michaels observes of these interac-tions, 'there is a curious process of accounting going on' in his intimate relationships, one that contradicts any wish we might have to believe that these communications are natural, spontane-

ous, uninvested (28). The language of accounting applied here
to gestures that convention codes as spontaneous expressions of
feeling suggests that there exists an alignment of all of these acts
with the dehumanizing tidiness imposed by institutions of hospital, university, and immigration department: like the institutional
spaces that define Michaels's body as abject, it seems that these
generic forms also reflect a deep discomfort with his illness. Seeking to keep the thought of his disintegration at bay, these ritual-
ized genres of reconnection threaten to purge his life of its
specificity, depriving him of the identity he had constructed and
keeping his anger at a distance by rewriting his last days in terms
of sympathetic reciprocity.

   But the obsessive repetition of the words 'accounting' and 'calculation' throughout the diary suggests that there coexists with
this critique another possible reading of intimate relationships,
one in which all intimacy is thought of as implicated in relations
of power and dependency, and as open to reinvention. From the
vantage point of increasing vulnerability and dependency to others, Michaels subjects what he calls 'familialities' to ethnographic
analysis: his investigations suggest that while familial relations are
implicated in state power, they are not consistently reducible to it
(28). He dwells with melodramatic intensity on his estrangement
from his family in the United States, resisting the state's logic that
in lieu of being married he naturally belongs to – and is the
responsibility of – his parents and siblings. In a sense, it is this
family that is spectral, that intrudes itself, ghostly and undesired,
into Michaels's dying, as though the blood tie erased all other
chosen affiliations. Indeed, the diary is punctuated by a series of
visits from this long-since-distanced set of family members,
emphasizing the dissonance produced by their reappearance
under the sign of death. These visits, as they are anticipated and
analysed during and after the fact, foreground Michaels's distance from his father, brother, and sister in the United States,
and work to interrogate the naturalness and centrality of these

relations in the context of grieving, along with the renewed and threatening proximity that results from the family members' ambivalent desire for reconnection. Illness and looming mortality threaten to dissolve all the significance of his life and loves through the path of reabsorption into the nuclear family. Emphasizing his disconnection from his father and siblings, and suggesting that their relationships are characterized primarily by conflict, aggression, and misunderstanding, Michaels queries whether all that defines family for him now 'is reduced to "people who can get away with checking for dust on the top of the bookshelf"': What kind of intimacy is this but the assumed right to police another's tidiness and respectability? (104).

The visits of his family are not written off entirely, however; at times they are approached with a measure of curiosity as well as trepidation. While its designated role may be that of taking responsibility for him, Michaels presents the process of reconnecting with his family as inherently untidy, ambivalent, and unpredictable: and it is by approaching it as a lived, self-conscious experiment that he is able to find in the process an unanticipated sense of excitement and emotional possibility. His niece Melissa he understands as functioning as an 'emissary for the whole family (such as it is) to go halfway around the world to test the waters regarding faggot uncle dying of fatal disease in unknown land' (39). The objectification of his plight inherent in this process (and in Michaels's sentence) is diluted a little, however, by his recognition of her 'bravery' in the face of his determination to be 'blunt' (39). Similarly, despite being 'frightened' of the consequences of intimacy with his brother, Michaels also feels an empathetic connection: 'And yet, it's quite clear that Mark is taking my situation quite hard in some way and it would be worse than unfair to ignore or deny him some intimacy and some opportunity to talk about it' (106). These encounters with family in fact disappoint the expectation of a dramatic conflagration and resolution, the plot line, that is, of melodrama, which would release violently intense emotions while nonetheless working its way towards a happy ending (an outcome dependent on excising those rebels and villains who disturb the family unit's image of coherence). In Michaels's terms, whereas 'classical melodrama requires some grand scene at this point in the narrative: a confession, a revelation, an accounting of some dramatic sort, which then makes comprehensible the whole plot out of which the family and its interior relationships are constructed,' these familial encounters are distinctly unspectacular: 'We couldn't find a great deal to confess, and no such conventional ritual was enacted' (106). Michaels's speculative statement that 'if my family is to take any major responsibility for my care – i.e., if I return to the States – we will have to invent that family' is similarly ambivalent, asserting on the one hand that no family exists for him there, at least no family he can meaningfully connect with his adult identity as a gay man, but on the other that one could perhaps be invented if it were desirable or necessary to do so (39). That this invention of family can be imagined, even if tentatively, as a collective activity raises the possibility of rethinking family in a way that would allow family members to adopt some caregiving duties without automatically threatening to negate Michaels's identity.

As in Hoffman's *Hospital Time*, the critique of the reassertion of the nuclear family is accompanied in *Unbecoming* by attention to the network of friendships that provides practical and emotional care. While the assistance and comfort he longs for were 'once personified in the image of the Lover,' Michaels looks to a broader web of relations to meet his requirements for help (22–3). Leaving this community is what makes the prospect of departing from Australia so dire – it would mean being removed from the social network that sustains a sense of his life's meaningfulness: 'If I leave Australia, not only do I die, but I do so in some horrible, confused, totally alienated public welfare environment [in the United States], with no friends, no confirmation of my life and work – just hysteria, rather than any possible satisfaction, fulfillment which anyone, any human, I think, is entitled to at death's door' (126). But, like Hoffman, Michaels is circumspect about idealizing these chosen relationships. Rather than simply reversing and re-valourizing the two categories of family and friends, he complicates the distinction between them, showing how power, resentment, and guilt are at play in his friendships, a comparative linking of the two forms of kinship. Describing, for example, how irritations over differences in domestic habits escalate into resentments and painful arguments, he notes his tendency to undermine friendships by 'hacking' 'ever so painfully until all players in this tawdry domestic are drowning in blood and familial guilt' (22). Referring to his determination to preserve a friendship that is being tested and compromised by Michaels's growing dependency, and pointing in particular to the necessity of resisting 'recasting us in a drama,' Michaels observes of his efforts to maintain the relationship that

part of this is calculation, a calculation I am surprised my mother apparently failed to make until perhaps her very end – which is that, if one is to be required to develop dependent relationships, and rely on others, wouldn't one prefer to choose who should do this for you? And I suppose, in most instances, those friends, people whose company, ethics, and conversations you enjoy, are to be preferred. (22)

Analysing his friends 'in terms of suitability for the role of personal butler, nurse, secretary, companion, cook, etc.' seems 'impossible and quite unfair, because, if nothing else, these were not the terms on which our friendships were based or grew' (22). Such deliberate, calculated attempts to mobilize a system of support that meets his particular needs and specifications can be seen as a strategy born out of the recognition of his dependency on others and the determination to structure actively the form that this support network will take. In appraising his actions and analysis as calculations, Michaels claims a proud pedigree, for, as he points out, 'it is the profound moral imperatives and ethical calculations that ultimately do drive great gay queens throughout this century and beyond' (25). Employing a register that vacillates between proclaiming a manifesto and dissolving his declaration in sarcasm, Michaels appropriates the language of morality, just as he appropriates the right to define 'familialities.' In his understanding, moral and ethical conduct in the context of living with AIDS encompasses a number of working principles for resisting containment and exercising agency: namely, the imperative to find emotional and material support; the necessity of testifying to his experience; and the refusal to give in to the cultural pressure to quietude. While the sexual practices and fantasies that have constituted his identity as a gay man are disintegrating with his body's dissolution, he retains the practice of negotiating between the law and his idiosyncrasies, continuing to mediate actively and passionately his relation to social collectives.

Comparing the mourning rituals he detects are at work in his most intimate circles to those he has observed among the Warlpiri, Michaels is able to interrogate further the implications of these rituals as cultural forms embodying relations of power – and shaping collective and individual memory. Against a view of culture as static, he asserts a way of thinking about the law governing mourning as always vulnerable to adaptation. Among the four taboos that television and film representations of the Warlpiri risk violating, most important is the mortuary taboo that restricts the reproduction of the images and names of the dead, a taboo that, as Michaels notes, tends to draw more attention to the dead person through the structure of disavowal, its 'elegant contradiction': what ensues from the prohibition is a series of complex erasures and negotiations that speak of the vexed intensity of loss (9). But Michaels wonders

whether [Francis] Jupurrurula – on hearing of my death – will burn my Texas cowboy boots which I will send him next week, or whether, as I

hope, he will find and invoke some dispensation, some loophole in the
'law' to permit him to wear them for a while. For years, he eyed them
with such obsessive fervour! It's these little researchable questions I'm a
bit disappointed not to be able to test any further. (10–11)

Approaching his death as replete with 'little researchable questions' that test the limits of identification and of the social body's
capacity for change, Michaels embraces the unpredictability of
the future. He may try to 'stage-manage his own posthumosity' to
some extent, but he knows – and in fact is counting on – the
hope that the future cannot be entirely scripted, predetermined,
coded. Indeed, if the logic of abjection at work in Western culture could be said to work performatively, in that it must be constantly reiterated, then so too do the calculations Michaels
applies to the category of the family. His references to the familial constitute repeated strategic interventions, with possible,
although far from guaranteed, performative effects, effects that
might cumulatively alter the law of abjection. Ultimately, however, the consistent privileging of familial and pair bonds by the
state in the interests of maintaining the symbolic cleanliness and
propriety of the body politic is more threatening to Michaels,
and more difficult for him to imagine reinventing, than are
everyday relations and practices.

A Small History of Photography in the AIDS Epidemic

The photographic portrait that prefaces *Unbecoming* extends
Michaels's investigation of the psychic and cultural meanings of
HIV and AIDS into the dimension of the visual. It powerfully performs his resistance to the law of abjection and its aggressive
efforts at assimilation and redemption by presenting readers with
a disturbing conjuration of our latent assumptions, fears, and
prejudices (124). The photograph, taken by Michaels's friend,
photographer Penny Taylor, is significant in the first place for
establishing the authenticity of Michaels's testimony. It offers a

visual point of reference for the medically ill body, a compressed communication of the overwhelming bodily disintegration documented in the diary, invoking, in the sense of Barthes's *punctum*, as Chambers has pointed out, a visceral personal confrontation with an other we recognize as lost and dead, but who lives on as a spectre in the photographic record of a real body that once existed (*Facing It* 105). At the same time, the composition and placement of Michaels's portrait attest to his awareness as a media theorist and anthropologist of the increasing centrality of visual representation in constituting subjectivity and in creating shared cultural meanings: I am thinking in particular of the prevalence of visual images in the construction of both biomedical and familial meanings and identities (Mirzoeff 5–6).[20] Chambers suggestively reads the photograph as the book's 'mise-en-abyme' – an image that confronts readers with the 'wild man' of AIDS (*Facing It* 105–8). But the photograph's significance can be developed somewhat further with reference to Walter Benjamin's writings on photography and allegory. By generating a series of readings that comment on and qualify one another, Michaels's photographic portrait asks its 'confused investigators' to hold in suspension the desire to redeem Michaels, or, more specifically, our image or memory of him, to propriety or a singular meaning (*Origin* 176).[21]

The project of specifying the nature of the entanglement of autobiographical texts and photography in twentieth-century culture has become one of the key preoccupations of theorists of autobiography. Critics concur that the complex contingencies of autobiographical writing are brought into sharper focus by the introduction of photography to written texts. As Marianne Hirsch argues, 'The illusion of the self's wholeness and plenitude is perpetuated by the photographic medium as well as by the autobiographical act: both forms of misrecognition rest on a profound misprision of the processes of representation' (84). Conversely, 'autobiography and photography share, as well, a fragmentary structure and an incompleteness that can be only partially concealed by narrative and conventional connections' (84). As elements of autobiographical texts, then, photographs thus underscore autobiography's vacillations between wholeness and fragmentation, and between the denial and awareness of meaning as constructed, conventional, and contextualized. In *Unbecoming*, while there is something peculiarly materializing or substantiating about the photograph of Michaels, the visual document also serves to heighten our awareness of disintegration – and of the reader and viewer's uncomfortable empowerment in the process of making meaning out of the scattered clues that remain of Michaels's bodily experience.[22]

In addition to being remarkable for its materializing effects, *Unbecoming*'s prefatory photograph is striking for its radically decontextualized status. This process of decontextualization has a long history. As has been the subject of much critical and historical discussion, beginning in the nineteenth century, criminals, the insane, and the sexually deviant were all subject to such cataloguing, as were cultures that seemed to exist, for the moment, just outside the civilizing influence, but not the gaze, of European empires. As Dick Hebdige emphasizes, for example, the nineteenth century inaugurated an official documentary use of photography that 'embod[ied] a desire and a will to know the alien-in-our-midst, the Other, the victim, and the culprit' ('Hiding in the Light' 33). Thinking of the history embedded in photographic conventions in this way, we can see how the torso shot of Michaels echoes the standard distance and composition of a medical textbook photograph or an ethnographic photograph, genres that take fragments of human bodies out of context, providing partial but authoritative evidence of the existence of degenerate underworlds – or primitive other worlds – that needed to be disciplined, either by being stigmatized as abject or by being integrated definitively into modernity.[23] The use of photography for medical, anthropological, and colonial purposes

overlaps in significant ways with its range of official and unoffi-
cial employment in criminal surveillance. As Pratt argues of ethnographic texts from the colonial period, the aggression often
embedded in looking is denied by a logic of 'anti-conquest' that
contrasts the humanity and neutrality of its seeing with more
overtly violent forms of domination (*Imperial Eyes* 66). In a certain sense, then, decontextualization – and the opportunity for
the array of motivated recontextualizations for which it makes
space – is Michaels's photograph's most important context. Its
dramatic lack of context thus signifies the portrait's vulnerability
to a proliferating host of interpretative frameworks that would fix
its meaning and, in so doing, contain Michaels. Quoting an array
of visual discourses (familial, medical, ethnographic), and counting on the expected (voyeuristic, horrified, tantalized) and unexpected (mindful, resistant) ways in which people might confront
such images, the photograph's placement as the frontispiece to
such a confrontational memoir foregrounds how the text forces a
critical encounter with the representation of the abject body of
HIV infection and AIDS for even the most casual of readers.

Such de- and re-contextualization is a key element in the ideological framework of popular, documentary, and 'high art' representations of Aboriginal peoples in Australia, images that have
had a wide popular circulation (in the form of postcards and
magazines) throughout the twentieth century. The portrait of
Michaels emphasizes the stunning spectacle of his body's unre-
strained (metaphorically tropical and intemperate) 'overgrowth'
of skin, and hair, and beard, a portrayal that signals both popular
and high art images of Aboriginal people produced by Europeans beginning in the nineteenth century and continuing
through much of the twentieth.[24] Mixed in with the curiosity
about exotic or primitive cultures expressed in such portraits was
'a nostalgic and melancholy regret for a race on the verge of
extinction' (Maynard 92). These photographs, like many visual
images of people living with AIDS, combine evocations of fascina-

tion, horror, and pity with an overriding fatalistic narrative that
anticipates the extinction of bodies defined as other or abject.[25]

That the Royal Brisbane Hospital where Michaels was several
times a patient misinterprets AIDS as a tropical disease, grouping
people with AIDS in wards where they are exposed to the very
diseases to which their compromised immune systems make
them more than ordinarily vulnerable, calls attention to the association of sexual deviancy with the degeneracy of the tropics and
to fears about the contaminating pathogenic power of the tropics
and tropical bodies to corrupt the clean and proper body, family,
and nation. Michaels's photograph can thus be interpreted as
staging a sighting of the savage and, in turn, of the ostensibly
uncivilized others existing (with varying degrees of visibility)
inside the body politic. By recirculating photographic conventions for documenting otherness, the portrait carries on a sustained, multivalent argument with the cultural construction of
the AIDS epidemic through visual as well as linguistic media in
Western democracies as well as globally, showing how pre-existing 'discursive dichotomies' – such as the opposition of self and
not-self, contagion and containment, normal and abnormal – are
remobilized in the context of AIDS discourse (Treichler 149, 35).
But the photograph confounds the boundaries that the discourses of civilization and savagery encourage us almost instantly
to draw between the civilized and the degenerate or uncivilized.
The conceptual blurring works by mingling antithetical recogni-
tions: since we know that Michaels is the author of the text we are
about to read, or are in the process of reading, and that Michaels
participated in constructing and publishing this visual representation of his body, then he cannot also be construed as the 'savage' imaged in the photograph. The almost inevitable mistake we
make in interpreting the photograph introduces a shocking dissonance to the process of relating the picture to the text, making
even the most casual reader of this diary confront the difficulty
of making sense out of it.

By extension from this demand that viewers confront the assumptions we bring to the process of making meaning, the photograph also raises the question of race, critically correlating the visual construction of the body with AIDS (and, in turn, the body of the male homosexual) to the visual process of racialization. The photograph's emphases and composition encourage us to read Michaels's ostensibly white body as racially other: the exaggerated abundance of his body hair; his nakedness, which allows us to inspect his body's lesions and markings; his extended tongue; and his defiant or suspicious gaze (implying discomfort with photographic technology by suggesting a visceral resistance to it). Michaels draws attention to stereotypical conflation of blackness and deviance, both sexual and criminal, as well as the tendency of these categories mutually to reinforce one another. In the process of defining degeneration against a cultural ideal of bodily purity, sexualities in excess of the heterosexual norm are represented as both pathological and pathogenic. Intersecting with and reinforcing the discourse of deviant sexuality, colonialist discourse defines racial others as physically degenerate as well as sexually excessive and uncontainable. In creating this alignment in their photographic portrait of AIDS and Aboriginality, Michaels and Taylor thus gesture towards a conclusion similar to the one arrived at by Radhika Mohanram in her recent exploration of postcolonialism, gender, and space: that 'race, like gender, is written on the body and is most often visible. The body classified as black need not necessarily be always black ... Race is a classification and is in the eye of the (white) beholder' (202). The photograph of Michaels powerfully evokes the intersecting discourses of sexual and racial deviance, demanding engaged speculation about the generic assumptions of documentary photography and about the consequences of how such photographs are made and read for the subjects who become objects in the process of being photographed. More specifically, Michaels's testimonial project suggests that the gaze of the notional metropolitan beholder of turn-of-the-century images of Aboriginal people corresponds to and overlaps with the phantasmatic general public of AIDS discourse: both forms of addressing the viewer seek to classify, distance, and disidentify the viewer from an abject, potentially contaminating other, while simultaneously positing that other as belonging to a diseased and dying race. By bringing to consciousness the embedded discourses of sexuality, degeneracy, and racialization that structure our encounter with his ill and dying body, Michaels refuses to allow us to evade confronting our fears, a desire that mirrors, as Chambers points out, the mixed motivations behind the persistent substitution of bourgeois 'concern' for some kind of real 'engagement' with people who are constructed and perceived as 'other' (*Facing It* 108).

Composed during the same time (1987–8) as the celebration of Australia's bicentenary, Michaels's diary and photograph are, it is essential to note, influenced by, and collaborate with, the projects and protests organized by Aboriginal peoples to contest this official celebration of colonial history. One such project was, in fact, organized by Penny Taylor, with Eric Michaels acting in the role of adviser. In *After 200 Years: Photographic Essays of Aboriginal and Islander Australia Today* (1988), Taylor brings together photographs of Aboriginal peoples present as well as past, emphasizing the importance of their undertaking to appropriate visual technology in order to represent themselves. While supported by arts funding made available by the bicentenary, the aims and methods of Taylor's project were revisionist and exploratory.[26] Seeking to put into practice 'a genre of collaborative documentary photography,' it focuses on representing the 'diversity' of 'everyday worlds' (xv); positioning itself against the historical antecedents of romanticization, exoticization, and doom, this photographic archive also effectively highlights the problems of poverty and continuing racism. The year 1988 also saw protests on the part of Aboriginal peoples from across the continent; for example, at the same time as the official ceremonies marking the bicentenary on January 26, a peaceful march was held leading away from the metropolitan centre of Sydney and towards an

Aboriginal community, a protest that attempted to enact resistance to the symbolic 'reenactment of their obliteration' by 'massacre and epidemic' in the interests of national unity (T. Smith 635–6; see *Unbecoming* 44–8). Such protests constitute cultural interventions in the symbolic construction of the nation and the role to which indigenous cultures have been recruited in relation to the nation, asserting at the same time 'other practices of sociality' against the logic of modernity and progress that would fix Aboriginal peoples as anachronistic artifacts of a vanished past (T. Smith 636). As a theorist of visual culture himself, Michaels was well aware of the necessity of engaging with visual representations of the epidemic. Combining a meditation on visual representation with testimonial writing multiplies the conundra as well as the stakes involved in redirecting the circuit, somehow, of the gaze. By implicitly referring to the history and the changing uses of documentary photography in Australia, *Unbecoming* signals its affinity with Aboriginal people's strategies for self-definition and political resistance and powerfully criticizes the comfortable reiteration of national, racial, and sexual identities.

Michaels borrows from the conventions that have governed the visual representation of Aboriginal peoples and from the emerging genre of critical documentary photography in Australia in order to signal, in a highly compressed fashion, then, his project's affinity and sympathy with these cultural interventions. He implicitly argues that people with HIV/AIDS occupy a relation to the state that parallels (and intersects with) the dilemma of Aboriginal peoples, although he is quick to clarify that he is by no means equating disparate struggles.[27] Michaels's lack of residency status in Australia echoes the dilemma of Aboriginal peoples confronting their relation (or non-relation) to the state. In the context of the denial of Michaels's application for permanent resident status, the radically decontextualized single photograph, showing only the torso, can also be thought of as invoking – and interrogating – the grammar of the passport photo, the material referent on which the meaning and usefulness of modern identification papers depend in order to fix our identities and to determine where our bodies belong. This connection highlights the link between photography, the mechanisms of identity, and the determining power of the state. As Benedict Anderson argues of the 'high-truth claims' of passports, they 'are also counterfeit in the sense that they are less and less attestations of citizenship, let alone of loyalty to a protective nation-state, than of claims to participation in labor markets' ('Exodus'; qtd in Kumar 40–1). The Kaposi's sarcoma lesions in Michaels's picture are by far the most visible marks on his body, but (tellingly) they hardly convey the essential particularity of an individual: rather, they generalize his identity, rendering him readable, at the state's border, as a body with AIDS. In all of these ways, *Unbecoming* links the photograph (and the entire text) to the scene of state control and violence, and foregrounds how our imaginings of the body with AIDS as contaminating inform policies that shape how the pandemic is lived and experienced by affected people.

Finally, the photograph (and its readerly expectations, its effects, and its motivations) stands metonymically for, and amplifies, an analogous textual effect that is my central concern in this book: namely, testimonial accounts' melancholic struggles to reshape how the epidemic is pictured and, in particular, to re-imagine the concept of family. To read Michaels's photograph as indirectly signalling the context of family photographs may at first glance seem counter-intuitive. The inclusion and deliberate arrangement of family photographs to produce a narrative of happy cohesion (at least on the surface) is a prospect resisted by Michaels, who resents that his brother, Mark, arrives from America armed with 'the unavoidable snaps of the family' (*Unbecoming* 104), and who would probably concur with Benjamin's famous formulation that such scenes combine the 'boudoir and the torture chamber,' emphasizing the painful objectification involved in being photographed for purposes of intimate display, a per-

sonal realm no less imbricated in power than other forms of photographic documentation (*Berlin Childhood*; qtd in Rugg 168–9).
Photographs made by and for familial viewing participate in a
melodramatic paradigm that tends to reinforce a conservative
ideology of the family: they are overwhelmingly disposed towards
constructing the family as a cohesive unit, excluding or minimiz-
ing evidence that contradicts a sense of harmony. By contrast,
Michaels, with his bare torso, unkempt hair, and extended
tongue, presents an image that is utterly alien to conventional fictions of familial coherence. Michaels thus foregrounds what is
excluded from the picture of familial cohesion, what it would
prefer to sanitize or omit: his symptomatic body as it appears –
but also as it is imagined – beneath the screens of clothing and
words. This image of the marked, porous, vulnerable body – this
'flawed countenance' that 'can't,' or won't, be 'managed' (*Unbecoming* 44) – represents 'the optical unconscious' of the conventions of family photography, formulas that are invested in
managing dissension, grief, and anger, as well as the memory of
the body's eroticism, its flesh and desires (Benjamin, 'A Small
History' 243). As in Benjamin's analysis of melancholy, 'it is no
accident that the subject is a torso' in Michaels's portrait, an
image deprived of hands and feet, lacking any capacity to push
back or run away, frozen in time and space, vulnerable to viewers'
temptations to redeem it (*Origin* 176). In its foregrounding of an
undesired and disturbing intimacy that unsettles the idealized
intimacies of family, Michaels's project bears a strong affinity with
the influential portraits of Nan Goldin, whose serial photographs
of her friends, many of whom are HIV-positive, extend by proxy
to her audience an almost intolerable but compelling intimacy
with them, and thus try to 'change the nature of photography
itself from the act of voyeur to that of a witness' (Mirzoeff 81).
Rather than reliably reconciling the contradictoriness of memory in the context of death and loss, the photograph returns
the past to us as a shocking revenant. Defiantly unbeautiful,
Michaels's photographed body is situated 'in the field of allegori-

cal intuition,' 'a fragment, a rune,' that 'wounds' us, but that is also still responsive, somehow, obscurely, to our efforts to interpret it (Benjamin, *Origin* 176).

A more powerful, utterly transfixing photographic encounter it is difficult to imagine, and I am rendered speechless, shocked, and then overwhelmed by its suggestibility each time I open the page to this photograph. Allegorically speaking, the self-image Michaels provides evokes the iconography of a death's head. Thinking of the image in these terms helps to clarify the significance of its resistance to any single interpretive strategy. In suggesting that Michaels's portrait can be seen as a death's head, I am following Benjamin's analysis of baroque allegory, in particular his observation that in the German Trauerspiel

everything about history that, from the very beginning, has been untimely, sorrowful, unsuccessful, is expressed in a face – or rather in a death's head. And although such a thing lacks all 'symbolic' freedom of expression, all classical proportion, all humanity – nevertheless, this is the form in which man's subjection to nature is most obvious and it significantly gives rise not only to the enigmatic question of the nature of human existence as such, but also of the biographical historicity of the individual. (166)

As Eduardo Cadava explains of the importance of photography to Benjamin's conceptualization of history, the death's head or Medusa's gaze 'stalls history in the sphere of speculation. It short-circuits, and suspends the temporal continuity between a past and a present' (99). By freezing history in this manner, Michaels's portrait of his own face becoming skull, decaying from recognizable humanity to an obscure ruin, invites our contemplation of the ghostly or spectral character emanating from the photograph, a dimension that history conceived of as progressive or redemptive encourages us, rather, to forget, to abject. Staging itself as at once familiar and alien, the image of Michaels resists the pressures of both domestication and civilization.

The photograph 'sets the scene,' in Benjamin's phrase, 'for a salutary estrangement,' giving 'free play to the politically educated eye, under whose gaze all intimacies are sacrificed to the illumination of detail' ('A Small History' 251). Evoking a state of melancholy self-regard and introspection, the photograph substitutes Michaels's face for the reader's gaze at a self-image in the mirror, and creates a moment of frantic oscillation between identification and disavowal in that each one of us, in looking at him, looks, in fact, at ourselves, at a projection of our own fears and desires. In turn, and despite our awareness of the active role of Michaels in composing this picture, we simulate each time we confront it the intrusiveness that complicates the intimate space of friendship or familiarity in this act of recording and fixing Michaels's face. Moreover, if photographic portraits are made and viewed in the awareness of death, and thus comprise a kind of cemetery in miniature, a place where memories are cultivated, Michaels's portrait situates him as still existing (as well as having existed during his illness) between death and life. This is a death's head with an extended tongue, and whether motivated by defiance or a delight in display, or both, this performance puts a distinctly postmodern twist on the early modern iconography it plays with. The extended tongue renders the portrait inassimilable to the desire to picture a peaceable death by emphasizing both its untoward capacity to speak, to continue to recontextualize itself, to read itself, to speak its own unending series of captions, as well as the obscurity of its message (the possibility that the utterance may not form words, or convey a recognizable syntax).[28] Thus, while in the photograph we encounter a material index of Michaels's ill and dying body, this visual remainder refuses to be located, to be definitively buried elsewhere. It remains disturbingly unmoored, generating, in tandem with the diary it accompanies, an endless horizon of allegorical possibilities that refuse our desires for redemption.

CHAPTER FOUR

Angels in Antigua

The Diasporic of Melancholy
in Jamaica Kincaid's *My Brother*

*The tradition of the oppressed teaches us that the 'state of emergency' in which we
live is not the exception but the rule. We must attain to a conception of history
that is in keeping with this insight.*
– Walter Benjamin, 'Theses on the Philosophy of History' (257)

Postcolonial Melancholy

Adopting a strategy of seeming frankness in her accounting for
facts, Jamaica Kincaid, in her 1997 memoir of the life and the
AIDS-related death of her half-brother Devon Drew, foregrounds
the intersection of grief with postcolonial and racial concerns,
emphasizing her conflicted feelings about death and loss and
about the 'privilege and power' she holds as a now-celebrated
writer living in the United States.[1] Faced with the emergency of
the AIDS epidemic, and with the ways in which it locates Devon's
dispossession, Kincaid finds that she must address her estranged
brother and the particularities of his world in the context of her
painful awareness that the events and images she recalls have
'meaning only because my life can make [them] have [mean-
ing]' (*My Brother* 128). It is especially urgent for Kincaid to
address her changed relation to her country of origin, Antigua,

and to her family there, given that she writes about a man,
Devon, whom she can barely claim to know, although they are
blood relations. (Kincaid left Antigua for the United States when
Devon was three years old and she was sixteen [20].) The result is
a melancholic text that, read as a self-theorizing document,
offers a rethinking of the politics of grief that is relevant and
bracing for theoretical discussions of postcolonial and racial
mourning, as well as for coming to grips with the cultural impact
of the AIDS pandemic as it continues to follow the fault-lines of
globalization.

Throughout *My Brother* Kincaid displays melancholic exasperation with Devon and a range of other affective responses associated with melancholia – namely, anger at herself, guilt, and self-
berating: 'My talk was full of pain, it was full of anger, there was
no peace to it, there was much sorrow, but there was no peace to
it. How did I feel? I did not know how I felt. I was a combustion of
feelings' (51). Kincaid's observation that grief has destabilized
her ability to account for her feelings in language corresponds,
for instance, to Kristeva's description of melancholia in *Black
Sun*, published in the same year as Ross Chambers's *The Writing of
Melancholy*: 'depressed speech,' she says, is 'built up with absurd
signs, slackened, scattered, checked sequences' and thus 'conveys
the collapse of meaning into the unnameable,' while at the same
time making the depressive text 'hyperlucid' (51–2). Kincaid's
references to the 'large vapor of sadness' that she feels she is
being 'swallowed up in' (20, 23), and to her pain, anger, confusion, and sense of meaninglessness, key her memoir to the current critical definition of melancholy and emphasize that if we
are to grapple with the contortions of *My Brother,* then the workings and unworkings of melancholy need to be examined, their
entwined psychic and political dimensions closely scrutinized.

Through an analysis of the memoir's pattern of botanical metaphors, as well as Devon's place in familial and colonial history
and the descriptions of his dying and of his corpse, I will explore

how Kincaid's melancholic commitment to Devon extends and complicates the politicized 'family romance' of her earlier autobiographical works by acknowledging for the first time the significant absence of her brothers from the life story she has presented.[2] Weighed down and consumed by his affliction, Kincaid traces the ways in which Devon – the object of her writing or, rather, her memory of him – somehow possesses independent powers of articulation in her text, forcing her to confront her own implication in the political, social, and economic contexts that shape his suffering.

My Brother's expressions of pain, bewilderment, and even anxiety about these feelings (feelings not in Kincaid's control) are not gratuitous but knitted, in a sustained, self-reflexive, and yet sometimes bafflingly oblique way, into a political context. In the first few pages of the memoir, for example, Kincaid admits that 'I don't know my brothers very well, but I am pretty sure that a condom would not be something he would have troubled himself to use,' and suggests that this is because he is poor, uneducated, and a victim of his macho attitude, which makes him unable to perceive himself as being at risk, or as a potential risk to others. She notes a conversation years earlier: 'I told him to protect himself from the HIV virus and he laughed at me and said that he would never get such a stupid thing ("Me no get dat chupidness, man")' (8). In introducing this kind of commentary, the memoir testifies to the demographics of the disease in Caribbean countries. Certainly, the asymmetrical relation between Antigua and the United States, allegorized here in the brother-sister relationship, is exemplified by the epidemiology of HIV infection and AIDS in the Caribbean. According to the Joint United Nations Program on HIV/AIDS, the incidence of HIV in the Caribbean is almost four times that in North America, making the rate of HIV infection in the region second only to that in sub-Saharan Africa.[3] The elevated rate of infection in the region can be connected to neocolonial economic and social factors: poverty, intravenous drug use, the stigmatization of homosexuality, and economic reliance on tourism.[4] While Eric Michaels's diary and its accompanying photograph try to tease out how the stigmatization of bodies with AIDS crosses over with cultural processes of racialization, in the case of Kincaid's memoir these questions are of even more central importance. Moreover, if Michaels works with tropical nature and tropical thinking about disease as figures or concepts, Kincaid, by contrast, cannot escape addressing the tropics as an actual as well as an imagined location: Antigua, as a Caribbean country, may be conceptualized by North Americans and even by the World Health Organization as one of the elsewheres or lost places of AIDS discourse, but it is also a place that she identifies, to some extent, as her home. She draws attention to the disturbing social and geographical inequities behind the statistics she cites, noting that 'most people suffering from the disease are poor or young, not too far away from being children.' HIV infection finds the precondition for a particularly rapid and intense regional outbreak in the 'vulnerability and powerlessness' that already afflict many young people and poor people in the Caribbean world, especially a man such as Kincaid's brother, who is further encumbered with the illusion of his virility, even as he lacks economic and cultural power (*My Brother* 32).

Still, even as she testifies to these inequities, the ironies of her complicity in Devon's infantilization are not lost on Kincaid as she vacillates between statements of 'judgement' (8) and her unwelcome awareness that she 'knew nothing about his internal reality' and thus may have 'misread anxiety when it appeared on his face,' not as suggesting that he 'despaired that the walls separating the parts of his life had broken down' but rather 'as another kind of suffering, a suffering I might be able to relieve with medicine I had brought from the prosperous North' (164). The power of the sadness that Devon inspires moves the memoir back and forth between, on the one hand, satisfaction with the sufficiency of empathy and help and, on the other, an emergent and troubling recognition of how much distance there is between brother and sister along with the ways their lives are implicated in and mirror each other's. Her position is not an entirely altruistic one in strict contrast to that of the tourist who travels to Antigua motivated by curiosity, pleasure, and recreation, an opposition to which she gestures in *A Small Place*, her 1988 critique of the tourist economy, with a reference to 'an Antiguan black returning to Antigua from Europe or North America with cardboard boxes of much needed cheap clothes and food for relatives' (4). Emphasizing the ambivalence that she feels towards Devon and the intrusion of his illness into her life, she reports a conversation with a fellow traveller who asks why she has come to Antigua and why she does not take her brother home with her so he can be treated in the United States. Kincaid candidly records that she misled the woman by suggesting that (although she had no information on the topic) immigration policies would prevent Devon's entry into the country, when what she 'really meant was, no, I can't do what you are suggesting – take this strange, careless person into the hard-earned order of my life' (*My Brother* 49).

From the beginning of the memoir it is implied that Kincaid's uneasiness is connected to the cultural and economic gulf that has emerged between her and her brother. Recalling an attempt years earlier to encourage Devon to practise safe sex, Kincaid reflects in a self-critical way on the inefficacy of her advice:

But I might have seemed like a ridiculous person to him. I had lived away from my home for so long that I no longer understood readily the kind of English he spoke and always had to have him repeat himself to me; and I no longer spoke the kind of English he spoke, and when I said anything to him, he would look at me and sometimes just laugh at me outright. You talk funny, he said. (8)

This imaginative reconstruction of Devon's evaluation of his sister's advice suggests that Kincaid's long absence has engendered gaps in language, communication, and experience. As she becomes aware of the distance that has emerged between them, as exemplified in the contrast between her well-intentioned warning and Devon's view that this lecture on the dangers of disease is 'stupid' or irrelevant to him, Kincaid begins self-consciously to consider the difficulty of testifying to Devon's life and death, for his story is both hers and not or no longer hers. The problem of her right to represent Devon is especially fraught now that Devon has died and can no longer directly voice his objections to his sister's interpretation of the significance of his life, illness, and death. Certainly, however, the question of what it means for Kincaid to speak on her brother's behalf, and as someone who lives a much more materially and intellectually privileged life than he did, does occur to her, and from the beginning of the memoir works to roughen any temptation for Kincaid or for her readers to believe that she possesses an uncomplicated claim on the story of Devon Drew.

This chapter endeavours to clarify the proliferating paradoxes of Kincaid's grief in *My Brother* as well as to suggest the pertinence of her enquiry into melancholic subjectivity to critical understandings of melancholia as a postcolonial thematic. Through its relocation of melancholic subjectivity at the intersection of postcolonial and racial anxieties, *My Brother* overlaps with and complicates current theoretical understandings of mourning and melancholia. Thinking of melancholia as inspired by compensatory guilt and nostalgia helps to account in part for the complexities of Kincaid's position as returning outsider-insider. But is the equation of her melancholy with compensatory guilt for having escaped her brother's fate the only possible interpretation of *My Brother*'s affective intensity? Anne Anlin Cheng identifies a theory of melancholia as a significant gap in critical race theory; namely, she suggests the need for 'a willingness to confront the psychic implications of the haunting negativity that has not only been attached to but has also helped to constitute the very category of the racialized,' suggesting that the legacy of 'racial melancholia for the raced subject' entails 'the internalization of discipline and rejection – and the installation of a scripted context of perception' (25, 17). As Cheng's argument suggests, then, it is also possible that the decentred quality of melancholic subjectivity, far from being motivated by a cynical evasion of responsibility, constitutes an inescapable 'mechanism of memory'[5] that, although it may fuel nostalgia, is not reducible to it.[6]

Cheng's articulation of melancholy as a constitutive mechanism of memory is corroborated and extended by Derrida's explorations of mourning and memorialization in *Specters of Marx*. Like Kincaid's memoir, Derrida's work of social and political theory is concerned with pinpointing the exorcisms that would exonerate the powerful from the responsible to recognize and change conditions of social inequity: 'triumphant mourning work' would absolve the powerful from obligations to address the conditions of powerlessness (*Specters* 52). As Derrida argues of the aims and methods of 'effective exorcism,' as they have been brought to bear on Marx and his legacies 'in the ideological supermarkets of a worried West' (68), exorcism 'pretends to declare death only in order to put to death' (48); and while it may seem passive to the extent that it is presented as inevitable, exorcism is an *active* form of forgetting, a motivated (because guilt-ridden) kind of erasure, and one that distorts even when it does not 'put to death.' As I suggested in the introduction, Derrida asks whether people living in conditions of privilege in the West are unable to see, and even actively work to hide from ourselves, the relation between definitions of 'delinquency' and the conditions of social marginalization. Such an overlapping of 'delinquency' and 'powerlessness' is exemplified perhaps in the person of Kincaid's brother. In this light, Kincaid's self-conscious 'willingness to confront' the dangers her memories represent to her (Cheng 25) and the threat posed by her desire to exorcize them, may be said to politicize or render her text oppositional in some measure, in the 'decentred' sense, between 'resistance' and 'retreat,' described by Chambers (*The Writing of Melancholy* 59).

My Brother's self-consciously melancholic textuality makes it possible, in other words, to glimpse the hitherto hidden political subtext of the autobiographical self that Kincaid has constructed. Devon emerges as her political unconscious or, to borrow Homi K. Bhabha's evocative construction of the haunting of the affluent by those they have left behind, as 'the "missing person" that haunts the identity of the postcolonial bourgeoisie' ('Interrogating Identity' 43). If Kincaid's brothers are the underwritten story of her novels *Annie John* and *Lucy*, appearing only as the shadowy threat to the protagonist's childhood paradise (their births push the family into economic disarray [*My Brother* 141]), then here, with the social and temporal rupture of the AIDS pandemic, which magnifies their marginalization, they can no longer rest beneath the surface of her prose. Reverberating with North American panic about AIDS, it seems that doom, shame, and rejection are the unavoidable fate of those who contract HIV in Antigua. Devon embodies his sister's political unconscious in that he represents an extreme example of the vulnerability of those who remain in the place that Kincaid has left, a vulnerability that remains profound even when it is masked by a performance of masculine bravado and indifference. Devon's presence and voice haunt his sister's text, compelling her to evaluate her complicity, from a distance, in his suffering, and motivating her to criticize his ignorance and the social and economic conditions that have produced it.

Gardening in the Tropics: Nature in Ruins

Gardening in the tropics, you never know
what you'll turn up. Quite often, bones.
In some places they say when volcanoes
erupt, they spew out dense and monumental
as stones the skulls of *desaparecidos*

– the disappeared ones. Mine is only
a kitchen garden so I unearth just
occasional skeletons.
                    – Olive Senior, 'Brief Lives' (*Gardening in the Tropics* 83)

By examining the motif of gardening in *My Brother*, we can begin
to grasp the extent of the destabilizing power of Kincaid's melancholic relation to Devon and, in turn, to Antigua. As Jamaican-
Canadian poet Olive Senior's poem 'Brief Lives' emphasizes,
colonialism has left an archaeology of destruction behind the
land's cultivation, even in the most innocent-seeming personal
garden. In the first few pages of her memoir, Kincaid offers the
detail that the news of Devon's illness interrupted her reading of
a book on gardening, *The Education of a Gardener*, by Russell Page,
a book she at first did not like for its posture of servitude (10).
Yet afterward, when she has returned to Antigua to see Devon,
she views it nostalgically, for its apparently simple pleasures. In a
moment of ambivalent irony, she attempts to read her current
experience through it: 'And when I picked up that book again, ...
I looked at my brother, for he was a gardener also, and I wondered, if his life had taken a different turn, might he have written
a book with such a title?' (11). The irony is levelled lightly, however, and blends with a self-consciously judgmental comment
regarding her shame that Devon did not have a productive life.
Lamenting that their mother has cut down a tree that Devon
planted, Kincaid remarks, 'That lemon tree would have been one
of the things left of his life. Nothing came from him; not work,
not children, not love for someone else' (13). These negations,
because they are so emphatic, suggest that his life is not (quite)
nothing, that it possesses enough significance to prompt the creation of this elaborate, self-excoriating text. Speaking of Devon,
Kincaid knowingly speaks more of herself, projecting onto him a
hypothetical version of herself and seeing in him a wasted potential for heterosexual and economic productivity.

In a series of articles on gardening written for the *New Yorker* beginning in the early 1990s, Kincaid continues the scathing tone of her previous essays, which exposed the ongoing effects of colonialism in an independent Antigua. Her reflections in the gardening essays on her relative privilege help illuminate her self-positioning in *My Brother*.[7] Breaking with the middle-class decorum of a conventional gardening column – that is, with the dispensing of descriptions and advice – she asks, in an essay titled 'Flowers of Evil': 'And what is the relationship of gardening to conquest?' (159). To summarize: gardening, especially the aesthetic cultivation of non-food plants, provides the ruling class with the fantasy of a paradoxically natural *and* controlled luxury, one that allows for the retrospective minimization of the ecological devastation and agricultural exploitation that characterized the European conquest of the Caribbean. Most striking in 'Flowers of Evil' is that, referring to her elaborate Vermont garden, Kincaid implicates herself in the dynamic of conquest she is criticizing: 'And I thought how I had crossed a line; but at whose expense? I cannot begin to look, because what if it is someone I know? I have joined the conquering class: who else could afford this garden – a garden in which I grow things that it would be much cheaper to buy at the store' (159).[8] In *My Brother*, she begins to look at the question of 'at whose expense' she has 'joined the conquering class': Devon may well be the someone she knows whom she has in effect conquered by leaving behind. Her rhetorical question may also be self-referential, suggesting that she has crossed the line at her own expense, that she has lost her closeness to her family and her 'native land.' She cannot 'look' because she would discover herself ('someone I know') and the consequences of those losses. Yet she must look. *My Brother* is to some extent an act of examining her conquering self as a split and devastated being.

The allegorical connections I am drawing among power relations, the AIDS pandemic, and the motif of gardening in *My Brother* are far from arbitrary. Alfred W. Crosby argues in *Ecologi-*

cal Imperialism that, just as the persistence of European plants
ensured agricultural and economic conquest of the Americas,
the imperialists' 'germs, not these imperialists themselves, for all
their brutality and callousness, ... were chiefly responsible for
sweeping aside the indigenes and opening the Neo-Europes to
demographic takeover' (196). Crosby points specifically to the
role of 'Old World pathogens' such as smallpox in killing so
many Amerindians, especially Arawaks, during the early years of
Caribbean colonial contact with Spain (198–9). In 'Flowers of
Evil,' Kincaid identifies the renaming of local flora and fauna by
the Europeans as part of the process of conquest in which she
has begun to implicate herself. Commenting on the European
names assigned to indigenous plants, Kincaid calls the 'naming
of things ... crucial to possession – a spiritual padlock with the
key thrown irretrievably away – that it is a murder, an erasing.'[9]
For these reasons, she suggests, 'it is not surprising that when
people have felt themselves prey to it [conquest] among their
first acts of liberation is to change their names' (159).[10] She thus
opens up the possibility that her use of botanical metaphors in
My Brother may allow her to dominate Devon through narration,
by telling a self-interested version of his story.

By writing about Devon, Kincaid risks the 'conquest' of his
story – that is, she risks participating in the 'renaming' that she
identifies as 'possession,' 'murder,' and 'erasing,' and therefore
in the history of epidemics as the vanguard of imperialist takeover (159). She worries that by cultivating his story, she may
obfuscate this act of conquest, masking it as her endowing of
Devon's story with proper values and a proper teleology. But
might there be another implication in her writing about Devon?
As Bhabha argues:

To *see* a missing person, *to look* at Invisibleness, is to emphasize the subject's *transitive* demand for a *direct* object of self-reflection, a point of
presence that would maintain its privileged enunciatory position *qua*

subject. To see a *missing person* is to *transgress* that demand; the 'I' in the position of mastery is, at *that same time*, the place of its absence, its re-presentation. ('Interrogating Identity' 47)

Bhabha indicates the possibility of displacing the imperative that the dispossessed other be a passive, self-reflecting object of the privileged subject's gaze. If the radical alterity of the other is recognized, then this calculus no longer obtains, and the 'I' of the representation loses the security of its authority. Kincaid for her part struggles to acknowledge the gap between brother and sister, and in the process allows into her account some sense of her emotional irrelevance from Devon's perspective: 'That night as he lay dying and calling the names of his brothers and his mother, he did not call my name' (*My Brother* 174). She must admit that 'I had never been a part of the tapestry, so to speak, of Patches, Styles, and Muds' (175). She explains the family nicknames (for Devon, Joe, and their mother) but does not or cannot use them. As she muses on her exclusion from the circuit of communication that has arisen in her absence, her readers are momentarily drawn into Devon's point of view, and we start to consider the possibility that perhaps it is Kincaid, ironically enough, who is the Drew family's missing person, and that it is her own lost self who haunts her, interrupting her self-coherence.

In the first of the memoir's two sections, however, Kincaid attempts to do the opposite of negating her position of mastery: she seeks to reframe Devon's 'delinquency' through the terms of an imagined identification as gardeners, a shared identity that extends into the fantasy of an alternative, indigenous paradise, a space that is beyond imperial/colonial knowledge. There is a tenacious idealism in this section of *My Brother*, one that is paralleled momentarily in the gardening essays when Kincaid sets aside her critique for a moment to imagine what 'the botanical life of Antigua consist[ed]' of before the arrival of Europeans;

she gestures towards an Edenic past, one retrospectively purged
of the taint of colonialism: 'What herb of beauty grew in this
place then? What tree? And did the people who lived there grow
anything beautiful for its own sake? I do not know; I can only
make a straightforward deduction: the frangipani, the mahogany
tree and the cedar tree are all native to the West Indies, so these
trees are probably indigenous' ('Alien Soil' 48–9). Nature promises to rewrite their relationship as one of pleasing symmetry and
mutuality, despite her simultaneous awareness, as in Walter Benjamin's analysis of melancholy, of the absence of any 'guaranteed
economics of salvation' that would restore the 'collapse of the
physical, beautiful, nature' and the 'spiritualization of the physical' it promises (216, 176, 187). Ultimately, however, Kincaid's
impulse to turn towards the natural world, like Derek Jarman's, is
complicated and qualified by an emerging sense that modern
nature is a realm of ruins that cannot, no matter how hard we
work to cultivate it, mirror back to us a sense of wholeness and
console us in our grief.

When Devon's illness is in remission as a result of the drugs
that Kincaid brought with her from the United States, drugs to
which he would have no access without her intervention,[11] the
two take a walk in the recently restored botanical gardens near
their mother's home:

But then we came to a tree that we could not identify, not on our own,
not from the book. It was a tree, only a tree, and it was either just emerging from a complete dormancy or it was half-dead, half-alive. My brother
and I became obsessed with this tree, its bark, its leaves, its shape; we
wondered where it was really from, what sort of tree it was. (*My Brother*
79–80)

Kincaid wants to see Devon, similarly, as 'coming out of a dormancy,' whether 'a natural sleep' or 'a temporary death' (81). In
her urgency to revivify him through the power of her incanta-

tions, though, she does not seem to be able to relinquish the possession of things through naming, and because of the strength of her desire, his lack of affirmation is framed as irrelevant ('Flowers of Evil' 159). She speaks on behalf of both of them, just as the memoir's title teasingly does, saying 'we' and 'my brother and I.' But she also admits that this identity may not have been acceptable to him: if he thought that the tree 'bore any resemblance to him right then and there, he did not say, he did not let me know in any way' (*My Brother* 80).

Towards the end of the first half of *My Brother*, Kincaid associates Devon with a mahogany tree, one of the few plants she can name as being indigenous to Antigua ('Alien Soil' 49), and this metaphor seems to console her by re-valourizing his life. The fruit of the mahogany tree stands for their shared appreciation of indigenous plants, and almost succeeds in presenting a purified image of Devon:

It was a marvel to us then, so perfectly shaped like a pear, the Northern Hemisphere fruit, not the avocado pear, but hard like the wood of the tree from which it comes. I brought it back to the Vermont climate with me and placed it on a windowsill, and one day when I looked, it had opened quietly, perfectly, into sections, revealing an inside that was a pink like a shell that had been buried in clean sand, and layers upon layers of seeds in pods that had wings, like the seeds of a maple. (80–1)

Observe, however, the comparisons in which Kincaid indulges: 'shaped like a pear, the Northern Hemisphere fruit,' 'like the seeds of a maple.' These awkward distinctions call so much attention to themselves that they seem intentionally alarming, especially since the comparisons are all to First World plants, and thus designed to foreground Kincaid's projection of her perspective onto her brother in recounting this anecdote of brother and sister as united in their passion for gardening and shared appreciation of indigenous plants. The possibility that the mahogany fruit might suggest genitalia is (in this context) almost thoroughly repressed, as though to foreclose the unbeautiful memories of Devon's decaying flesh, particularly the anxiety-inducing display of his penis, which is covered with fungus and 'looked like a bruised flower that had been cut short on the stem' (91). Kincaid cannot escape being haunted by lost possibilities, exclaiming: 'This feeling that his life actually should have provided such a metaphor' – of a flower that blooms, dies, and regenerates itself by producing seeds – 'so ordinary an image, so common and so welcoming had it been just so, could not leave me' (168). If anything, this trope of regeneration is more appropriate to her own process of storytelling and of memory than it is to Devon's sense of his life, for the mahogany fruit, pear-shaped and pink-shelled, may best refer to herself, to her female body, and to her disseminated memory: 'And in the *unfolding* were many things, all *contained in memory* (but without memory what would be left? Nothing? I do not know)' (163; emphasis added).

The last detail in the botanical-gardens episode is similarly jarring and makes apparent the discrepancies between Kincaid's imagining of Devon and the realities of his world, although these differences remain hypothetical until the final forty pages of the memoir, when, in a distorted and delayed way, Kincaid registers her already existing awareness that Devon was 'a participant in homosexual life' (161). Remembering the continuation of their walk, she recalls how, as they passed 'the Recreational Grounds, the public grounds where major public events are held,' Devon 'pointed to a pavilion and told me that when he was a student at his school, he and a friend used to take girls under there and have sex.' Devon's actual phrasing is recorded in parentheses, as though she cannot process his statement: '("Mahn, me used to bang up some girls under there")' (81). This statement directs her and the reader's gaze away from pastoral possibilities and towards an aggressively sexualized male body, one that defies public civility and conformity to conventional English. The description 'recreational grounds' generates, moreover, multiple meanings, signifying colonial and masculine aggression (using women and the land for recreation, in the sense of pleasure but also in the sense of self-fashioning) and Kincaid's desire to re-create an idealized indigenous past that would mollify such a history of aggression. The ironies of this passage are only redoubled once she starts to interpret Devon as closeted, for she begins to see that his bravado masks a deeper nonconformity, 'his secret of not really wanting to seduce them, really wanting to seduce someone who was not at all like them, a man' (164). The parentheses function prophylactically as though they might (if they could) protect the narrator and her readers from the dangerous, pathogenic power of her brother's sexuality and his lack of power. And yet the bracketing off of Devon's voice from his sister's narrative also preserves the very language and memories against which the narrative struggles to institute boundaries: Kincaid refuses (by staging her failure) to speak for Devon in any language but the one she remembers him using.[12]

Subsequently, when Kincaid quotes Devon as using 'conventional English,' she identifies dialect as 'the English that instantly reveals the humiliation of history, the humiliations of the past not remade into art' (108), suggesting that she attributes this dimension of unfathomable shame evidenced in language to the 'real,' uncensored Devon, the one whom she has so much difficulty in recording. She rewrites this nostalgic mahogany-fruit metaphor in a way that acknowledges how 'the humiliations of the past' and, indeed, of the present – as embodied in Devon's plight, his illness, poverty, ignorance, closetedness, and above all, his language – similarly resist being 'remade into art' (108). Echoing the image of the layers of the mahogany fruit when it opens on her Vermont windowsill to reveal its seeds, she recalls her first meeting with Devon on her return to Antigua: 'When I first saw him in the hospital, lying there almost dead, his lips were scarlet red, as if layers and layers of skin had been removed and only one last layer remained, holding in place the dangerous fluid that was his blood.' The metaphor and the narrative (suggested by the focus on Devon's mouth), like Devon's blood, are thus revealed simultaneously to be held in place by only the thinnest, most fragile of membranes, a membrane beneath which the dangerous fluid-becoming-vapour of his being is visible. In being transformed into a more literal reference to Devon's HIV infection and his illness, the metaphor ceases to bear the fruit of consolation. If Devon's life can be called emblematic of anything, it is of his unending, untransmutable suffering, not his beauty, for the description continues: 'His face was sharp like a carving, like an image embossed on an emblem, a face full of deep suffering, beyond regrets or pleadings for a second chance' (83). Devon has, it seems, ossified, his face becoming 'like a mask' as he exists in an almost dead state that 'still amounted to something called being alive' and taking on a deeper blackness, a darkening that connects him perhaps with the dark redness of mahogany wood (150). He has become an artifact, the subject of human work and interpretation, not simply a blossom, fruit, or leaf, though the images of his mouth and penis 'abloom with thrush' present us with the hint of an organic reality – but one that has gone awry, so that blackness returns, disturbingly, as a symptom of disease (156). Mahogany, a deciduous hardwood, is precious and irreplaceable, but the imperative to consume pays this irreplaceability no mind; likewise, Devon, potentially 'brilliant' and 'important,' becomes a victim of neocolonial economics (59).

Rewriting the Family Romance

While the memoir's stated purpose is to 'understand' his illness and thus avoid 'd[ying] with him' (196), there is a marked tension between Kincaid's desire to reinvent the relationship and the ways in which Devon eludes her narrative grasp, undermining what she refers to as 'my now privileged North American way (my voice full of pity at the thought of any kind of destruction, as

long as my great desires do not go unmet in any way)' (*My Brother* 125). Near the end of the memoir, Devon's spectral presence seems to have prompted a change in her judgment of his life: 'The source of the sadness was a deep feeling I had always had about him: that he had died without ever understanding or knowing, or being able to let the world in which he lived know, who he was' (162). By what path does Kincaid arrive at this revised perspective, and what are its conditions and complications? For the most part, it seems that the memoir is describing the devastation of the situation from above: despite her horror she cannot turn away and continues to bear witness. Looking 'towards the past,' Benjamin's angel of history, that is, of materialist historiography, contemplates rather than reconstructs the past: 'Where we perceive a chain of events, he sees one single catastrophe which keeps piling wreckage and hurls it in front of his feet' ('Theses on the Philosophy of History' 257). Kincaid rejects the practice of writing a 'journal,' 'a daily account of what occurs during a certain time,' and instead relives in memory the 'time' of Devon's illness, that 'short time' between when 'he became sick and the time he died,' the time that 'became a world' (*My Brother* 91–2).[13] The project is profoundly unsettling, for it reveals the connections among life and death, power and powerlessness:

To be so intimately acquainted with the organism that is the HIV virus is to be acquainted with death; each moment, each gesture, holds in it a set of events that can easily slide into realities that are unknown, unexpected, to the point of shock; we do not really expect these moments; they arrive and are resisted, denied, and then finally, inexorably, accepted; to have the HIV virus is to have crossed the line between life and death. On one side there is life, and the thin shadow of death hovers over it; and on the other, there is death with a small patch of life attached to it. This latter is the life of AIDS; this was how I saw my brother as he lay in his bed dying. (95–6)

Unlike smallpox, which, according to Alfred W. Crosby, in the early decades of conquest drew distinct lines between the conquerors (who were immune) and the indigenes (who were not), the HIV virus extends immune status to no one. Kincaid cannot escape the evidence she faces of Devon's vulnerability and struggles with her desire to distance herself from him as a way of repudiating the fragility of her own life. By exploring how the hospital and family embody and reproduce structural inequities that reflect cultural attitudes towards gender, race, and history (familial and colonial), Kincaid investigates the archaeology of her ambivalence about Devon. In looking at the stigma, secrecy, and denial that exacerbate Devon's plight, Kincaid finds that her grief for Devon enhances the prismatic, analytical potential of her already melancholic relation to her 'native' place, Antigua.

My Brother's obsessive attention to the conditions in which Devon Drew lives and dies pinpoints the health care system's inadequate and inconsistent approach to addressing the medical and social needs of HIV-positive people. The placement in Antigua of people with AIDS 'in rooms by themselves' (21–2) exemplifies a logic of panic, doom, and denial (Singer, *Erotic Welfare* 28–9). *My Brother* connects this logic to the lack of medical resources for the underprivileged and to a deeply ingrained homophobia; thus, the Antiguan situation reflects the inequities of the higher-income countries of the northern hemisphere, such as the United States, where HIV infection and AIDS are also increasingly shown to be linked to racial inequities, social marginalization, and poverty.[14] When Devon becomes ill he is placed alone in the hospital in a small room, and we quickly become aware, as with Eric Michaels's critique of the misplaced energies of the discourse of 'tidiness,' that rather than connoting the privilege of privacy, Devon's placement in isolation is a manifestation of fear and neglect. The room lacks basic amenities: there is no table lamp, the television is broken, the floors and walls are dirty (22). Considering that Devon has 'trouble breathing,' the fact that 'pieces of dust' would frequently 'become dislodged' from 'the blades of the ceiling fan' seems a preposterous risk (27). The condition of Devon's room expresses the view that if AIDS is a death sentence, then health care resources should not be 'wasted' on prolonging doomed lives. Kincaid mimics a dispassionate bureaucratic voice to emphasize this problem as well as to criticize it: 'It is felt in general, so I am told, that since there is no cure for AIDS it is useless to spend money on a medicine that will only slow the progress of the disease; the afflicted will die no matter what; there are limited resources to be spent on health care and these should be spent where they will do some good, not where it is known that the outcome is death' (31).

This dismissive attitude is the culmination of the despair generated by an underfunded and badly organized health care system. In the late 1980s, when Kincaid asked the tourist/reader of *A Small Place* to imagine the consequences for her or his own health of Antigua's dilapidated health care system, she identified the hospital as an indicator of the economic and medical precariousness of the lives of ordinary Antiguans in that country after independence:

Will you be comforted to know that the hospital is staffed with doctors that no actual Antiguan trusts; that Antiguans always say about the doctors, 'I don't want them near me'; that Antiguans refer to them not as doctors but as 'the three men' (there are three of them); that when the Minister of Health himself doesn't feel well he takes the first plane to New York to see a real doctor; that if any one of the ministers in government needs medical care he flies to New York to get it? (8)

Those without the means to travel to the United States, or who require emergency care, are left to the mercies of a decrepit system, and those in power are not motivated to improve the situation because for them the best of American health care services are only a quick plane ride away. An additional cause for frustration in the context of HIV infection and AIDS in the early 1990s is the unavailability of up-to-date drugs that might produce some improvements for patients, for 'even if a doctor had wanted to write a prescription for AZT for a patient,' as Devon's physician, the kind Dr Ramsey, clearly would like to do, 'that prescription could not be filled at a chemist's; there was no AZT on the island, it was too expensive to be stocked, most people suffering from the disease could not afford to buy this medicine' (*My Brother* 31–2). Kincaid's provocative gesture in her gardening essays that the indigenous knowledge of plants might hold some real medicinal possibilities for treating opportunistic infections associated with AIDS (such as the use of the cancanberry bush to treat thrush) suggests that reliance on imported treatments and faith in Western medicine tends to preclude looking for local and immediately available ways of treating illness ('Alien Soil' 50); widespread 'public concern, obsession with the treatment and care of the AIDS-suffering community by groups in the larger non-AIDS suffering community does not exist' (*My Brother* 31).

The interpretation of people with AIDS as doomed contributes, according to Kincaid's analysis, to individual as well as institutional denial of the epidemic and avoidance of responsibility to take preventive measures. Devon's refusal to regard himself as a potential source of infection for others exemplifies the widespread cultural attitude of denial, panic, and self-interest. The social worker assigned to his case discovers that during his remission Devon 'had been having unprotected sex with [a] woman and he had not told her that he was infected with the HIV virus' (66). The one warning that registers with him is the false but persuasive statement 'that HIV infection was dose-related, that is, the more of the virus you have received, the quicker it kills you' (67). Devon seems to her to be impervious to appeals to altruism: only the thought that he might need 'to protect himself from other people' has any impact on him. Despite the fact that he is very ill, he continues to see himself as 'a powerfully sexual man,' invincible and irresistible, who 'could not go two weeks without having sex,' making it unlikely that he will follow through on practising safe sex (67).

Kincaid sees Devon's life as having been compromised by his continuing childlike role in their shared family of origins, which she reads as a microcosm of Antiguan society. She sees a long history of destruction and shame in the triangular configuration of mother, sister, and brother, and in the relations of power among them. Take, for instance, the secrecy in which Devon's illness is initially cloaked: 'At first he did not tell our mother the truth, he told her he had lung cancer, he told someone else he had bronchial asthma' (23). Only through institutional prejudice, ironically, does the truth become known, though it remains unacknowledged: 'But he knew and my mother knew and anyone else who was interested would know that only people who tested positive for the AIDS virus were placed in that room in isolation' (23). Devon's final dwelling is a temporary 'coffinlike' addition to his mother's home, a detail that highlights the stinginess of the arrangements made to accommodate his illness in both familial and institutional settings: the space the family makes for him is no improvement after all on the dirty, dilapidated hospital room to which he was previously confined, and both situations are read by Kincaid as predetermining Devon's doom, sealing him off from the rest of the community with a certain 'aloofness, at-arm's-lengthness' (172, 31, 46). Mrs Drew's welcoming back of the prodigal into her home, and even, for lack of other options when he first returns, into her very own bed (54), creates an appearance of intimacy, but Kincaid implies that the arrangement is mutually parasitic and debilitating for Devon, 'another example of the extraordinary ability of her love for her children to turn into a weapon of destruction' (53). Kincaid views the over-closeness of the bond between mother and son as creating a situation of dependency in which Devon has not had to take on the responsibility of an independent, adult life. Allowances are made for Devon and the other boys in the family that were never made for their sister: 'He would lie on his bed in a drug-induced daze. His mother would not have allowed him to do this if he were female; I know this' (44). The household arrangements made in response to his illness thus appear as an intensification of the dependency and childlike state that have characterized Devon's life thus far, for, previously, Devon lived in a shack adjoined to his mother's house, a building that '*resembled* an actual house; it had three windows that had working shutters, it had a door that could be bolted' (55; emphasis added). Devon may, in a certain sense, perform separation from his mother by shutting the door to his apartment, but in reality he remains dependent on her. In all of these ways, Devon's place in his mother's household represents, metonymically, all of the ways in which maleness, homosexuality, and infantilization are entwined in this context: that is to say, Devon lives a prolonged adolescence, and at once depends on his mother and lives a life that remains secret from her.

Kincaid defines herself against her mother, criticizing Mrs Drew's powerful, destructive role as caregiver and mourner. She sets her own anxious preoccupation with mourning in contrast with that of her mother, whose claim to exemplary, final mourning seems to foreclose on knowing the complexities of Devon's life and desires (131–2). Past traumas and conflicts recur in present time, suggesting a causal or at any rate contributive relationship between Devon's neglected childhood and his HIV infection and AIDS-related illnesses as an adult. Mrs Drew, in her exhaustion and despair after Devon's birth, did not 'give his chemise the customary elaborate attention involving embroidery stitching and special washings of the cotton fabric,' making Devon vulnerable, symbolically at least, to 'evil spirits' (5). Later, he is attacked by 'an army of red ants' while sleeping in his mother's arms, an incident that Kincaid, out of her melancholy, sees as being repeated in the present: 'I was only wondering whether it had any meaning that some small red things had almost killed him from the outside shortly after he was born and now some small things were killing him from the inside' (6). Mrs Drew both denies this history and refuses to admit the serious-ness of Devon's illness. Kincaid observes how, from the time of Devon's relapse, 'the house had a funny smell, as if my mother no longer had time to be the immaculate housekeeper she had always been and so some terrible dirty thing had gone unnoticed and was rotting away quietly' (90). The passage implies criticism of the mother's abjection of Devon and his illness, as though her inattentiveness has a causal relation to the very 'rottenness' that disturbs her, and emphasizes by contrast Kincaid's self-conscious awareness that she is unable to 'find a simile for this smell, it was not a smell like any I am familiar with' (90). Even before his death, Devon begins to take a diffuse material form as an aroma of dirt or shame for the members of his family, a smell the dis-turbing memory of which cannot be cleared or cleaned, however, from the psychic space of anyone who is involved or implicated in Devon's dying.

Kincaid's criticisms of her mother may be read, however, as motivated by Kincaid's guilty and regretful feelings about her lack of closeness to Devon. She sceptically states of her mother that 'she mourns beautifully, she is admirable in mourning; if I were ever to be in mourning, this is the model, the example I would imitate' (132). While Kincaid constructs herself as a failed and contemptible mourner (and thereby implicitly as more faith-ful), her attitude in fact resembles her mother's in several ways: both have difficulty acknowledging Devon's sexuality, and both experience feelings of shame. Kincaid sees her mother's dis-avowal of Devon's sexuality and her refusal to use the word AIDS as exemplifying the contradictory attitude towards the epidemic in Antiguan society, where, from Kincaid's North American per-spective, the forms for mourning the dead seem to be given more energy than the labour of caring for the ill: Kincaid points out, for example, how ludicrous it is 'that when a person is ill no one mentions it, no one pays a visit; but if the person should die, there is a big outpouring of people at the funeral, there are bouquets, people sing hymns for the dead with much feeling' (146). And yet has Kincaid herself not returned to Antigua precisely under the force of a familial and social obligation to perform mourning, rather than purely by her own volition? Thus, if Mrs Drew has sustained a pattern of alternately neglecting and indulging Devon, symbolically as well as literally destroying her memory of him by cutting down the lemon tree he planted, then Kincaid creates this narrative in part because she wants to be able to see herself as representing some more faithful allegiance or identification with Devon, as preserving her brother's legacy. What is almost but not quite masked, however, by the melodramatic vilification of Mrs Drew is the fact that she has remained close to Devon and has participated in caring for him in ways that Kincaid herself has not. As Hoffman's and Michaels's representations of caregiving relationships and notions of family help to clarify, it is all too easy for Kincaid to castigate as pretended, deficient, or illegitimate the caregiving arrangements that have arisen in her absence and in response to a crisis.

Moreover, this troubling of the relative status of Kincaid's grieving in relation to that of her mother highlights how the anxiety that Devon's death instigates painfully holds open the question of what it might mean to mourn 'well,' when one can never escape the feeling of profanation that grieving – and especially writing about grief – entails. Here it becomes pertinent to wonder what lies in the shared past of sister and brother and to enquire into how their shared childhood informs their present relationship and, in turn, Kincaid's struggle to represent Devon. Kincaid is haunted by the memory of her resentment of the disarray into which Devon's birth pushed the Drew family as well as her neglect of her sisterly responsibility to care for him. Devon, who has read his sister's books, asks her if he is the 'throw-way pickney,' the unwanted and overlooked child she mentions in several places in her fiction (174). While the red-ants incident may be attributable to their mother, Kincaid's guilt about her own neglect of Devon, her wish 'that he had never been born,' also haunts the memoir (141). Questioning her mother about the charred remains of a soursop tree, and remembering her mother's capacity for unleashing destructive anger on the outside world, violently destroying what gets in her way, in this case the parasitically infected tree, Kincaid faces how a similar scene of maternal destruction remembered from childhood pitted her interests against those of Devon (125–8). She recalls that there is one story that 'no one ever told my brother, an incident that everyone else in my family has forgotten, except me': left in charge of her infant brother as a young girl, she gets so caught up in her reading that she forgets to change his diaper; enraged, Kincaid's mother burned her books (128–34). The scene encapsulates for Kincaid the family's destitution, and crystallizes her determination to escape it: 'And in [his diaper], this picture of my brother's hardened stool, a memory, a moment of my own life is frozen; for his diaper sagged with a weight that was not gold but its opposite, a weight whose value would not bring us good fortune, a weight that only emphasized our family's despair' (131). Devon, in his vulnerability and helplessness, represents everything that Kincaid has escaped, and suggests that the interests of sister and brother are pitted against one another in this colonial family romance. As Kristeva argues of the significance of bodily waste in the structure of abjection, 'dung signifies the other side of the border, the place where I am not and which permits me to be' (*Powers of Horror* 3). Now, with Devon's illness, with his body disintegrating, literally liquefying, even 'evaporating' (*My Brother* 124), refusing to form a coherent visual image, Kincaid can no longer abject from her consciousness the 'corporeal waste' with which she associates her brother, as dung returns in another instance of traumatic and unsettling repetition, forc-

ing her to consider his suffering on its own terms: 'My brother
was in great pain. A stream of yellow pus flowed out of his anus
constantly; the inside of his mouth and all around his lips were
covered with a white glistening substance, thrush' (138).

That Kincaid may sometimes be more similar to than different
from her mother in her desire to bring the process of mourning
to completion – and thus seeking after the power and authority
to assert her reconstructed, self-interested view of the past – is far
from easy to admit. The memoir registers again and again
Kincaid's exhaustion and exasperation, her wish for some resolution: she resents his 'weighing on my sympathy, at times preying
on my sympathy,' and even says that 'I was sick of him and wanted
him to go away, and I didn't care if he got better and I didn't care
if he died' (169). Kincaid tries to grapple, however, with the
aspects of Devon's identity that she finds particularly threatening
and difficult to admit, namely his marginalization as a poor black
man in Antigua and his sexuality.

As is evident from an early story printed in *At the Bottom of the
River,* Kincaid has been preoccupied for a long time with the melancholic suspension of selfhood, which she describes in terms of
'blackness':

The blackness enters my many-tiered spaces and soon the significant
word and event recede and eventually vanish: in this way, I am annihi-
lated and my form becomes formless and I am absorbed into a vastness
of free-flowing matter. In the blackness, then, I have been erased. I can
no longer say my own name. I can no longer look at myself and say 'I.' In
the blackness my voice is silent. First then, I have been my individual
self, carefully banishing randomness from my existence, then I am swallowed up in the blackness so that I am one with it ... ('Blackness' 46–7)

'Blackness' is melancholy formlessness and a suspension of language's ability to confer stable meaning, but the term also necessarily has a historical, familial, and racial resonance in the

context of Kincaid's writing. In *My Brother*, Devon's increasing 'blackness' leads Kincaid to invoke the following strategy of containment: the baffling assertion that he (her half-brother, as opposed to her?) 'was descended from Africans mostly' (150). On what grounds, she seems to ask, but on those of the distance implied by a quasi-objective labelling of the source of Devon's blackness in this sentence can she disavow their shared ancestry? Does she not share a familial and racial history with her brother, however fractured? She thus raises difficult questions about racialization and racial prejudice as internalized phenomena, suggesting a desire (one she struggles with and against) to dissociate herself from Devon's body marked as 'black' and to assert her own identity as unmarked, free from the process of racialization.

Kincaid struggles with the difficulty of acknowledging love and attachment to a man deemed 'unlovable' and 'ungrievable' by a homophobic society and a troubled family: in this, Kincaid must travel, however, a somewhat longer distance to reach her recognition of Devon's sexuality than Amy Hoffman does to embrace Mike Riegle as her kin in *Hospital Time*. Ultimately, it is only when a stranger, a woman friend of Devon's who was part of the gay and lesbian community in Antigua, informs Kincaid when they meet at a book signing in Chicago that Devon was 'a participant in homosexual life' that this gap is filled in (164–7). Until this point, when the knowledge becomes unavoidable even if it is still deflected by her oddly distancing phrase, Kincaid is confused by Devon, struggling to assure herself of his vibrancy and intelligence and unable to understand his struggle with sexuality:

He was not meant to be silent. He was a brilliant boy, he was a brilliant man. Locked up inside him was someone who would have spoken to the world in an important way. I believe this. Locked up inside him was someone who would have found satisfaction speaking to the world in an important way, and that someone would not have needed to greet every passerby, that someone would not have time for every passerby, that someone would have felt there isn't enough silence in the world. (59)

These seem to be more Kincaid's own feelings; she is someone who finds 'satisfaction in speaking to the world in an important way.' Devon's promiscuity, not only his sexual promiscuity but his indiscriminate way of conducting his life, contrasts with the value his sister places on publicly recognized achievement. If something is 'locked up' or hidden, she tends to read this missing piece according to her own anxieties as negative evidence of his stifled ambition. She remembers how Devon assented to her projection of another more important life for him:

It is I who told him this and he agreed with me at the moment I told him this, and he said yes, and I saw that he wished what I said were really true, would just become true, wished he could, wished he knew how to make the effort and to make it true. He could not. In his daydreams he became a famous singer, and women removed their clothes when they heard him sing. (59–60)

Both from her own sense that her projections always miss the mark and from the information about Devon's 'homosexual life' that she eventually receives, Kincaid is compelled to adopt a characteristic pattern of undercutting her own projections, a pattern that challenges her idealized image of Devon, including this secondary definition of homosexual, the other of herself as heterosexual. As with her botanical metaphors, Kincaid vacillates between, on the one hand, judging Devon according to a straight and middle-class concept of productivity and, on the other, struggling to acknowledge to herself the existence of a more complicated reality, one that she, disconnected from her family in Antigua and trying to remember Devon after he has died, will never fully know.

She confronts her feeling of disturbance about the association of sexuality with disease in the context of her brother's illness. Paralleling Hoffman's references to Mike Riegle's penis, Kincaid dwells specifically on Devon's genitals as the locus of their new, unsolicited, and disturbing intimacy. Her memory of his showing her his infected penis, which, 'covered with sores' and 'fungus,' 'looked like a bruised flower that had been cut short on the stem,' both violates her sense of propriety and seems to invite a conflation of his illness with a fearful reading of sexuality as inherently pathogenic. The image of Devon's penis seems to corroborate other images she has seen of venereal disease and her visceral reaction that 'these images of suffering and death were the result of sexual activity, and by the end of Dr. Ramsay's talk, I felt I would never have sex again, not even with myself' (91, 38). In recalling these disturbing memories and exploring what they mean for her own sense of sexuality, Kincaid is pushed towards the recognition that she has lost control over the process of memory: 'I could not think about him in any purposeful way' (157).

In its focus on Devon as 'embodied subject' and Kincaid as struggling 'universal subject,'[15] *My Brother* restages the usual gender polarity of the body-mind split and points out how gender, race, geography, and economics overlap, complicate, and contradict the relation of the privileged to the marginalized. The passage I cited from *At the Bottom of the River* ends on a note of self-assertion, suggesting the deliberate, self-conscious adoption of an identity that both rejects and compensates for the body's material vulnerability: 'I was not made up of flesh and blood and muscles and bones and tissues and cells and vital organs but was made up of my will' (79). It is through this strategy of self-possession that Kincaid's autobiographical narrators attempt to 'banish' 'randomness' – and the subject's vulnerability evidenced in the history of racial oppression – from 'existence' (47). But *My Brother* anxiously questions Kincaid's desire to dissociate herself from Devon's material vulnerability and to retrieve a sense of coherent selfhood from the 'blackness' that threatens to swallow her up along with him. Attempting, similarly, to retrieve an identity from the abyss of colonial and familial history, Devon insists on constructing himself as ultra-masculine, defined by his will, identifying with 'the great hero-thieves of English maritime history: Horatio Nelson, John Hawkins, Francis Drake.' He asserts his powers of self-determination in flat denial of reality, without recognizing the irony of 'lik[ing] the people who won, even though he was among the things that had been won' (94–5). His fantasies of heroism, like his sister's belief in her own will to surmount and transform circumstances, amount to a 'life that was not real, not yet a part of history; his reality was that he was dead but still alive; his reality was that he had a disease called AIDS' (95).

Postcolonial Melancholy and Critical Memory

Lacking a historical or biographical framework into which Devon can be written and perhaps redeemed, Kincaid cannot avoid looking at Devon's dying body and his corpse: these are the only materials from which she can try to make meaning. But in confronting the material traces of Devon's body-in-ruins, she rediscovers time after time that she cannot assimilate his remains or her memories of him to a pastoral vision. The passages describing his dying body and corpse are indicative of the process by which the aspects of his existence that Kincaid tends to exclude from her consciousness haunt the boundaries she constructs for her relationship with him; they haunt as a ghost that activates all kinds of unwelcome memories, not least of which is her own role in perpetuating Devon's infantilization, a state she obsessively seeks to assure herself she has 'avoided or escaped' (176).

In the second half of the memoir, where Kincaid faces her childhood memories and Devon's corpse simultaneously, her first viewing of Devon's dead body contrasts with her viewing of

him in his coffin after his body has been remade by the under-
taker. Once 'the people still in life arranged him,' Devon 'looked
like an advertisement for the dead, not like the dead at all': 'his
hair was nicely combed and dyed black,' 'his lips were clamped
tightly together,' and 'eyes had been sewn shut' (180–1). Kincaid
repeats the words 'sewn shut' – 'I have to say it again, sewn shut' –
as if out of disbelief that the orifices of his body could or should
be closed in this way (181). Kristeva suggests the corpse is the
ultimate 'jettisoned object,' what is most 'radically excluded'
from culture. As 'the utmost of abjection,' Devon's dead body
puts Kincaid in a state of mind where language has lost all reference and she can speak of nothing (*Powers of Horror* 2–4; *Black
Sun* 51). Yet when she faces the corpse before it is made over,
while it is still unadorned, enclosed in its 'plastic bag,' a complex
dynamic of recognition and estrangement is initiated (*My Brother*
180). Devon does not look like himself, but neither does he look
'arranged' as an 'advertisement for the dead' (181):

His hair was uncombed, his face was unshaven, his eyes were wide-open,
and his mouth was wide-open, too, and the open eyes and the open
mouth made it seem as if he was looking at something in the far distance, something horrifying coming toward him, and that he was
screaming, the sound of the scream silent now (but it had never been
heard, I would have been told so, it had never been heard, this scream),
and this scream seemed to have no break in it, no pause for an intake of
breath; this scream only came out in one exhalation, trailing off into
eternity, or just trailing off to somewhere I do not know, or just trailing
off into nothing. (179)

Caught in the caesura in time produced by her initial viewing of
the corpse, Kincaid holds on to this non-image of Devon in the
face of social and familial pressure to keep his mouth, and the
rest of his speaking body, 'sewn shut.' The language of negation
('uncombed,' 'unshaven,' 'I do not know,' 'trailing off into noth-

ing') and of paradox ('silent' combined with 'sound' and 'scream') suspends the work of mourning, drawing attention to the unclear boundary of Devon's living death. While his wordless exhalation can be registered only as a blank within the terms of symbolic language, on a semiotic level it brings us into contact with everything we would rather suppress: a close-up, extreme view of the moment of death, of the body's becoming corporeal waste and lapsing into passivity. His dead body is further described as 'unreal': 'his eyes, closed, shut, sealed, like an envelope, not a vault: his body was delicate, fragile-seeming, all bones' (190). The embedded metaphors suggest that Devon's corpse has become a hieroglyph, that it bears an encoded message that is compelling but inscrutable: his 'farawayness' is 'so complete, so final,' and yet he continues (paradoxically) to speak to her, 'though not in the everyday way that I speak of speech' (190). Her narrative voice is enfolded in the silent voice of Devon's pain, overwhelmed by the unstable boundary of his 'living death,' which entails that neither the unpredictable, fluid forces of memory nor those of the body can be staunched. Thinking retrospectively, in the shadow of these recollections, Kincaid has to recognize, from the beginning of her memoir, that the 'plantsman in my brother will never be, and all the other things that he might have been in his life have died; but inside his body a death lives, flowering upon flowering, with a voraciousness that nothing seems to be able to satisfy and stop' (19–20). Writing about Devon, she becomes, as suggested by this weird trope of death's (rather than life's) bloom, the gardener of a strange and fecund death.

In the midst of the overlapping of illness and homosexuality in the context of the AIDS pandemic, the sovereignty of masculinity – the hierarchy of privilege against which the young Kincaid rebelled by choosing her books over the role of proxy caregiver for her brother – is shown to be interrupted by Devon's powerlessness, both in the past, when he was an infant and brought close to death by his family's neglect, and in the present, because of his illness and his sexual orientation. In this transformed context, she begins to grasp that there may be more than one meaning attributed to the anxiety that underlies his bravado. And it is here that she speculates, as I suggested previously, that his anxiety may have been a reaction of anguish at the loss of privacy (164). His thin, broken skin and his silent vocative of agony in death gesture not just towards physical pain, then, but also towards his grief in response to the disintegration of the life he constructed, however ramshackle it was. Identifying with Devon's secrecy and sense of exposure, Kincaid implies that there exists for her simultaneously a sense of connection (their struggles against oppression possess similarities) and a sense of disjunction (through what she calls her own 'cold and ruthless' actions [69], Kincaid 'avoided or escaped' the vulnerability and powerlessness that remain Devon's lot [176]). As she mournfully repeats, while Devon's 'homosexuality is one thing, and my becoming a writer is another altogether, ... this truth is not lost to me: I could not have become myself while living among the people I knew best, I could not have become myself while living among the people I knew best' (162). The memoir is thus written out of the interruption of Kincaid's autobiographical 'I,' for, as she seems to discover each time she attempts to assert an explanatory metaphor, it is only through self-annihilation that she can write responsibly about the disaster or emergency that is Devon's life and death.[16]

Desperate and overwhelmed by this recognition, Kincaid reasserts the privilege of textual comprehension as the memoir goes haltingly towards its conclusion, though at this stage the impossibility of masking her horror seems clear to her: 'When I heard about my brother's illness and his dying, I knew, instinctively, that to understand it, or to make an attempt at understanding his dying, and not to die with him, I would write about it' (195–6). Even more astonishingly belated is the homage she pays in the final pages of the memoir to the late William Shawn, the *New*

Yorker editor and her mentor and father-in-law. If Kincaid cannot close the 'open wound' that is Devon's body, then what are the implications of adopting another dead man, Shawn, as a replacement addressee (a white American intellectual father figure [196–8])? What does it mean for her to call Shawn the 'perfect reader' (198) in a text that supposedly addresses Devon Drew? In some senses, Shawn symbolizes everything that Devon is not: at the centre of the metropolis, sophisticated, and supportive (indeed one of the crucial agents) of Kincaid's career as a writer. Turning to her memories of him might furnish a point of stability that can release her from melancholy. Her memoir sustains, nonetheless, a critical distance from the 'impatien[ce] with memory' on which, she believes, the American 'order thrives' ('Alien Soil' 51). Her attachment to the material realities of Devon's experience is one that her yearning for understanding, her substitution of an alternative addressee, and her statements about protecting the integrity of the life she has built with her own family in the United States cannot exorcize, for the supplements, introduced with such delay and in the context of so much grief, do not cohere and point only to 'the law of endless supplementation' that characterizes melancholy (Chambers, *The Writing of Melancholy* 168).[17] Indeed, Kincaid theorizes early in the memoir, preparing us for this dynamic of unfolding and refolding, that precisely what most enrages her family, 'the people I grew up with,' about her is her dedication to the necessity of remembering and her awareness of memory's incompleteness. Never content with a single memory's sufficiency, 'I always say, do you remember?' (*My Brother* 19).

My Brother continually circles back to the unanswerable question, 'Which Devon was he?,' a question that summarizes Kincaid's sense that she is responsible for recognizing who he was and her doubled sense of loss at the realization that she never will, that she has missed her opportunity to 'know' him (191). Though 'it is the end,' 'yet so many things linger' (156).

She holds on, melancholically, to Devon in his complexity and in
the complexity of her feelings about him and about the family
and the place of their shared origins. In so doing, she affirms her
bond to him. But because 'the dead never die' (121) and so continue to haunt those who attempt to record their lives and
deaths, what Devon's life, illness, and death mean remains open-
ended. The ephemeral is held 'parenthetically' in the textual,[18]
implying that there may not be a 'life' (her own or Devon's) to
reconstruct as would ordinarily be conceived of in the conventions of Western biography or autobiography: 'In his life there
had been no flowering, his life was the opposite of that, a flowering, his life was like the bud that sets but, instead of opening into
a flower, turns brown and falls off at your feet' (162–3). Without
progress, only demonstrating decay, Devon's living and dying
compel Kincaid to take up a position of authorial passivity, the
role of a disoriented, grief-stricken, self-berating observer, one
who has (by her own analysis) a tendency aggressively to compensate for this lack of power by asserting authority. She is at once
overwhelmed by and bereft of significant facts, attempting to
balance between bearing witness to Devon's life and making
meaning out of it. *My Brother*, through its shifting melancholic
identifications, keeps watch and suddenly, surprisingly, in the
same moment that so much anguish is being registered, suggests
that there coexists with all the disavowals of love the possibility,
however tenuous, of a radical and loving identification with a
missing person: 'I said to him that nothing good could ever come
of his being so ill, but all the same I wanted to thank him for
making me realize that I loved him' (21). The melancholic
dynamic of *My Brother*, its self-implication in abjection, in impossible mourning, thus powerfully, though not unambivalently, contests the panic and compartmentalization through which AIDS is
associated with delinquency, and contests also the retrospective
idealization of the lives of the dead. In these senses, the book
counters the logic that confines people living with HIV and AIDS

(narratively and socially speaking) to 'rooms by themselves' (21–2), to the medical, social, familial, and memorial closets in which triumphant mourning would confine them. Through the enunciative situation of melancholic anxiety and uncertainty, *My Brother* brings its critique of the technologies of AIDS, sexuality, family, coloniality, and nation forward for our uneasy inspection.

Melancholic Reparations

Images of the natural world's beauty and decay – and of its cultivation by people in the form of gardens and memorials – are a
crucial recurring element in testimonial writing about the AIDS
epidemic, and it is by meditating on one specific example, Derek
Jarman's garden at Prospect Cottage, the physical, visual analogue to *Modern Nature*, that I wish to bring together, by way of
conclusion, my thoughts on AIDS testimonial writing, mourning,
and kinship. Casting himself as a latter-day Kentish 'saint' – and
indeed canonized as Derek of Dungeness by the gay group Sisters
of Perpetual Indulgence in 1992 – Jarman created Prospect Cottage as a retreat to be sure, but also as a work of art with a cultural
register. The cottage and its immediate surroundings stand as a
self-mythologization or self-memorialization that would ensure
his survival on something like his own terms beyond the event of
his death. But Prospect Cottage has also, as the journals explain,
been the scene of confrontations between Jarman and the media
and other prying strangers, with people, that is, who expressed
surprise to find him still there. That there exists a record of these
uncomfortable encounters forces the question of mourning
upon any visitor. And certainly my own journey to Dungeness has
raised the question of what needs, desires, and fears I bring with
me and that shape my reading of the place. Like Sedgwick edit-

ing the writings of her friend, Gary Fisher, I have found myself struck by a feeling of profanation around my visit. Was it a kind of tourism? voyeurism? an act of memorialization? an attempt at exorcism? Clothes flap on the line, the wind filling them as though giving them bodies. Keith Collins, Jarman's surviving partner, tends the garden, listens to top of the charts radio while transplanting, trimming, keeping the plants at bay in this strangely fertile desert. I arrive for a mere hour to watch someone else's grief.

But there are other lingering responses, too, besides this feeling of trespass. The intense suspicion that I had no right to be there has given rise subsequently to a series of questions about memorials and their (im)permanence – and to the crucial ongoing cultural work performed by written memoirs, which insist on these same questions and demand that readers engage with them in perpetuity. The 'fragments of memory' that make up *Modern Nature* have a corollary in Prospect Cottage, and, in both cases, Jarman's text foregrounds the imbrication of his project of reparation in hostile surroundings and draws attention as well to its tenuousness. The plants flourish in the midst of industrial debris, and under the minimal dispensation of the wind and sun, with the sea kale, broom, and poppies set amid Jarman's beachcombing finds – driftwood, shingle, an anchor, a weather-beaten boat – appearing as an intensification of what is already present in the local environment, such that the garden both resembles and contrasts with the ordinary randomness of the decay that surrounds it. Intimating a lurking danger, and creating the impression of entering a military compound of some kind, munitions fields line the road to Dungeness. All the more astonishing then the somehow slight, transient-seeming row of fishermen's cottages dotted along the coast. And on the day of my visit an amateur fashion shoot took place on the beach south of the main road, a bizarrely appropriate apparition of photographic technology in the midst of this barrenness, an apparition reminiscent, too, of

Jarman's film record of Dungeness, *The Garden*, a film that, like *Modern Nature* and Prospect Cottage, also foregrounds its own making.

But perhaps the most striking way in which Prospect Cottage draws attention to its ephemerality is the melting of the inscriptions written in tar, particularly the citation from John Donne's love poetry on the building's west wall. Jarman's rendering of Donne's words enacts a knowing and morbid calculation, as the 'busie Sunne' performs the work of time against which the poem complains. The effect of this melting is to make the text increasingly illegible as time passes. Can these words even be considered inscriptions, given the impermanence of the materials and their placement, exposed as they are to the very element to which they are most vulnerable? Tar, Jarman's symbol of choice for representing majority culture's torture and excoriation of people readable as queer (as in 'tar and feathers'), is shown to be in this context subject to the 'unworking' powers of time and the elements. The history of violence fades, melting into a material that strengthens the dwelling's ability to withstand the ravages of this weather, though it, too, will ultimately be subject to the same disintegrative process.[1]

Another reading: looking at the blurred, dripping lines of text, my companion offered the remark that the garden is bound ultimately towards disintegration or to become a National Trust Property, with gift shop and parking lot. I shot back heatedly that being designated 'National Trust' was a very unlikely future for this place. Caught amid the rush of my feeling at once that I had no right to be there at all, and my sense of being so immersed in thinking about Jarman – even thinking as him – I assumed the right to ventriloquize what I had internalized as his likely opinion on such a proposal. I have found myself wondering since about the future of Prospect Cottage. How long will Collins continue this work of maintaining the garden, a labour I imagine can be incredibly lonely? Under what conditions should it be preserved and what would preservation mean? Would preservation mean precisely the destruction of the spirit of the cultural critique that the cottage embodies and enacts? As Jarman's railing against the mausoleum-like gardens at nearby Sissinghurst underlines, public institutions for perpetuating memory are tied up with forgetting, with the streamlining imperatives of majority culture and the politics of heritage that allow only love across genders to count as 'a love and loss worthy and capable of being grieved, and thus worthy and capable of having been lived' (Butler, *Psychic Life* 138). On the other hand, can Jarman not be thought of precisely as extending the reparative, improvisatory project of Vita Sackville-West and Nigel Nicolson, in a manner that is only slightly less elitist and only a little less caught up in preserving inherited privileges and reinvigorating a pastoral vision of England? These are some of the ways in which we may read Sissinghurst, framed as it is by its own weird amalgam of disavowals of and prurience about what has been left out of its owners' famous performance of compulsory heterosexuality.[2]

Jarman's legacies persist, albeit in a sometimes ambivalent way, in his copious body of literary and filmic texts. As Sedgwick observes, commenting on the disruptive potential of literary representations in the context of a culture that would forget AIDS by declaring (repeatedly) an end to the epidemic: 'That's the wonderful thing about the printed word – it can't be updated instantly. It's allowed to remain anachronistic in relation to the culture of moment' ('This Piercing Bouquet: An Interview with Eve Kosofsky Sedgwick' 253). Still, although the textual gestures by which Jarman posthumously perpetuates his legacy are perhaps less likely to disintegrate completely than the cottage, the inassimilable remainders his texts constitute are still vulnerable to assertive revisions, to the projection of readers' desires for consolation. But the four texts I have read closely in this study anticipate and exploit their potential for their anachronistic disruption of the narrative that would declare the epidemic already to be over and, more specifically, for the insufficiencies and aggressions they identify in the discourses of redemption. I have accordingly attempted to read these examples of AIDS testimonial writing with attention to their staging of discord and of contradiction.

More specifically, I have emphasized the memoirs' incoherence – their strange mixing of narrative frameworks with distinctively non-narrative impulses – with the aim of elaborating, to return to Derrida's phrasing, 'this respect for justice for those who *are not there*' (*Specters of Marx* xix). I have sought, in other words, to perform a melancholic reading 'strategy' that might correspond to the melancholic opposition of these texts to the discourse of AIDS. The abjected spectres that haunt the boundaries of the 'clean and proper body' (and, in turn, of the 'clean and proper body politic') are, in the context of Hoffman's, Michaels's, Kincaid's, and Jarman's accounts, neither silenced nor made into spectacle. Rather, they are shown as haunting the boundaries of what is deemed proper to the self (and thereby to the social or national body), stalling its restoration, and even, at certain moments, revoking the belief in the possibility of redemption. Most crucially perhaps, what these memoirs show is that the pressures exerted by this domain cannot and should not be regulated or resolved by invoking the proprieties of gender relations and the primacy of the nuclear family, those conventions that David Halperin describes as promulgating various 'versions of pastoral' (145). The correlation between duty and women's self-sacrificing labour is a set of cultural assumptions that these texts seem to be asking us to reject, or at least to suspend, as we imagine other ways of relating, where responsibility could be acknowledged as complicated, as loving, as difficult, as replete with viscerally felt gaps, as predicated on unresolvable differences.

Furthermore, as in the case of Kincaid's relation to her brother, Devon, there is no legitimacy conferred by the intimate proximity to the epidemic that I explored in my discussion of Jarman – and perhaps nothing more than a series of potential pitfalls. If I have emphasized Jarman's reparative impulses – the 'arts of existence' that his memoir seems to be modelling – might this reading emerge from my own grief for a personal loss, my grief for the loss of my uncle, and specifically for his role in introducing nonconformity, urbanity, and a sense of the powers of performance into what was otherwise, in most ways, a sealed-off rural childhood? Still, there is a curiosity – as well as a morbid, sentimental, and paranoid potential – in the situation of grieving for someone who is neither parent, husband, lover, or brother to me, a curiosity that makes me doubt the knowledge I thought I had about what marks certain relations as significant and others as marginal. As Michaels writes anticipating his niece's visit from the United States, 'It will be interesting to see what gaps we can bridge and which distances we enforce during this week or so of a sustained encounter of mutual admiration, but comparative mystery' (*Unbecoming* 28). Subsequently, Michaels registers his suspicion of these differences, observing that 'she seems sensitive and perhaps might hurt easily, only I don't know how to go about calculating these sorts of things so I was blunt' (39). This discourse or posture of forthrightness constitutes perhaps less an innocent blundering than it does another kind of calculation, a performed experimental articulation of 'the profound moral imperatives and ethical calculations that ultimately do drive the great gay queens throughout this century' (25). And what I can't help but read into Michaels's comments is an awareness of 'the space for nonconformity carved out by the avunculate,' its adumbration of 'a less hypostatized view' not only 'of what and therefore how a child can desire' but of what bonds kinship and friendship, and perhaps reading or writing, might entail and enact (Sedgwick, 'Tales of the Avunculate' 63).

Michaels's and Jarman's reparative strategies are not a backtracking on the diaries' and memoirs' collective questioning of the ethics of a rush to consolation. On the contrary, they emerge in the midst of unresolved grief, out of a persistent attachment to bodies that a heteronormative, sexist, and racist culture would banish, would cut off from nurturance, would, in a word, exorcize. Reparation may be, so my reading of Jarman insinuates, the perpetuation or fulfilment of melancholic subjectivity: What is melancholy but a complicated, rending love, above all else? What is possible for Jarman and Michaels in this regard seems less so for Amy Hoffman, however, who worries about being consumed by her grief: reparation, if there is any, must it seems be read very much between the lines in *Hospital Time*, although Hoffman's disavowal of the kaddish does strike me now as perhaps a more knowing calculation than my initial encounter with the text suggested. And Jamaica Kincaid, in grappling with a person and a place deeply compromised by social and geographical inequities, raises perhaps more questions about the temptations of consolatory fictions than she does strategies for thinking and living differently. Nonetheless, *My Brother* also keeps in play a nagging hypothesis that Devon's life might have been more valued and more visible had he more access to the 'arts of existence' to which Kincaid herself has recourse, as Jarman, Hoffman, and Michaels do, in the project of shaping her life and various affections.

Reading these memoirs and diaries with a focus on their melancholic powers of estrangement – and their diverse and incoherent powers of reparation – may provide leverage for seeing, thinking, and writing differently about the affective and the bodily in the context of HIV and AIDS. These are historical, cultural, and political projects of great urgency, for they unfold in the midst of a crisis that is far from over, whether in terms of the increasing numbers of people infected and affected worldwide or in terms of the personal and cultural traumas the pandemic has permanently established for everyone, though this ostensible universality is inescapably crossed by many differences, disadvantages, and disavowals. The fragility of these texts' questioning of consolation may, furthermore, be the very index of their value to us in that they probe (though in fits and starts) 'to what extent it might be possible to think differently instead of legitimating what is already known' (Foucault, *The Use of Pleasure* 9). If reading these memoirs might be described as burdensome, it is never predictably so. More than simply, or self-indulgently, depriving us of our usual strategies for coping, they push the limits of what we may be capable of imagining and remembering. If a burden constitutes a load, a duty, a responsibility, and especially one that is oppressive or worrisome, even one that threatens to become parasitical and to impinge upon the self's integrity, it refers also (in an older, technical sense of the term) to the *capacity* for carrying that burden. As Hoffman's, Michaels's, Kincaid's, and Jarman's memoirs explore, unresolved grief may destabilize the systematic disavowals by which we ordinarily sort out and order different kinds of love, and so make us test (and perhaps to expand) our various capacities for love. In turn, these texts ask readers to think again, and to think differently, about the social and institutional frameworks that shape the lived and felt experience of HIV infection and AIDS, although they offer no unambiguous models and no guarantees.

Notes

Introduction

1 Here I am drawing on Paula Treichler's important and influential argument that 'the social dimension [of AIDS] is far more pervasive and central than we are accustomed to believing' and her more specific point that the meanings of AIDS, in both popular and scientific realms, are constructed by 'a series of discursive dichotomies,' which the discourse of AIDS 'reinvigorates' (15, 35).

2 As Cindy Patton contends in *Globalizing AIDS*, 'The way that the story of AIDS is told has a potentially great effect on the acceptability of policies that are promoted within that story's narrative reach' (50).

3 In a 1995 article on AIDS and photography, Watney emphasizes that the 'requirement that AIDS be [portrayed as] painful, hideous, and uniformly fatal' is still with us, even in the face of 'changing medical information' ('"Lifelike"' 65).

4 There have been a number of other trenchant analyses of the discourses shaping the representation of HIV infection and AIDS, especially with respect to media representations. Some helpful sources from the 'early' years of cultural analysis that I will refer to in the course of this study include essays by Douglas Crimp, Julia Epstein, Josh Gamson, Jeff Nunokawa, Cindy Patton, Susan Sontag, and Paula Treichler. Relatively recent accounts include book-length analyses by Robert Ariss, Ross Chambers, Alexander García Düttmann, Lee Edel-

man, William Haver, Katie Hogan, Steven Kruger, Cindy Patton, Marita Sturken, Paula Treichler, and Thomas Yingling.

5 As Linda Singer outlines, the gendered assumptions reproduced in these stories have several implications for public health policy. First, 'in a climate induced by epidemic, it becomes reasonable to intervene into the bodies of others' (28–30). Second, the AIDS epidemic has furnished opportunity for 'the remarketing of the nuclear family as a prophylactic social device,' although 'history reveals that the family has never been a particularly safe place for women and children' (69). And it is particularly unsafe in the context of the epidemic. Patton argues, regarding public health discourse and policy, that 'because the initial "risk behaviors" were thought to be the exclusive domain of the "risk groups" the public health strategies inadvertently fused the two types of approach,' and therefore policymakers tend to work with skewed definitions, which tend to correlate vulnerability to the virus with deviant sexuality and social delinquency ('"With Champagne and Roses"' 167). Patton notes, moreover, the prevalence of 'a kind of patriarchal self-obsession that has still not been able to admit that biologically speaking, women are indeed at far more risk of contracting HIV from men than vice versa' (169). The central concern of much of her work is to highlight how these systematic denials of the risks of unsafe heterosexual intercourse endanger women: 'The elision of a realistic subject position from which to assess what personal risk meant became the linchpin of the reconstruction of heterosexual identity, first by degendering women who had contracted HIV – pictured as women who shared needles – and second by reinforcing the idea that "normal" sexual intercourse between "ordinary" [i.e. non-kinky] heterosexuals required no modifications, specifically, no condoms' (171). Katie Hogan has shown, furthermore, that, in popular filmic and literary representations of the epidemic, women have been overwhelmingly associated with selfless, sacrificial caregiving, in effect rendering women's own sexual and other health care needs a secondary and all too often sidelined concern: the 'bad,' sexualized, and at-risk or infected woman is eclipsed by the image of her 'good' opposites, the innocent victim and the selfless nurturer. Reactivated as a way of ameliorating feelings of terror, the ideal of feminine sacrifice in

caring for others draws on long-standing ideological assumptions that caregiving does not constitute real labour and that women – especially women of colour and lesbians, who tend to be seen as desexualized and positioned as being in service to others' needs – are naturally suited and inclined to perform the role of caregiver (*Women Take Care* 3). See also Paula Treichler's chapters on AIDS and gender.

6 Even the most progressive developments in Western science – such as a year 2000 study that projects the 'immediate and substantial' bene-fits of using antiretroviral drugs prophylactically in the Third World by targeting HIV-positive pregnant women – remain enmeshed in prejudicial discursive and economic systems. A study published in the *Lancet* projects, for example, that between the years 2000 and 2005 '110 000 HIV-1 positive births [in South Africa] could be pre-vented by short course anti-retroviral prophylaxis' (Wood et al.). This proposition – and the story the study narrates between the lines – raises at least a couple of ethical problems. First, given the difficulty of confidentially identifying which pregnant women are HIV-positive, the scenario was modelled on 'universal treatment without testing or counseling,' a tactic that defines women on an instrumental basis, not as dealing with HIV themselves, but first and foremost as carriers of fetuses at risk. Second, the advantage of prophylactic use is weighed against the cost per year of life gained were 25 per cent of HIV-positive people in South Africa given the most up-to-date drug treatments available to prevent the onset of AIDS (the difference being $19 for prophylactic use of nevirapine and $15,000 for triple-combination treatment use, all taking into account UN-brokered price reductions). These calculations and the study's conclusion that 'interventions other than triple-combination treatment will probably be more cost effective' illustrate the contingency of treatment and public health policy on tropical thinking. Governments' and corpo-rations' perceptions of what they can afford to give are structured by a pre-existing belief that the problem exists elsewhere and affects lives construed as already lost.

7 Yet, as Josh Gamson observes, because the object of protest is not a particular state figure or institution but rather an 'abstracted, disembodied, invisible' enemy, namely, social 'control through the

creation of abnormality,' the focus of groups such as ACT UP has sometimes seemed 'hazy' and 'abstract' and has sometimes had difficulty changing to reflect the changing demographics of the disease (352).

8 See also, for instance, Rob Baker's *The Art of AIDS: From Stigma to Conscience* (1994) for an overview of the impact of AIDS activism on North American and European culture (music, drama, dance, movies, and media) and Stephanie Nolen's article 'The Art of the Positive,' which despite its thesis that art about AIDS is 'evaporating' actually provides a thorough survey of the continuing impact of the epidemic on a wide variety of cultural productions (2000).

9 Although Hawkins occasionally makes some insightful remarks, her vehement rejection of postmodernism rings hollow in the context of autobiographical writings about HIV and AIDS. Particularly bewildering is her argument that 'there seems to be a radical contradiction between the proliferation of literary narrative and the prevalence of deconstructive practice and theory in literary criticism' (188) and her insistence that 'in narratives describing illness and death, the reader is repeatedly confronted with the pragmatic reality and experiential unity of the autobiographical self' (17). She draws the hasty and defensive conclusion that 'pathography [lifewriting about illness based in what she calls "mythic thinking"] challenges the skepticism of critics and theorists about the self, making that skepticism seem artificial, mandarin and contrived' (17). Hawkins entirely ignores the critique of medical discourse that has been an integral part of AIDS activism and its related cultural productions; even Susan Sontag's wrist is slapped for presuming to suggest that metaphor has ideological valences. My study will demonstrate on the contrary that AIDS memoirs, written out of a rupture in the ontology of self, engage a set of concerns about representation and ethics that correspond to and complicate several strands of current theoretical discussion.

10 Along with the continuing devastating impact of HIV and AIDS in sub-Saharan Africa, recent statistics suggest that the increase of HIV infection worldwide follows patterns of pre-existing social and economic instability, and exacerbates those conditions. Eastern Europe and Central Asia are seeing HIV incidence rise faster than anywhere

else in the world as IV-drug use and sex work become more common (Joint United Nations Program on HIV/AIDS 9). And in higher-income countries (Australia, Canada, the United States, Japan, and Western Europe), 'HIV is moving into poorer and more deprived communities, with women at particular risk of infection' (16). Prevention fatigue and the hope inspired by the promise of public consciousness of new treatments means that 'young adults belonging to ethnic minorities (including men who have sex with men)' are now at greater risk of infection than they were in the early 1990s (16).

11 A few words on the parameters of this study. Limitations of space, and my particular interest in how written memoirs and diaries constitute themselves as reflections on narrative processes, prevent me from discussing personal accounts of the epidemic in visual form, including films such as Nan Goldin's *I'll Be Your Mirror* (1997) and Tom Joslin and Peter Friedman's *Silverlake Life* (1993). And while this study addresses some of the social, racial, and economic asymmetries of HIV infection and AIDS, particularly in the context of Jamaica Kincaid's invective against the inadequate social infrastructure in her country of origin, Antigua, I recognize that in some ways my discussion touches all too briefly on the geopolitically diverse dimensions of culture and the pandemic. Indeed, there are now many powerful films that address the topic of HIV/AIDS in its specific and disproportionate geographical and economic manifestations, providing an important critical window into these issues. I am thinking, for example, of films such as Tsitsi Dangarembga's *Everyone's Child* (Zimbabwe, 1996), Marlon Riggs's *Tongues Untied* (United States, 1991), Allan Bibby's *The Long Walk* (Canada, 1998), and the films about HIV and AIDS in southern Africa produced by the *Steps for the Future* collaborative documentary project (International, 2000–present).

12 While in the past seven years there have been studies published by Alexandra Juhasz on the alternative AIDS video movement (1996), by Melissa Zeiger on illness and elegy (1997), and by David Roman on gay culture, AIDS, and theatre (1998), autobiographical prose texts remain underanalysed. Chambers's *Facing It* is the only book-length study that significantly overlaps with mine. Work on pathography (illness narratives) by Anne Hunsaker Hawkins (1993, 1999) and G. Thomas Couser (1997) does not discuss AIDS memoirs in the con-

text of contemporary critical theory; moreover, Hawkins's dismissal of the erotic as decadent in the context of AIDS constitutes a serious limitation for her readings of texts about HIV and AIDS. Finally, Susanna Egan's *Mirror Talk* (1999), while it discusses illness and testimony with attention to autobiographical films about HIV and AIDS, namely Derek Jarman's *Blue* and Tom Joslin and Peter Friedman's *Silverlake Life*, casts a much wider net in the course of defining autothanatography as a genre than does my study.

13 The category of the diary should not be taken as an unmediated one: both Jarman's and Michaels's diaries were revised for publication with outside editorial involvement and contain considerable conventionally autobiographical reflection on childhood and adolescence.

14 In his study of the impact of AIDS on gay life in the United States, John-Manuel Andriote addresses the issue of 'disenfranchised grief' in the context of AIDS, with particular reference to the dynamics of family. Not only does American culture lack conventions for mourning the death of a same-sex partner, but disagreements about legal responsibility, financial legacies, and funeral arrangements can spark emotionally shattering conflicts among survivors – lovers, friends, and family members – who often inhabit radically separate parts of a gay man's life (346–7).

15 Doty's elaboration is evocative. He emphasizes that 'the work of the living is remembering, and the collective project of memory is enormous; it involves the weight of all our dead, the ones we have known ourselves and the ones we know only from stories. It is necessary to recall not just names, but also faces, stories, incidents, gestures, tics, nuances, those particular human attributes that distinguish us as individuals' (8).

16 For a summary of elegiac conventions, see Peter M. Sacks, *The English Elegy: Studies in the Genre from Spenser to Yeats*. Sacks notes that the form and topoi of the elegy have been influenced perhaps most profoundly by 'the rituals associated with the vegetation gods,' rituals that comprise part of a working through of grief and relinquishing of erotic attachment by 'seeming to place the dead, and death itself, at some cleared distance from the living' (19). In turn, he provides a reading of the role of nature in elegiac poetry as more than merely sentimental, arguing that the elegy's focus on the correspondences

between nature's decline and the mourner's grief is not so much an expression of 'self-pity' but driven in equal measure by 'the motives of mastery and revenge' (21).

17 Resistance to the confrontational strategies of AIDS activist art is well encapsulated in Arlene Croce's 1995 'non-review' of choreographer Bill T. Jones's piece *Still/Here*. Croce refused to see the piece on the grounds that it constituted 'victim art' (22). 'By working dying people into his act,' writes Croce, 'Jones is putting himself beyond the reach of criticism' (20). But this stance did not prevent her from publishing, in place of a review, a long, and unintentionally revealing, disquisition on her discomfort. Referring to the ideal of 'disinterested art,' Croce castigates Jones's work as 'an aggressively personal extension of the anti-conventionalism of the sixties, when you were manipulated into accepting what you saw as art' (23–34). I would suggest that witness art does not make the critic expendable but rather demands a different kind of critic, one who could think through the resistance to forgetting that such a personal and confrontational art practice enacts; but this is a kind of criticism that Croce is unable to imagine (28).

18 If, even with a 'resisting text,' there remains a 'danger' 'that it survive its author's demise only to be read complacently' (Chambers 112), then it is more than likely that more ambivalent texts should be even more vulnerable to complacent, resistant, or normalizing readings. *Gary in Your Pocket: Stories and Notebooks of Gary Fisher* (1996) can be categorized 'a resisting text' in that the journals and stories collected here consider how HIV intertwines with and intensifies the social exclusions to which Fisher is already subject as a black gay man, exclusions that are complexly caught up, too, with his desires. So much could and should be said about this important text, but here I want to comment specifically on the chain of relations that bring Fisher's writings to us posthumously in published form and that literally contextualize it in the form of an editorial framework, with an introduction by Don Belton and an afterword by Eve Sedgwick. On the one hand, Belton and Sedgwick's collaborative work on and with Fisher's textual remains constitutes an attempt to model the 'reweaving of sustaining relations' (Butler, *Psychic Life* 145), a crucial project when, in the context of the spectacle of AIDS, and perhaps especially

'when subjected to hospitalization,' 'one occupies the paradoxical
position of losing one's usual site of validation in a system of gazes
and regards' (Singer 104). But Fisher's writing proves itself to be
unamenable to being recuperated into such a 'system of gazes and
regards.' With its emphasis on masochistic sexuality – what Fisher
calls 'self-slaughter' and tries to understand as an analytical act of
'decreation' – his writing blurs the boundary between analysis of
oppression and its internalization even as he seems to begin to make
such distinctions, leaving his readers traumatized and bereft of a liberated individual at the core of his writings (Fisher 188). Contrasting
with Belton's readerly embrace, which emphasizes the bond of a
shared identity as black men and a politics derived from that stand-
point, Sedgwick painfully confronts how her own writing about
Fisher threatens to become 'a defense against reading' the complexities of her friend's life and writings (*A Dialogue on Love* 128).
Ultimately, it seems that no amount of critical working through by
Belton and Sedgwick can fully repair the feelings of shame, loss, and
exclusion that permeate Fisher's self-representations.

19 The broader context for this comment in *Specters of Marx* is the fate of
the 'Marxist reference' in current theoretical discourse, which would
read Marx in a purely scholarly fashion, as philosophy, rather than as
a theory of revolution; the reference to Marx's thought is routinely
weakened 'by putting on a tolerant face, to neutralize a potential
force, first of all by enervating a *corpus*, by silencing in it the revolt
[the return is acceptable provided that the revolt, which initially
inspired uprising, indignation, insurrection, revolutionary momen-
tum, does not come back]' (31).

Chapter One

1 Derek Jarman's autobiographical productions demand to be
acknowledged for their full multiplicity in a dizzying array of genres:
memoirs, diaries (published and unpublished), film, painting, and
gardening. So, while I focus on *Modern Nature* and make some
extended references to *At Your Own Risk* and Prospect Cottage (the
visual and material counterpart to *Modern Nature*), it is worth noting
the sheer volume of Jarman's self-productions: it suggests his com-

pulsion to make the text of his life grow, shift, and shimmer, all, one suspects, in the hope of eluding easy critical exegesis of his legacy. For my citations from the two key texts, I will use the abbreviations *MN* and *AYOR*.

2 In his recent authorized biography of Jarman, Tony Peake notes that 'in early 1990,' Jarman's diary 'had been accepted for publication by Mark Booth at Century'; it was 'between September, when he made a final entry, and the end of the year, [that] Jarman shaped the raw material into the book it would become' (463–4). Although he did not exactly write the book under commission, then, we may be certain that Jarman had thought of it from the outset as a public rather than a strictly private record.

3 On the allegorical aspects of Prospect Cottage, see Deborah Esch, '"The only news was when" (The Journals of Derek Jarman)' and Daniel O'Quinn, 'Gardening, History, and the Escape from Time: Derek Jarman's *Modern Nature.*'

4 *Dancing Ledge* (1984) is addressed (on a prefatory page) 'To the British Cinema' and stands primarily as a defence of his film *Caravaggio*, an imaginative queering of the life of the Renaissance painter. Jarman is adamant that 'the film will dig and excavate and make no attempt to hold the mirror up to reality' and acknowledges its autobiographical bent: 'The problem is I've written a self-portrait filtered through the Caravaggio story' (25, 28).

5 In films such as *Jubilee, The Tempest, Caravaggio, Edward II,* and *Wittgenstein,* Jarman engages the distortions and elisions of the historical record, countering, as Jim Ellis insists in his discussion of Jarman's queering of the Renaissance, 'the nostalgic, Thatcherite construction of England's glorious past in the cinema of the 1980s,' and 'resist[ing] homophobic constructions of the past and present' (290–1). Ellis argues that typically 'Jarman's refusal to provide the visual pleasures of period, whether through an aggressively antirealist mise-en-scène, or the pointed use of anachronistic props and language, both circumvents and implicitly critiques the trap that is almost constitutive of the genre' (290).

6 The shift in terminology we can note in Jarman's writings – from 'homosexual' in *Dancing Ledge* and 'gay,' but increasingly often, 'queer,' in *Modern Nature* and *At Your Own Risk* – is a telling indicator

(as it is for many other activists and writers over the same period) of his increasing politicization in the context of HIV/AIDS, as well as a complication of his sense of subjectivity. As he implies in *Blue* – describing himself at one point as 'a cock-sucking / Straight acting / Lesbian man / with ball crushing bad manners' – a recognition of the instability of gender identity categories and a scepticism about what counts as 'ideologically sound' politics are essential components in a strategy of queer performativity designed to test the boundaries of empathy and charity in the context of the epidemic.

7 Jarman's reference to Plato's *Symposium* and Shakespeare's sonnets as a 'cultural condom' protecting the community against hate points similarly to the irony my phrasing aims to capture here (163).

8 Esch comments on the representation of Jarman in the media and on his response to those representations in her chapter on *Modern Nature*; she draws particular attention to Jarman's confrontation with a member of this 'yellow press,' noting his assertion that journalistic reports will fade into obscurity, while his memoir will persist, and even accrue greater authority, beyond the present moment (120–7). He asserts the power of 'authorship' over the anonymous reportage that feeds a 'vulture culture' (120).

9 Peake suggests that this is one possible interpretation of *The Garden* (1990), the film Jarman made at Dungeness concurrently with his writing of *Modern Nature*. Specifically, Peake notes that the serpent in his leather harness is an overtly sexual – and nightmarish – figure: 'You wonder whether Jarman is asking himself if his own sexual appetite was not perhaps to blame for his illness. If sexual spontaneity is not as dangerous a force as repression' (459).

10 Sedgwick bases her claims on Melanie Klein's theory of object relations, noting the 'paranoid position' as one of 'terrible alertness to the dangers posed by the hateful and envious part-objects that one defensively projects into, carves out of, and ingests from the world around one' (8).

11 O'Quinn argues that Jarman's garden precipitates him out of history and time, and into an alternative archaeology of 'sacred somitical space' (115).

12 I use the word 'freedom' in the sense Foucault derives from his reading of the 'moral problematization of pleasures' in Greek and Greco-

Roman culture: 'more than a nonenslavement, more than an eman-
cipation that would make the individual independent of any exterior
or interior constraint; in its full, positive form, it [freedom] was a
power that one brought to bear on oneself in the power one exer-
cised over others' (*The Use of Pleasure* 80).

13 Jarman's sadness consistently contradicts the introduction of myths
that would organize his grief more economically. We may mark the
extent of Jarman's memoir's dissent from Anne Hunsaker Hawkins's
category of 'pathography' in *Reconstructing Illness*. Emphasizing the
abiding power of 'mythic thinking' (and citing myths of battle, journey, dying, and healthy-mindedness), Hawkins characterizes the
'"pathographical act"' as 'one that constructs meaning by subjecting
raw experience to the powerful impulse to make sense of it all, to
bind together the events, feelings, thoughts, and sensations that
occur during an illness into an integrated whole' (18).

14 The polemical register of *At Your Own Risk* is clearly signalled by the
title, which, as Peake notes, echoes the 'designation given in gay
guides to the more dangerous places to cruise or search for casual
sex' (488).

15 As Butler emphasizes in *Excitable Speech*, 'The possibility for a speech
act to resignify a prior context depends, in part, upon the gap
between the originating context or intention by which an utterance
is animated and the effects it produces' (14). The context provided
by the quilt, I am suggesting, might or might not be altogether too
close to the recuperative project of the family romance.

16 Contrasting the disruptions posed to American collective memory by
the AIDS epidemic with those of the Vietnam War, Sturken argues
that the 'AIDS epidemic will not be historicized and rescripted as the
Vietnam War has been, to smooth over its rupture' (179). Though
she admits the danger of the 'translation of a disruptive narrative
into familiar clichés,' this does not stop her from praising the 'radical steps' taken by films such as *Philadelphia* and *And the Band Played
On* (177). Against Sturken's attempt to be even-handed, I would
insist that 'simple narratives' continue to take hold, especially in
mainstream narrative film and television, even as memory is acknowledged in some critical contexts to be 'complicated' and 'tangled'
(182).

17 As Eric Michaels argues, contra Marshall McLuhan, 'Conceptual and process art did not conquer the world,' and 'what persisted [instead] was narrative, character, nationalism' (*Unbecoming* 38).

18 Jarman here performs a strange projection of what he perhaps fears are the implications of his own work onto other cultural projects. His criticism of Keith Haring's art as 'domestic,' and perhaps feminine, for example, echoes quite closely the dismissive reviews of Jarman's own work, as documented in *Modern Nature*. The critical response to *The Garden* was mixed, and the particular criticisms expressed by Vincent Canby in the *New York Times* are tinged (according to Jarman's recitation of the them) with a homophobic and gender-inflected bias: '*Derek Jarman has made a movie of epic irrelevance that, when it rises to the occasion, is merely redundant ... Mr. Jarman, whose films include* Sebastiane *and* Caravaggio, *has a weakness for the kind of baroque imagery that is utterly beside the point.* The last line: *Mr. Jarman decorates a film as much as he directs it*' (234).

19 'White Glasses' predates Sedgwick's working out of the distinction between 'paranoid' and 'reparative' reading in her introduction to *Novel Gazing*, of course, but we can well label this particular line of questioning 'paranoid' for the worry and rage it evokes.

20 As Sturken summarizes, 'The implied patriotism and connotations of family heritage implicit in the quilt form threaten to rescript those memorialized in the AIDS quilt into a narrative of Americana in a country that has systematically marked them as outsiders' (215).

21 Though he is perhaps best known as a film-maker and writer, Jarman began and ended his career as a painter, having also worked as a set designer during the 1970s. From a technical point of view, Jarman's use of 'collage and object trouvés' in painting is paralleled by 'superimposition and complex editing in film' along with his incorporation of his own and his parents' Super-8 footage (Roger Wollen, 'Introduction: Facets of Derek Jarman' 15). As Jonathan Hacker and David Price point out, 'Jarman's aesthetic impulse centres on the value of art, not for the viewer but for the creator,' and accordingly he emphasizes 'process' rather than 'product' and embraces the 'collaborative nature of film-making' ('Essay on Derek Jarman' 232). Peake emphasizes Jarman's incorporation of the results of his beachcombing into his art during his years living in London's docklands, tracing

this back, in turn, to his childhood habits: 'The boy who had stared so fixedly at flowers had become a man who could stare with equal intensity at the detritus in his path and isolate its beauty ... Now, by giving new life to the discarded and the decaying, he was questioning what should be valued, what rejected' (150). Overall, as Peter Wollen summarizes, 'there is a lasting tension in his work between a delirious neoromantic Englishness and a pop modernism, always in touch with "street culture"' ('The Last New Wave: Modernism in the British Films of the Thatcher Era' 248). In the late paintings, 'the visual field becomes a complex densely worked site of simultaneous overlay and excavation,' where the mark of the artist's hand is visible in the finger-painted text superimposed on canvases that might be considered 'pastiches' of Abstract Expressionism (Stuart Morgan, 'Borrowed Time' 114–15). Titles among this group of paintings (most of which were completed in 1992) include *Toxo, Sick, Letter to the Minister,* and *Queer.*

22 Ellis, Esch, and O'Quinn all comment at some length on Jarman's technique of massive, often unmarked quotations from his wide readings in art history and Renaissance writings.

23 This contrast sheds light on abjection as an intersubjective relation. Viewed at second hand, the failures of 'the most ordinary capacities of the body' are (almost inevitably) viewed with horror. Accounted for by a subject experiencing the process of a body's failure to sustain itself, the shift is just as dramatic, but, here at least, it is not regarded with repulsion.

24 In *At Your Own Risk,* Jarman documents the passage of these pieces of legislation and explains what he sees as their installation of a kind of second tier of citizenship for gays and lesbians. As Peake and Esch both discuss, in 1993–4 proposed changes to the age of consent for gays and lesbians were to disappoint him further, as they promised to mitigate inequality but ultimately reinforced it by perpetuating a double standard in the adoption of the age of eighteen as a compromise position.

25 See also Peake, who notes Jarman's argument with Shaun Allen 'about whether or not to delete or tone down the passages describing Jarman's nocturnal visits to Hampstead Heath' (463).

26 The garden at Prospect Cottage is in some senses a reconstruction of

the gardens he associates with the happy times of his itinerant RAF childhood, for example, the garden at Villa Zuassa at Lake Maggiore in Italy and the one at Curry Mallet Manor, a Tudor house in Yorkshire (Peake 16–17, 31–2).

27 In these letters from April 1991, Jarman responds to film critic Alexander Walker's critical review of *Edward II* and, in particular, his attack on Jarman's Hampstead Heath passages as encouraging a kind of indulgence in 'revelry' that contradicts 'willingness to help foster more sensible attitudes to HIV' (127). Jarman's retort stresses that 'HIV is not linked to promiscuity ... if safer sex practices, which are widely known by gay men and ill publicised in the straight press, are adhered to' (128).

28 In this connection, Jarman's memoir mobilizes the remedy that Cindy Patton calls for in her indictment of the failures of safe-sex education in the 1990s: an acknowledgment of 'the practical logics of erotic survival that already exist in communities' (*Fatal Advice* 139).

29 Based on his reading of Jarman's unpublished papers and correspondence, Peake suggests that Jarman saw himself as 'writing specifically for the young men of the nineties,' but the reception of *Modern Nature* – particularly the slew of 'unbidden letters' Jarman received – indicates that 'Jarman's persona and message were starting to reach a wider much wider circle' (488, 479–80).

30 According to the Joint United Nations Program on HIV/AIDS, the countries of Eastern Europe, particularly the Russian Federation and other countries of the former Soviet Union, are now experiencing the fastest growing epidemic in the world. Contributing factors include economic instability and the disintegration of public health services (9).

31 As Ulf Hannerz observes, 'the varied kinds of linkage' produced by globalization – that is, by 'increasing long-distance interconnectedness, at least across national boundaries' but also 'between continents' – 'do no combine in the same way everywhere' (17–18).

32 As a child Jarman was drawn to what Dick Hebdige explains in reference to Jean Genet as 'the subversive implications of style,' to practices of 'Refusal' that, although they invoke suspicion and rage in authority figures, 'become forbidden signs of identity, sources of value' ('Introduction: Subculture and Style' 3).

33 Corroborating Butler's and Derrida's criticisms of the mournful determination to vanquish difference, Britzman argues that normality is 'built when the other is situated as a site of deviancy and disease, and hence in need of containment' (85). She rejects the strategy of encouraging an 'empathetic' response to difference, arguing that 'such hopes are able to offer only the stingy subject positions of the tolerant normal and the tolerated subaltern,' advocating instead that the category of normality is precisely what needs to be reconsidered (87).

34 See Peake's chapter 'School House and Manor House' (26–33) for detailed comparisons of Jarman's multiple retellings of these events. I shall, however, restrict my analysis to the accounts offered in *Modern Nature.*

35 In *My Brother* Kincaid describes the visceral impact of attending a public lecture on HIV and AIDS that is accompanied by a slide presentation showing the effects of fungal and other infections. Kincaid's account corroborates Jarman's view of the power that such visualizations have to construct our ideas about sexuality and disease and the correlation between the two. Overwhelmed by the message that 'these images of sex and death were the result of sexual activity,' Kincaid reports that 'at the end of the talk, I felt I would never have sex again, not even with myself' (37–8).

36 Jarman's school years were not entirely lacking, however, in more nurturing influences. Robin Noscoe, his art teacher at Canford School, made the school's art room a place of refuge for Jarman and others, and was the first in a line of influential, supportive teachers of art and architecture in whose orbit Jarman flourished (Peake 53–8).

37 Neither Britzman's nor Jarman's model by any means suggests that education should become a free-for-all. As Foucault argues in *The Use of Pleasure*, with the Greeks 'it is in the reflection on the love of boys that one sees the principle of "indefinite abstention" formulated' as an 'ideal of a renunciation' (245). Taking the Greek model of ethicized (as opposed to strictly rule-governed) subjectivity, understood as 'the elaboration of a form of relation to self that enables an individual to fashion himself into a subject of ethical conduct,' Foucault, like Jarman, advocates the adoption of 'an aesthetics of existence, the purposeful act of freedom as a power game' (251–2). I under-

stand Jarman's approach to these questions not as prescriptive, but as provoking thought about new kinds of exchanges and possibilities that will help to save and nurture lives in the time of AIDS, especially the lives of young people. But in all of this Jarman's reiterated claim that he wishes he had been initiated by an older man, in the Greek tradition, is a reconstruction of the past that I am not sure what to do with (*AYOR* 18). In *Dancing Ledge* he argues that 'the old Greek way of men and women initiating adolescents of their own sex, helping them to discover their own sexuality in an atmosphere of responsibility, contained much humane and practical wisdom' (50). Still, as Sedgwick implies in *Epistemology of the Closet*, this ideal of pedagogy in male-male pederasty is not one we can easily reconstruct, not least because it probably never existed in an uncomplicated, ethically neutral way. Foucault glancingly acknowledges that the so-called 'aesthetics of existence' were available only to 'the smallest minority of the population, made up of free adult males'; however, this paradox of 'legitimacy' is even more problematic in a contemporary context and may not be so easily sidestepped (*The Use of Pleasure* 245–52). As Sedgwick further argues, 'the "Hellenic ideal," insofar as its reintegrative power is supposed to involve a healing of the culturewide ruptures involved in male homosexual panic, necessarily has that panic so deeply at the heart of its occasions, frameworks, demands and evocations that it becomes not only inextricable from but even a propellant of the cognitive and ethical compartmentalizations of homophobic prohibition' (*Epistemology of the Closet* 138). And furthermore, as David Halperin stresses, 'pedagogy was not, even among the honorable members of that *beau monde* [in Ancient Greece], the essence of pederasty' (*One Hundred Years of Homosexuality* 91–2). Thus, 'despite modern appearance-saving claims to the contrary, the erotic excitement and bittersweet longing aroused in Athenian men (whether low- or high-minded) by attractive boys do not seem to have been primarily of a philosophic nature' (92); the possibility of acting on such erotic attractions was governed, moreover, by the laws of citizenship, which made it 'extremely difficult and hazardous for a male resident of Athens in the classical period to gain sexual access to any person of citizen status' (92).

Chapter Two

1 Within these four sections are arranged anecdotes, stories, and reflections, each with its own subtitle. I have chosen to italicize the section titles to distinguish them from the subtitles of the individual anecdotes and essays. The memoir also includes an introductory essay on the subject of the disorientation of living in 'hospital time.'

2 Melancholia 'behaves like an open wound, drawing to itself cathectic energies ... from all directions, and emptying the ego until it is totally impoverished' (253).

3 Steven F. Kruger distinguishes 'epidemiological or population' AIDS narratives from personal narratives, pointing out that in the domain of popular culture and media 'both narratives present the picture of a "battle" already lost: the individuals and populations affected by HIV and AIDS are irretrievable' (80). John Greyson's critique in the film *Zero Patience* of Randy Shilts's 'epidemiological narrative,' *And the Band Played On*, pinpoints the potential such narratives have to distort. Shilts's invention of 'Patient Zero' in the person of Gaetan Dugas, a promiscuous Québécois airline attendant who, it is suggested, was responsible for bringing HIV to North America, plays on exactly the kind of cultural fantasy Sedgwick, Singer, and Epstein are identifying. Greyson's film explores the genealogy of this fantasy, investigating, through its parodic reinvention of the Victorian explorer and sexologist Richard Burton, in the role of besieged museum curator and eventually the lover of Zero/Dugas, the role of 'tropical thinking' in shaping how we imagine both disease and sexuality (Patton, *Globalizing AIDS* 37).

4 Edelman interrogates, for example, the way in which the slogan 'Silence = Death' 'enacts a metaphorical redefinition of "silence" as "death,"' and thus 'configures the activity of life with the (re)production of discourse (however oppositional) and thus plays out the logic that privileges procreative intercourse over homosexual sex by aligning the former with active production and the latter with "murder of the race"'(89).

5 Chambers argues that the melancholic subject may be read as oppositional, despite being resistant to alignment with a stable political

position, for 'between these extremes of resistance and retreat, the decentered self of the melancholic subject – that vaporized, faltering, lacking subject of a new textuality – occupies a precarious middle ground of semiresistance and semiretreat, a ground neither of resistance nor retreat, which is that of the oppositional and the "depolitified"' [*sic*] (*The Writing of Melancholy* 59).

6 Elsewhere Abraham and Torok distinguish the sense of 'phantom loss' characteristic of 'transgenerational haunting' from an individual's own repressed experiences, noting that 'what haunts are not the dead, but the gaps left within us by the secrets of others,' particularly the secrets of family members. These inherited gaps and elisions 'wreak havoc ... in the coherence of logical progression,' producing a disconnected melancholic subjectivity (*The Shell and the Kernel* 171–5).

7 Doty's text has been quite widely heralded as the major memoir to emerge from the 'later phase' of the pandemic (Jarraway 121–5). Perhaps it has been read as such in part because of the consolation it offers. Painfully aware of the kind of melancholy out of which Hoffman writes, Doty refers to it from a certain remove, although melancholy does enter the text in the form of the personal letters that Doty intersperses among his retrospective reflections.

8 Zeiger argues of AIDS elegies that 'such poems inscribe a double vision: they summon ghosts while insisting upon the finality of death. The living poets do not want the dead to be buried *in* AIDS elegies, nor, endangered as they are themselves, can they see the dead as wholly other. The poems are filled with ghosts and revenants, while the relations of the living with these revenants are intimate, unforeclosed' (131).

9 And yet these polarities are shown to be highly unstable. Hoffman's reference to Mike as a 'radical fairy' probably refers to the complicated allegiances signified by the practice of radical drag, where some gay men sought to identify themselves with the feminist movement by dressing up in 'hairy' drag. As Andrew Ross points out in his discussion of the politics of camp, radical drag was 'worn by some [gay men] as a way of directly and publicly experiencing the oppression of women, and by others as a way of ridiculing traditional gay male roles,' but it has also been criticized by feminists on the

grounds that 'it exploited female oppression to make its point' ('Uses of Camp'163). As she mulls over questions of gender identification, Hoffman suggests that Mike strongly identified with his lesbian friends, while also failing to have divested himself of some commonplace masculinist assumptions: she recounts, on the one hand, the story of Mike having received an anonymous note 'addressed to Mike Riegle: Male Lesbian,' but, on the other, she questions his reliance on her 'feminine intuition,' his trust that 'he wouldn't have to explain himself' but rather 'simply be' (and be free to be difficult), 'and we [his support network of women friends] would simply understand' (72).

10 There are numerous examples of this dynamic in traditional elegies, as Celeste Schenck suggests in her study of women elegists.

11 A similar pattern is at work in the context of women's contributions to activism and caregiving in the AIDS emergency. See Jeannine de Lombard ('Who Cares? Lesbians as Caregivers') and Halina Maslanka ('Women Volunteers at GMHC') for analyses of the gendered aspects of caregiving in the context of AIDS. De Lombard reports that while 'many lesbians see their AIDS caregiving as a form of gay activism,' many also express 'mixed feelings' that the expectation for women to become involved replays conventional gender roles and suspicion that care would not be fully reciprocated were the circumstances reversed (350–2). In this context, Patton's critique of the narrow definitions of women's roles in the AIDS crisis is also relevant. According to Patton, women who choose to be active as volunteers enact a conventional gendered (and class-specific) pattern of providing support, nurturance, and even redemption (exemplifying 'the compassionate member of the general public'), while HIV-positive women are generally visible not as sexual agents of any kind, but as either innocent or delinquent ('"With Champagne and Roses"' 170).

12 Revising Hegel, particularly his aside labelling 'womankind – the everlasting irony in the life of the community' (496), Jacobs contends that 'what Antigone performs is no supplement to a natural process, no addition of the movement of consciousness ... no "positive *ethical* action," rather an eternally possible irony' (911). Hegel's implication that woman's valuing of the individual constitutes 'the

contradiction and the germ of destruction, which lie hid within that very peace and beauty belonging to the gracious harmony and peaceful equilibrium of the ethical spirit' may be read as a precise, if unintended, analysis of the disruptive force of 'feminine' melancholic attachment (498).

13 In her analysis of *Boys on the Side* (1995), the first Hollywood film to address women and AIDS, Katie Hogan focuses on the narrow role assigned to Whoopi Goldberg's character, Jane. While it is no surprise to hear that a mainstream studio movie grants women stereotyped roles, fails to represent women as having complex psychic lives, and inscribes a conservative conclusion to the narrative, still Hogan draws from her analysis of this film an instructive point, one that resonates with Amy Hoffman's frustration about the lack of cultural recognition and respect for her friendship with Mike: 'The only role available to [Jane] is as a devoted, celibate, lesbian friend/mammy and second-class citizen' (92–3).

14 I am thinking, for instance, of how the closing scene of Jonathan Demme's *Philadelphia* restores the protagonist to the family of his birth and insists on the primary importance of these connections. As Eva Cherniavsky observes, 'The infusion of infants and children into this final scene [particularly the focus on his sister's baby] works to suture Beckett's fate to the reproductive social destiny he has declined' (388).

15 Zeiger argues that because they are 'not required to integrate female figures sacrificially into their cultural dynamic, AIDS poems [by gay men] are free to include them in roles previously foreign to elegies by men. The poems are marked by expressions of love, intersubjectivity, and identification with women absent from almost all earlier depictions' and with 'an ironic awareness of its [femininity's] traditional representations' (113).

16 In another section that considers Mike's clothing, 'Mike's Coat,' Hoffman alludes to the documentary *Brother's Keeper*, making an analogy between the four brothers in that film, poor farmers in upstate New York, one of whom is accused of murdering another, and Mike's increasingly dilapidated appearance. *Brother's Keeper* turns on the question of whether the alleged confession of Delbert Ward was coerced, whether, under pressure, he signed documents that he was

unable to read; and it focuses on the way in which the brothers come under the voyeuristic gaze of the media and even a local community that construct them as exotic in their primitiveness, and in their supposed 'queer' relation, one to the other. The allusion thus identifies the traps in approaching stories of marginalization from the assumption that there could be anything like objectivity, or a method that would have no impact on the subject of the story. Hoffman also emphasizes the recalcitrance of her subject in this scene: Mike Riegle quickly tires of the new coat that his friends coerce him into buying and returns to wearing his dirty, worn-out jacket, the one that he chose.

17 Indeed, the opening lines offer praise, and seemingly no hint of rage: 'May His great Name grow exalted and sanctified in the world that He created as He willed' ('The Mourner's Kaddish' 177).

18 Sarah Schulman emphasizes the threat this move poses to the claims of friends and caregivers to grieve their losses to AIDS in her novel *People in Trouble*. Recalling how 'stiff' and 'out-of-place' the 'contingent of relatives' looks at the memorial service for a friend who died of AIDS, Molly describes their relieved response to the traditional funerary script: 'Then the family moved to the front and brought in a rabbi who got to stand up at the end and say, "Yiskadol veh yiskadosh shemay rabah," which seemed to be the only part of the whole event they could understand. That was when they cried' (94).

19 Hoffman's reference to the kaddish competes with Allen Ginsberg's poetic version, which also attempts to reinvent the prayer for the dead. His 'Kaddish,' written for his mother, addresses an overwhelming, unresolved, and materially specific grief for a deteriorated life: 'Towards education marriage nervous breakdown, operation, teaching school, and learning how to be mad, in a dream – what is this life?' (8). His recollection of her final advice to him ('Get married Allen don't take drugs – the key is in the bars, in the sunlight in the window') (31), like the irony of 'Hymmnn,' which heaps up a demented discourse of exaltation (36), registers his anger and sense of discord. Still, there is a romantic celebration of self and body implied in this rewriting of kaddish. As Ginsberg's note on the back cover suggests, these are meant to be 'hymns laments of longing and litanies of triumphancy of Self over the mind-illusion mechano-

234 Notes to pages 114–25

universe of un-feeling Time.' There is an intention to elevate, some-how, 'the beatific human fact.' For Ginsberg, writing, unlike Hoff-man, before HIV and AIDS, there is a truth residing in the self and the body; the Hebrew tradition celebrates this vitality.

20 Towards the end of *Cancer in Two Voices* Sandra Butler records the loss of two male friends to AIDS, suggesting the importance of communal 'recognition' for loss and grief in contexts where dominant cultural definitions for significant relationships predetermine invisibility. After Barbara's death they clean up her garden, performing 'an act of recognition for a neighbor, a friend, a comrade in a time of plague'; Butler in turn helps to care for them as they become ill (173).

Chapter Three

1 For accounts of Michaels's academic career, with emphasis on his work with the Warlpiri, see Jay Ruby's 'In the Belly of the Beast: Eric Michaels and Indigenous Media' and Michael Moon's preface to *Unbecoming*.

2 According to Treichler, such narratives strive incessantly for contain-ment even while 'strongly urg[ing] compassion, medical rationality, intelligence, and tolerance' (181). Treichler focuses on *An Early Frost* (1985), 'the first feature-length drama about AIDS on network televi-sion,' and *Our Sons* (1991) (176).

3 The family melodrama has been read by film and literary critics as signifying far more than a naive investment in the nuclear family or uncritical endorsement of a conservative status quo. Family melodra-mas offer fantasies of the nuclear family as capable of securing the legibility of moral values in the face of a post-sacred era where reli-able systems of truth and ethics are perceived to be lacking; at the same time, such narratives explore the family not only as riven with conflict and unhappiness, but also as an institution in crisis. As the patriarchal nuclear family seems to fall apart, the genre of the family melodrama tries to repair familial discord (and in this way symboli-cally also to repair social disorder), even as it continues to gesture emphatically towards elusive existential and moral truths. For more on melodrama, see Peter Brooks's study of the melodramatic imagi-nation, Thomas Schatz's overview of family melodrama in 1950s Hol-

lywood film, and Paula Treichler's and Eva Cherniavsky's discussions of melodramatic paradigms as they come into play in television and film narratives about HIV and AIDS. While Treichler emphasizes the power of melodramatic expression to close off the complexities of the epidemic as it is lived by individuals and their partners, friends, and families, Cherniavksy argues that 'the subject of HIV/AIDS ... overtaxes melodrama's narrative apparatus: the subject of HIV/AIDS remains only partially and provisionally assimilable to melodrama's familial narrative design of loss and (re)generation' (377).

4 This discussion of consumerism appears in an untitled essay appended to Michaels's diary entries by editor Paul Foss (126–9). The essay, found among Michaels's papers after his death, constitutes, as Foss suggests in his prefatory note, 'an apostil to certain remarks made in the diary about defining gayness, gay political sensibility, and the prehistory of contemporary gay culture' (126).

5 Employing a reader-response approach, Ross Chambers's chapter on Michaels in *Facing It* focuses on the 'difficult patient' performance and its potential for subversiveness, and the problematic of a text that survives its author to be read 'complacently,' effecting a double death for the author (81–114). Reading the phrase I gloss here ('first principles'), Chambers specifies Michaels's principles as 'a principle of immanence, a principle of resistance, and a principle of continuity or survival' (88–9). I suggest instead that 'first principles' probably refers to Michaels's strategy of applying methods and critical questions drawn from anthropology to the dilemma he faces in representing his illness. My approach to *Unbecoming* thus differs from and expands on that of Chambers's by turning in more detail to Michaels's intellectual context in order to get a sense of the principles informing his textual practices, and by commenting at greater length on the question of the difficulty of resisting the hospital's 'Foucauldian horror show,' the need to 'invent family,' and the contexts and functions of the photograph of Michaels that accompanies the diary (91).

6 Writing and publishing his essays in the mid-to-late 1980s, Michaels belongs to the cohort of scholars such as Mary Louise Pratt, Michael Taussig, and James Clifford who were also publishing work on auto-ethnography, ethnographic writing, and postcolonial concerns about metropolitan domination.

7 In the context of the AIDS epidemic there has been much incisive work in anthropology and cultural studies on the meanings of HIV infection and AIDS as culturally constructed, as in the work of Treichler (who is heavily indebted to Michael Taussig's essay 'Reification and the Consciousness of the Patient,' which emphasizes that the body is not only an 'organic mosaic of biological entitites' but 'also a cornucopia of highly charged symbols' [86]) and Cindy Patton, whose writing is devoted to teasing out the cultural assumptions and meanings built into public health discourse. Consider, in addition, the insights provided by critical work on immune system discourse. Medical anthropologist Emily Martin's fieldwork suggests, for example, that anxiety-laden representations of immune system failure, including the 'startlingly graphic images of the devastation wrought by HIV' (133), are connected to people's worries about the threat that the virus presents to 'the integrity of their own body systems,' systems increasingly perceived, in the postmodern world, as being in 'flux' by virtue of being 'a loosely coupled system' (136, 142). At the same time, Martin draws attention to the *limitations* of literary and anthropological analyses of the cultural meanings of illness, insisting that first-person accounts locate the meanings of illness in ways that differ radically from the meanings constructed by observer accounts, be they journalistic, medical, anthropological, historical, or literary critical. She challenges third-party analysts of the meanings of illness to interrogate the position of 'immune witness,' the position that is occupied by many, if not all, professional or academic commentators (140).

8 Pratt uses the term 'autoethnography' in her survey of travel writing to summarize the strategies employed by 'colonized subjects' when they write back to the metropolitan centre 'in ways that *engage with* the colonizer's own terms' (7).

9 One of the only models for the practice of autobiographical narrative that meets with Michaels's approbation is Derek Jarman's *Caravaggio*, which he observes 'is hysterical, at least in the sense that is absolutely about what being gay is about: maleness, femaleness, competition, status, class, art and artifice' (50).

10 See also 'If All Anthropologists Are Liars ...' (1987).

11 For a more sympathetic reading of *My Place* as an attempt to 'embody

history,' particularly the occluded 'history of miscegenation,' that restructures autobiography's tendency to disembody the individual and to displace (and hence to naturalize) racialization, see Mohanram's *Black Body*, Chapter 5: 'Place in *My Place*: Embodiment, Aboriginality, and Australia' (122–3).

12 I am taking 'ethnicity' in this context as a term that can be extrapolated to indicate 'cultural identity,' a broader concept that can also encompass Michaels's 'counter-cultural' affiliations. Admittedly, these terms serve to indicate some important differences among cultural domains, but from an anthropological perspective, as Robert Ariss notes, homosexuality has been 'refram[ed] ... in recent decades in less pathological constructs [than the biomedical one], injecting it with a greater legitimacy by positioning it in relationship to developing concepts of human rights, lifestyle choice, and social (ethnic) identity' (18–19).

13 I am suggesting that Michaels writes against the logic of 'salvage' ethnography, which endeavours to prevent its object from disappearing, but sets about saving the other in self-interested terms, rewriting the gazed-upon other to suit the observer-writer's agenda. As James Clifford has pointed out, 'the very activity of ethnographic *writing* – seen as inscription or textualization – enacts a redemptive Western allegory' ('On Ethnographic Allegory' 99).

14 His rejection of the model of textuality seems also to function as a determinate negation, that is to say, as a disavowal that foregrounds the extreme self-consciousness about the relationship between writing and meaning, all of these 'morbid reflexivities' that he not only cannot fend off but actually elaborates and embellishes (4).

15 For a more detailed application of Kristeva's concept of abjection to the public rhetoric of AIDS, see Karen Zivi, 'Constituting the "Clean and Proper" Body: Convergences between Abjection and AIDS.' Zivi's analysis addresses how laws, state police power, and media images attempt to entrench 'public order and public safety' by invoking AIDS as 'abject' (39–40).

16 As Cathy Waldby suggests of *Unbecoming*, with reference to Kristeva, the 'confrontation ... with the prospect of immanent death' shows how linear temporality is implicated in the image of the self as 'clean and proper': the 'day-to-day accounts of the dissolution of the author's

body' in *Unbecoming* initiate an 'anti-teleology of self-investigation which seeks the discontinuities of an "I" in time, treating the self as an accident of history' ('AIDS, Death and the Limits of Identity' 209).

17 According to Kristeva, 'depressed persons' reject the arbitrariness of the linguistic sign; they *'disavow the negation'* that makes symbolic language possible, or, in other words, 'they cancel it out, suspend it, and nostalgically fall back on the real object (the Thing) of their loss, which is just what they do not manage to lose' (43). In Kristeva's writings, we encounter a rereading of melancholia in terms of what Tilottama Rajan describes as 'semiotic materialism,' which 'is concerned with how this *real,* even though it is unsignifiable *in* language, can nevertheless be seen transversally *through* language' ('Trans-Positions of Difference' 221). Resistance to the symbolic order (of the ego and, in a related way, of the social) comes from the semiotic (conceived of in a 'de-idealized sense' [Rajan 221], that is, as an hypothesis of excess rather than as essence). Kristeva has been criticized for a strain of biological essentialism in her work. See, for example, Butler's critique of Kristeva's feminism in 'The Body Politics of Julia Kristeva.' However, Rajan's phenomenological reading of Kristeva puts this criticism into perspective: 'Her work in semiotics, culminating in her theory of the genotext, is an attempt not just to see the unconscious as structured like a language, but also to read language as a body. This is in no sense a return to a myth of presence, since the body is conceived in terms of differential pulsions that preclude its being the site of any prereflective immediacy' (Rajan 216).

18 Ariss cites the lobbying efforts of the Australian Medical Association in the late 1980s 'to grant health care workers the right to refuse service to the infected,' and a 1989 case 'when a widely publicized legal action against the medical profession by a gay man who had been refused surgery ended in favor of the accused health-care worker' (42). For more on the management of HIV and AIDS in Australia, see Waldby, *AIDS and the Body Politic* (85). Australia's policies are not exceptional, but reflect international trends. As Patton emphasizes, Australia was only one among many countries to try to limit the entry of HIV-positive individuals: 'By 1990, as many as fifty-five countries, including the United States, Canada, the United Kingdom, and Australia, had imposed HIV-related travel-restrictions on incoming trav-

elers, despite clear policy and human rights statements from the
WHO, the International Red Cross, the United Nations, and the
Council of Europe' (*Globalizing AIDS* 108).

19 The published diary reprints these documents (110–16).

20 W.J.T. Mitchell argues similarly that contemporary culture has
undergone a 'pictorial turn,' namely 'a postlinguistic, postsemiotic
rediscovery of the picture as a complex interplay between visuality,
apparatus, institutions, discourse, bodies, and figurality' (16). And
Treichler links visual representation to the staking out of 'regimes of
truth' in the representation of AIDS: 'Media accounts of AIDS conform to such regimes; they come to seem familiar, true, because they
simultaneously reinforce prior representations and prepare us for
similar representations to come' (139).

21 The capacity of Michaels's photographic portrait to wound us does
not depend solely on an idiosyncratic, personalized identification
with the photograph's details but is generated, rather, in dialogue
with cultural and historical contexts that we share (although we are
certainly differently affected by them). Michaels's photograph thus
upsets to some extent Barthes's oft-cited distinction between *punctum*
(the level of a particularized, personal viewing) and *studium* (the
level of cultural or historical interpretation, available to anyone),
showing the mutual imbrication of these categories.

22 See also, for example, Susanna Egan's *Mirror Talk* (1999) and Linda
Haverty Rugg's *Picturing Ourselves* (1997). Egan argues that photography is a resource for representing the self dialogically. Because
visual media 'open possibilities for grounding a viewer's experience
in a life before and beyond the text,' while also 'rais[ing] questions
simultaneously about the subjectivity-in-representation of that life,'
autobiographers can draw on film and photography 'to define and
represent subjectivity not as singular or solipsistic but as multiple and
as revealed in relationship' (19–20). Rugg takes a more sceptical
approach: looking at autobiographical writing as interrogating the
ideology of photography, she focuses on the reactions of Walter Benjamin and Christa Wolf 'against the dangerously objectifying power
of photographs in their autobiographical narratives, which pointedly
omit actual photographic images but embrace photography as a metaphor for history and memory' (7).

23 'These mugshots,' notes Hebdige, in his survey of contemporary photographs of working-class youth, are 'as carefully cropped as the heads of the skins themselves,' rendering them all to easily as either 'victims' or 'culprits,' in either case 'objects of our pity, fear and fascination' ('Hiding in the Light' 22–3). See also Judith Williamson, who argues that in the sphere of education 'photography occupies a position somewhere between the family album [and its ideology of managed pleasure] and criminal surveillance' (237).

24 Nineteenth- and early twentieth-century anthropology subjected Aboriginal peoples to 'a gaze that was at once comparative and classificatory,' approaching them as 'survivors of an early and "primitive" stage in the evolution of mankind' (Donaldson and Donaldson, 'First Sight' 17). Photographs of Aboriginal people in a romantic vein typically involve 'a decontextualization of people by photographing them against blank backgrounds or recontextualizing them in formal poses in their "natural surroundings"' (Peterson 168).

25 For an extended critique of the assumptions embedded in the photographic representation of people living with AIDS, see Watney, '"Lifelike."'

26 Based on a model of embeddedness in community (involving extensive consultation and participation on the part of community members), Taylor's project also adopted the principle of employing a diverse group of photographers, including 'insiders, Aboriginal outsiders, and non-Aboriginal outsiders,' so that 'differences between photographs' might be foregrounded (xvii–xviii). The fact that the project was funded by the Australian Bicentenary Authority prompted some groups to decide not to participate, but many others took advantage of the opportunity to make their own views of contemporary life and history publicly visible (xvii–xix). As she describes it, 'The principle aim was to represent the diversity of Aboriginal Australia, to move into everyday worlds of Aboriginal work, play, home and neighbourhood. These are the areas excluded from a photographic obsession which has focused on the exotic, the "authentic" and the traditional' (xv).

27 The literature accompanying the recent show 'Re-take: Contemporary Aboriginal and Tores Strait Islander Photography' argues that

the 1988 bicentenary 'was an obvious point of dissension and led to a body of documentary photography that deals very directly with [contemporary Aboriginal life]' (Gellatly 1–2). 'Access to public education,' including 'art school education,' produced a generation of artists who, beginning in the 1980s, 'explo[ded] ... onto the Australian art scene' (1).

28 Benjamin emphasizes the importance of 'captions,' which 'turn all life's relationships into literature.' All pictures demand to be 'read' and 'interpreted,' or, in other words, they ask us to generate captions (256). But here we find ourselves in a double bind: on the one hand, there is the imperative to interpret photographs, but, on the other, the ready availability of the camera 'to capture fleeting and secret moments' creates images that 'paralyse the associative mechanisms in the beholder,' refusing our interpretive capacities (256).

Chapter Four

1 In an interview given during the writing of *My Brother* in 1996, Kincaid indicated that she was particularly preoccupied with 'the distinction between privilege and power and no privilege and no power' ('Jamaica Kincaid: Interview' 326, cf. 330).

2 Kincaid refers to her eldest brother's story as 'another big chapter,' thus suggesting that she conceives of her autobiographical fictions as an ongoing family biography (*My Brother* 81). It is also possible to trace connections between *My Brother* and Kincaid's earlier autobiographical fictions, *At the Bottom of the River, Annie John,* and *Lucy*: from the focus on the mother-daughter relationship as an analogy for colonialism, to the narrator's preoccupation with death, illness, and melancholy, similarities of detail and of intonation abound. For a discussion of these earlier texts, see Gilmore, *Autobiographics* (104–5) and *The Limits of Autobiography* (96–116) and the book-length studies of Kincaid by Moira Ferguson and Diane Simmons. Gilmore's discussion of *My Brother* in *The Limits of Autobiography* focuses primarily on Kincaid's critique of her mother's legacy; she argues that the mother-daughter relationship is as central in *My Brother* as it is in the earlier texts (116–19). My reading instead prioritizes Kincaid's self-question-

ing in the context of the sister-brother relationship and draws attention to her own problematic desire to evade responsibility for her
brother or to blame others for his illness.

3 At the end of 2000 the Joint United Nations Program on HIV/AIDS
estimated that there were approximately 390,000 people in the
Caribbean region living with HIV/AIDS out of a total population of
36 million people (Joint United Nations Program on HIV/AIDS 4).
Thus, the rate of incidence among adults is 2.3 per cent, or almost
four times that of the North American rate of 0.6 per cent (4). And
the annual number of AIDS cases in the region is on the increase,
whereas numbers have remained relatively stable in North America.
See 'AIDS in Latin America and the Caribbean,' ICAD, December
1998, and Kovaleski, 'Poverty, Drug Abuse Fuel Caribbean AIDS Outbreak.'

4 Citing 'labour migration' and 'tourist travel' (and the associated
issue of the sex trade) as major elements in 'the migration of HIV
infection' in the Caribbean, Bond et al. contend that 'the development of tourist industries' has been a particularly egregious example
of how 'U.S. capital as a replacement for the decline of profits from
older colonially established sources such as sugar cane ... has traced
the routes for HIV to follow' ('The Anthropology of AIDS in Africa
and the Caribbean' 6). Moreover, it has also been suggested that 'at
the beginning of the epidemic, some countries [in the region] did
not want to recognize an AIDS problem out of fear that tourism
would be adversely affected' (Kovaleski).

5 I borrow this phrasing from Chambers, who notes that melancholy
'appears as the mechanism of memory itself, and of the production
of meaning, when it is experienced as a phenomenon of unfinished
and interminable "thought"' (*The Writing of Melancholy* 168).
Similarly, in *Memoires for Paul de Man*, Derrida points to 'an un-
controllable necessity, a *nonsubjectivizable* law of thought beyond interiorization,' and conjectures that it is this unavoidable 'mechanism'
of 'thinking memory' that makes '*true mourning*' 'impossible'
(35–7).

6 The book thus challenges Slavoj Žižek's recent assertion that 'the
rehabilitation of melancholy' in the context of 'postcolonial/ethnic'
criticism 'enacts' an 'objective cynicism' that would 'allow us to claim

that we remain faithful to our ethnic roots while fully participating in the global, capitalist game' (659).

7 In 1999 Kincaid republished these essays as *My Garden (Book)*. The two essays to which I refer, 'Flowers of Evil' and 'Alien Soil,' appear here with minor variations but under different titles (respectively, 'To Name Is to Possess' and 'What Joseph Banks Wrought'). The changed titles highlight more clearly perhaps Kincaid's interest in investigating her own implication as an expatriate in relations of conquest, but the original title 'Flowers of Evil' suggests Kincaid's affinity with the poet Charles Baudelaire, whose poetry, along with that of other early French modernists, forms the textual basis of Chambers's and Kristeva's analyses of melancholy. Although Kincaid began writing these essays on gardening for magazines with the intention of publishing a book, she only returned to their completion *after* addressing her brother's story. The intertwined publishing histories of these texts thus support my reading of Devon's story as an undesired and yet necessary interruption of an upper-middle-class writerly identity she might prefer to construct.

8 Erika J. Waters and Carrol B. Fleming point to the complexities of 'de-colonizing poetry dealing with the Caribbean landscape,' remarking that 'metaphors in [contemporary] poetry and fiction which utilize native fruits and vegetables' work to 'replace ... the language of the center in a discourse fully adapted to the colonized place' by emphasizing local knowledge, and especially a 'survival linked closeness with the earth' – in place of the 'malevolent connection' forged by European domination of the landscape (390–3). Kincaid is, I suggest, alarmed by her increasing distance from this 'survival linked closeness to the earth,' and begins to speculate that she may have aligned herself with the oppressors.

9 Crosby notes the 'sunny view' taken of 'imported diseases' by white colonial administrators: 'John Winthrop, first governor of Massachusetts Bay Colony and a lawyer by training, noted on 22 May 1634, "For the natives, they are neere all dead of small Poxe, so as the Lord hathe cleared our title to what we possess"' (208).

10 Kincaid's change of name, from Elaine Potter Richardson to Jamaica Kincaid, has been the subject of much critical commentary, most of it emphasizing self-liberation through reinvention. For example, Sim-

mons sees the conclusion of *At the Bottom of the River* as claiming an autonomous subjectivity through the process of renaming: 'I claim these things then – mine – and now feel myself grow solid and complete, my name filling up my mouth' (82).

11 Kincaid's gift to her brother is AZT – but it is also worth emphasizing that the optimism inspired in the 1990s by new antiretroviral drug 'cocktails' that promise to make HIV/AIDS into a manageable chronic illness comes into doubt in light of the reality that these drugs are not readily available to people in the Caribbean, Africa, and Latin America, among other parts of the world, in which rates of infection continue to increase dramatically. The barriers are economic as well as bureaucratic and informational. As Rafael Mazin and Fernando Zacarias report, for instance, 'the monthly cost of antiretroviral therapy is two to five times the monthly income of most families in Latin America and the Caribbean' ('Antiretrovirals: Reality or Illusion?' 28).

12 In her discussion of the non(role) of 'Caribbean language' in *Annie John*, Merle Hodge notes: 'These flashes of dialogue in Creole seem to come as part and parcel of certain intimate and unprocessed memories, preserved in such detail that the actual language used is indelibly recorded, resisting translation' (50–1).

13 Tony Kushner has made extensive use of Benjamin's idea of the 'angel of history' in *Angels in America*, and I allude to the play in this chapter's title. The influence of Benjamin on Kushner is discussed, for example, by David Savran, who argues that the politics of Kushner's play are 'ambivalent' (15), owing perhaps more to Mormonism than to 'Theses on the Philosophy of History' ('Ambivalence, Utopia, and a Queer Sort of Materialism: How *Angels in America* Reconstructs the Nation' 24–5). Savran argues that '*Angels* unabashedly champions rationalism and progress,' demonstrating 'the dogged persistence of a consensus politic that masquerades as dissensus' (21); thus, Belize, the black ex–drag queen, becomes not only the play's exemplary caregiver, but also its conscience and 'guarantor of diversity' (30). Kincaid's memoir, while also self-contradictory in certain ways, is, I argue, more self-consciously and self-questioningly ambivalent than *Angels in America* in that it examines more unsparingly 'what the tradition of the oppressed teaches us.'

14 In the preface to *Strong Shadows: Scenes from an Inner City AIDS Clinic,*
Abigail Zuger stresses how AIDS exposes social inequities in the
United States: 'No disease shows up the crazy quilt of American
medical care for the shabby thing it is among the sick-to-death poor
better than AIDS. In the infectious disease clinics of large urban
hospitals like mine, the much touted amenities of our health-care
system are not in evidence' (xii).

15 I borrow these terms from Sidonie Smith, who distinguishes the
'embodied subject' (female) from the 'universal subject' (male) in
theorizing the body in women's contemporary autobiographical
practices (*Subjectivity, Identity, and the Body* 5). Radhika Mohanram
reads this opposition in terms of race as well as gender, noting that
'the expunging of the body for the construction of subject status ... is
only possible for a select group of subjects. The rest remain the body
in excess, be it the black body, or the perverse female body' (*Black
Body* 49).

16 Kincaid's 'self-annihilation' in her autobiographical text contrasts
with what Joanne Braxton summarizes as the characteristics of black
women's autobiographies, namely the emphasis on the 'formation'
of 'black and female identity' and 'public voice' (205). It also seems
to contradict Julia Watson and Sidonie Smith's suggestion that autobiographical writing by ethnic minority women 'may constitute an "I"
that becomes a place of creative and, by implication, political intervention' ('Introduction,' *De/Colonizing the Subject* xix). In this, I agree
with Giovanna Covi's assessment of Kincaid as 'postmodern': Covi
argues that Kincaid's 'narrative [style], in fact, is a continuous
attempt to turn away from any definitive statement and to utter radical statements' and that 'Jamaica Kincaid, a black woman writer, is
radically postmodern precisely because she is also postmodern, but
not only so' (345–6). I suggest that *My Brother* extends Kincaid's radical postmodernity.

17 This inconsistency or, to refer to Benjamin's characterization of melancholy, apparently wasteful 'extravagance' (*The Origin of German
Tragic Drama* 184) is the price of *My Brother*'s melancholic engagement with Devon, as it veers headily between repudiation and identification. One might be tempted to criticize Kincaid for certain 'close-
minded' statements, but I would argue that these moments remain

tied to a process of identification and that the text's self-reflexive
quality emphasizes this paradox.

18 The interpolated quotation is from Levinas's essay 'Reality and Its
Shadow?' (131). Levinas's point – that the repoliticization of the aesthetic is the responsibility of criticism – resounds sharply in the time
of AIDS. If we only contemplate art and do not respond, such paren-
thetical presences will be at best ambiguous and, at worst, 'in a world
of initiative and responsibility, a dimension of evasion' (141). And, as
Chambers has argued recently of AIDS diaries, and as I think we can
extend also to other kinds of testimonial writing about the pandemic, perhaps the defining feature of this 'emerging genre' is the
tendency to offer a 'chain of confrontations' to which 'every reader'
must respond if he or she is not to be charged with 'indifference'
(*Facing It* 22–3).

Conclusion

1 Esch analyses Jarman's representation of his garden in light of
Derrida's essay 'Biodegradables,' arguing that Jarman seeks not to
transmit a message but rather to 'nourish' the future (133–4).
2 See O'Quinn's comments on Jarman's critique of the 'heritization'
of Sissinghurst as an example of 'monumental' history (120–1).

Works Cited

Abraham, Nicolas, and Maria Torok. *The Shell and the Kernel*. Ed. and trans. Nicholas T. Rand. Vol. 1. Chicago: U of Chicago P, 1994.

'AIDS in Latin America and the Caribbean.' Interagency Coalition on AIDS and Development. Ottawa: December 1998.

Andriote, John-Manuel. *Victory Deferred: How AIDS Changed Gay Life in America*. Chicago and London: U of Chicago P, 1999.

Ariss, Robert M. *Against Death: The Practice of Living with AIDS*. With Gary W. Dowsett. Amsterdam: Gordon and Breach, 1997.

Baker, Rob. *The Art of AIDS: From Stigma to Conscience*. New York: Continuum, 1994.

Barthes, Roland. *Camera Lucida: Reflections on Photography*. Trans. Richard Howard. New York: Hill and Wang, 1981.

Belton, Don. Introduction. *Gary in Your Pocket: Stories and Notebooks of Gary Fisher*. By Gary Fisher. vii–xii.

Benjamin, Walter. *The Origin of German Tragic Drama*. (1924–5). Trans. John Osborne. London: NLB, 1977.

– 'A Small History of Photography.' (1931). *One Way Street and Other Writings*. Trans. Edmund Jephcott and Kinsgley Shorter. London: NLB, 1978. 240–57.

– 'Theses on the Philosophy of History.' (1940). *Illuminations*. Ed. Hannah Arendt. Trans. Harry Zohn. New York: Shocken Books, 1968. 253–64.

Beverley, John. 'The Margin at the Center: On Testimonio.' *De/Colonizing the Subject: The Politics of Gender in Women's Autobiography*. Ed. Sidonie Smith and Julia Watson. Minneapolis: U of Minnesota P, 1992. 91–114.

Bewell, Alan. *Romanticism and Colonial Geography*. Baltimore: Johns Hopkins UP, 1999.

Bhabha, Homi K. 'Interrogating Identity: Frantz Fanon and the Postcolonial Prerogative.' *The Location of Culture*. London: Routledge, 1994. 40–65.

Bond, George C., John Kreniske, Ida Susser, and Jean Vincent. 'The Anthropology of AIDS in Africa and the Caribbean.' *AIDS in Africa and the Caribbean*. Ed. Bond et al. Boulder, CO: Westview, 1997. 3–9.

Braxton, Joanne M. *Black Women Writing Autobiography: A Tradition within a Tradition*. Philadelphia: Temple UP, 1989.

Britzman, Deborah P. *Lost Subjects, Contested Objects: Towards a Psychoanalytic Inquiry of Learning*. Albany: SUNY P, 1998.

Brooks, Peter. 'The Melodramatic Imagination.' *Imitations of Life*. Ed. Landy. 50–67.

Brown, Rebecca. *The Gifts of the Body*. New York: Harper Perennial, 1994.

Burton, Robert. *The Anatomy of Melancholy*. (1621). The Third Partition: Vol. 3. London and New York: Everyman, 1968.

Butler, Judith. *Antigone's Claim: Kinship between Life and Death*. New York: Columbia UP, 2000.

– *Bodies That Matter: On the Discursive Limits of 'Sex.'* New York: Routledge, 1993.

– 'The Body Politics of Julia Kristeva.' *Ethics, Politics, and Difference in Julia Kristeva's Writing*. Ed. Kelly Oliver. New York: Routledge, 1993. 164–78.

– *Excitable Speech: A Politics of the Performative*. New York: Routledge, 1997.

– *Gender Trouble: Feminism and the Subversion of Identity*. New York and London: Routledge, 1990.

– *The Psychic Life of Power: Theories in Subjection*. Stanford: Stanford UP, 1997.

Butler, Sandra, and Barbara Rosenblum. *Cancer in Two Voices*. San Francisco: Spinsters Book Company, 1991.

Cadava, Eduardo. 'Words of Light: Theses on the Photography of History.' *Diacritics*. Special Issue: Commemorating Walter Benjamin. Ed. Ian Balfour and Cynthia Chase. 22.3–4 (Fall–Winter 1992): 84–114.

Caruth, Cathy, and Thomas Keenan. '"The AIDS Crisis Is Not Over": A

Conversation with Greg Bordowitz, Douglas Crimp, and Laura Pinsky.'
American Imago 48.4 (1991): 539–56.

Chambers, Ross. *Facing It: AIDS Diaries and the Death of the Author.* Ann
Arbor: U of Michigan P, 1998.

– *The Writing of Melancholy: Modes of Opposition in Early French Modernism.*
(1987). Trans. Marie Seidman Trouille. Chicago: U of Chicago P,
1993.

Cheng, Anne Anlin. *The Melancholy of Race.* Oxford: Oxford UP, 2000.

Cherniavsky, Eva. 'Real Again: Melodrama and the Subject of HIV/
AIDS.' *GLQ: A Journal of Lesbian and Gay Studies* 4.3 (1998): 375–401.

Clifford, James. 'On Ethnographic Allegory.' *Writing Culture.* Ed. Clifford and Marcus. 98–122.

Clifford, James, and George E. Marcus. *Writing Culture: The Poetics and
Politics of Ethnography.* Berkeley: U of California P, 1986.

Couser, G. Thomas. *Recovering Bodies: Disability and Life-Writing.* Madison:
U of Wisconsin P, 1997.

Covi, Giovanna. 'Jamaica Kincaid and the Resistance to Canons.' *Out of
the Kumbla: Caribbean Women and Literature.* Ed. Carole Boyce Davies
and Elaine Savory Fido. Trenton, NJ: Africa World P, 1990. 345–54.

Crimp, Douglas. 'How to Have Promiscuity in an Epidemic.' (1987).
AIDS: Cultural Analysis/Cultural Activism. Ed. Crimp. Cambridge, MA:
MIT P, 1989. 237–71.

– 'Mourning and Militancy.' *October* 51 (Winter 1989): 3–18.

Croce, Arlene. 'Discussing the Undiscussable.' *Dance Connection* 20
(Summer 1995): 20–8.

Crosby, Alfred W. *Ecological Imperialism: The Biological Expansion of Europe,
900–1900.* Cambridge: Cambridge UP, 1986.

de Lombard, Jeannine. 'Who Cares? Lesbians as Caregivers.' *Dyke Life: A
Celebration of Lesbian Experience.* Ed. Karla Jay. New York: Basic Books,
HarperCollins, 1995. 344–61.

Derrida, Jacques. 'Fors.' Trans. Barbara Johnson. Foreword to *The Wolf
Man's Magic Word: A Cryptonomy.* Trans. Nicholas Rand. Minneapolis:
U of Minnesota P, 1986.

– *Memoires for Paul de Man.* Rev. ed. Trans. Cecile Lindsay, Jonathan
Culler, Eduardo Cadava, and Peggy Kamuf. New York: Columbia UP,
1989.

– 'The Rhetoric of Drugs.' *Points ... Interviews, 1974–1994.* Ed. Elisabeth

Weber. Trans. Peggy Kamuf and others. Stanford: Stanford UP, 1995.
228–54.

– *Specters of Marx: The State of the Debt, the Work of Mourning, and the New
International.* Trans. Peggy Kamuf. New York: Routledge, 1994.

Dixon, Melvin. 'I'll Be Somewhere Listening for My Name.' *In the Company of My Solitude.* Ed. Howe and Klein. 182–8.

Donaldson, Ian, and Tamsin Donaldson. 'First Sight.' *Seeing the First Australians.* Ed. Donaldson and Donaldson. 15–20.

– eds. *Seeing the First Australians.* Sydney: George Allen and Unwin, 1985.

Doty, Mark. *Heaven's Coast: A Memoir.* New York: HarperCollins, 1997.

– 'Is There a Future?' *In the Company of My Solitude.* Ed. Howe and Klein.
3–12.

Duncan, Derek. 'Solemn Geographies: AIDS and the Contours of Autobiography.' *a/b: Auto/Biography Studies.* Special Issue: Autobiographical
Que(e)ries. 15.1 (Summer 2000): 22–36.

Düttmann, Alexander García. *At Odds with AIDS: Thinking and Talking
about a Virus.* Trans. Peter Gilgen and Conrad Scott-Curtis. Stanford:
Stanford UP, 1996.

Edelman, Lee. *Homographesis: Essays in Gay Literature and Cultural Theory.*
New York and London: Routledge, 1994.

Egan, Susanna. *Mirror Talk: Genres of Crisis in Contemporary Autobiography.*
Chapel Hill and London: U of North Carolina P, 1999.

Ellis, Jim. 'Queer Period: Derek Jarman's Renaissance.' *Out Takes: Essays
on Queer Theory and Film.* Ed. Ellis Hanson. Durham and London:
Duke UP, 1999. 188–215.

Epstein, Julia. 'AIDS, Stigma, and Narratives of Containment.' *American
Imago* 49.3 (Fall 1992): 293–310.

Esch, Deborah. '"The only news was when" (The Journals of Derek Jarman).' *In the Event: Reading Journalism, Reading Theory.* Stanford: Stanford UP, 1999. 116–34.

Everyone's Child. Dir. Tsitsi Dangarembga. Harare: Media for Development Trust, 1996.

Feinberg, David. *Queer and Loathing: Rants and Raves of a Raging AIDS
Clone.* New York: Viking, 1994.

Ferguson, Moira. *Jamaica Kincaid: Where the Land Meets the Body.* Charlot-
tesville and London: U of Virginia P, 1994.

Fisher, Gary. *Gary in Your Pocket: Stories and Notebooks of Gary Fisher.* Edited and with an Afterword by Eve Kosofsky Sedgwick. Introduction by Don Belton. Durham and London: Duke UP, 1996.

Foucault, Michel. *The Use of Pleasure. Volume 2 of the History of Sexuality.* (1984). Trans. Robert Hurley. New York: Vintage, 1990.

Freud, Sigmund. 'Mourning and Melancholia.' *The Standard Edition of the Complete Psychological Works of Sigmund Freud.* Ed. James Strachey. Vol. 14. London: Hogarth Press and Institute of Psycho-Analysis, 1957. 243–58.

Gamson, Josh. 'Silence, Death, and the Invisible Enemy: AIDS Activism and Social Movement Newness.' *Social Problems* 36.4 (October 1989): 351–67.

Gellatly, Kelly. 'Re-take: Contemporary Aboriginal and Torres Strait Islander Photography.' <http://www.nga.gov.au/Retake/brochure. htm>. 1–4.

Gere, David. 'Applause and Anxiety in the Age of AIDS.' *New York Times* Sunday, 29 November 1998, Arts and Leisure: 1, 29.

Gilmore, Leigh. *Autobiographics: A Feminist Theory of Women's Self-Representation.* Ithaca and London: Cornell UP, 1994.

– *The Limits of Autobiography: Trauma and Testimony.* Ithaca and London: Cornell UP, 2001.

Ginsberg, Allen. *Kaddish and Other Poems, 1958–1960.* San Francisco: City Lights, 1963.

Golding, Sue. 'Pariah Bodies.' *Critical Quarterly.* Special Issue: 'Critically Queer.' 36.1 (Spring 1994): 28–38.

– 'Revenge.' *The Eight Technologies of Otherness.* Ed. Golding. London and New York: Routledge, 1997. 196–9.

Grosz, Elizabeth. *Jacques Lacan: A Feminist Introduction.* New York and London: Routledge, 1990.

– *Volatile Bodies: Toward a Corporeal Feminism.* Bloomington and Indianapolis: Indiana UP, 1994.

Hacker, Jonathan, and David Price. 'Discussion with Derek Jarman.' *Take Ten: Contemporary British Film Directors.* Ed. Hacker and Price. Oxford: Clarendon, 1991. 248–60.

– 'Essay on Derek Jarman.' *Take Ten: Contemporary British Film Directors.* Ed. Hacker and Price. Oxford: Clarendon, 1991. 231–47.

Halperin, David. *One Hundred Years of Homosexuality and Other Essays on Greek Love.* New York and London: Routledge, 1990.

Hannerz, Ulf. *Transnational Connections: Culture, People, Places.* London: Routledge, 1996.

Haver, William. *The Body of This Death: History and Sociality in the Time of AIDS.* Stanford: Stanford UP, 1997.

– 'Queer Research; or, How to Practice Invention to the Brink of Intelligibility.' *The Eight Technologies of Otherness.* Ed. Sue Golding. London and New York: Routledge, 1997. 277–92.

Hawkins, Anne Hunsaker. *Reconstructing Illness: Studies in Pathography.* (1993). West Lafayette, IN: Purdue UP, 1999.

Hebdige, Dick. Foreword. *Bad Aboriginal Art.* By Eric Michaels. ix–xxvi.

– 'Hiding in the Light: Youth Surveillance and Display.' *Hiding in the Light.* New York and London: Routledge, 1988. 17–36.

– 'Introduction: Subculture and Style.' *Subculture: The Meaning of Style.* London: Methuen, 1979. 1–4.

Hegel, G.W.F. *The Phenomenology of Spirit.* Trans., with an introduction and notes by J.B. Baillie. 2nd ed. London: George Allen and Unwin, 1964.

Hirsch, Marianne. *Family Frames: Photography, Narrative, and Postmemory.* Cambridge, MA: Harvard UP, 1997.

Hodge, Merle. 'Caribbean Writers and Caribbean Language: A Study of Jamaica Kincaid's *Annie John.*' *Winds of Change: The Transforming Voices of Caribbean Women Writers and Scholars.* Ed. Adele S. Newson and Linda Strong-Leek. New York: Lang, 1998. 47–53.

Hoffman, Amy. *Hospital Time.* Durham and London: Duke UP, 1997.

Hogan, Katie. *Women Take Care: Gender, Race, and the Culture of AIDS.* Ithaca and London: Cornell UP, 2001.

Howe, Marie, and Michael Klein, eds. *In the Company of My Solitude: American Writing from the AIDS Pandemic.* New York: Persea Books, 1995.

I'll Be Your Mirror. Dirs. Nan Goldin and Edmund Coulthard. U.S.A.: s.n., 1996.

Irigaray, Luce. *Speculum of the Other Woman.* Ithaca: Cornell UP, 1985.

Jacobs, Carol. 'Dusting Antigone.' *Modern Language Notes* 111.5 (December 1996): 889–917.

'Jamaica Kincaid: Interview.' With Eleanor Wachtel. *More Writers and Company: New Conversations with CBC Radio's Eleanor Wachtel.* Toronto: Knopf, 1996. 320–38.

Jarman, Derek. *At Your Own Risk: A Saint's Testament.* London: Hutchinson, 1992.

– dir. *Blue.* Basilisk Communications and Uplink in association with Channel 4, 1993.

– dir. *Caravaggio.* BFI in association with Channel 4 and Nicholas Ward-Jackson, 1986.

– *Dancing Ledge.* London and New York: Quartet Books, 1984.

– *Derek Jarman's Garden.* With photographs by Howard Sooley. London: Thames and Hudson, 1995.

– dir. *Edward II.* Working Title in association with British Screen and BBC Films, 1991.

– dir. *The Garden.* Basilisk in association with Channel 4, 1990.

– *Modern Nature: The Journals of Derek Jarman.* (1991). London: Vintage, 1992.

– dir. *Sebastiane.* Distac, 1976.

– dir. *War Requiem.* Anglo International, 1989.

– dir. *Wittgenstein.* Bandung for Channel 4, 1993.

Jarraway, David R. 'From Spectacular to Speculative: The Shifting Rhetoric in Recent Gay AIDS Memoirs.' *Mosaic* 33.4 (December 2000): 115–28.

Joint United Nations Program on HIV/AIDS. 'AIDS Epidemic Update 2001.' <http://www.unaids.org/epidemic_update/report_dec01/index.html#full>.

Juhasz, Alexandra. *AIDS TV: Identity, Community and Alternative Video.* Durham: Duke UP, 1996.

Kincaid, Jamaica. 'Alien Soil.' In the Garden. *New Yorker* (21 June 1993): 47–51.

– *Annie John.* New York: Farrar, 1985.

– *At the Bottom of the River.* New York: Farrar, 1983.

– 'Flowers of Evil.' In the Garden. *New Yorker* (5 October 1992): 154–9.

– *Lucy.* New York: Farrar, 1990.

– *My Brother.* New York: Farrar, 1997.

– *My Garden (Book).* Illustrations by Jill Fox. New York: Farrar, 1999.

– *A Small Place.* New York: Farrar, 1988.

– 'Sowers and Reapers.' *New Yorker* (22 January 2001): 41–5.

Kovaleski, Serge F. 'Poverty, Drug Abuse Fuel Caribbean AIDS Outbreak.' *Washington Post* 14 January 1998: A12.

Kristeva, Julia. *Black Sun: Depression and Melancholia.* Trans. Leon S. Roudiez. New York: Columbia UP, 1989.

– *Powers of Horror: An Essay on Abjection.* Trans. Leon S. Roudiez. New York: Columbia UP, 1982.

Kruger, Steven F. *AIDS Narratives: Gender and Sexuality, Fiction and Science.* New York and London: Garland, 1996.

Kumar, Avitava. *Passport Photos.* Berkeley: U of California P, 2000.

Kushner, Tony. *Angels in America. Part One: Millennium Approaches and Part Two: Perestroika.* (1992). New York: Theatre Communications Group, 1994.

Landy, Marcia, ed. *Imitations of Life: A Reader on Film and Television Melodrama.* Detroit: Wayne State UP, 1991.

Laub, Dori. 'Bearing Witness or the Vicissitudes of Listening.' *Testimony: Crises of Witnessing in Literature, Psychoanalysis, and History.* Ed. Shoshana Felman and Dori Laub. New York and London: Routledge, 1992. 57–74.

Levinas, Emmanuel. 'Reality and Its Shadow?' Trans. Alphonso Lingis. *The Levinas Reader.* Ed. Seán Hand. Oxford: Blackwell, 1989. 129–43.

Lionnet, Françoise. *Autobiographical Voices: Race, Gender, Self-Portraiture.* Ithaca and London: Cornell UP, 1989.

The Long Walk. Dir. Alan Bibby. National Film Board of Canada, 1998.

MacCabe, Colin. 'Derek Jarman: Obituary.' (First published in a shorter version, 21 February 1994 in *The Independent*). *Critical Quarterly.* Special Issue: 'Critically Queer.' 36.1 (Spring 1994): v–ix.

Martin, Emily. *Flexible Bodies: Tracking Immunity in American Culture – From the Days of Polio to the Age of AIDS.* Boston: Beacon, 1994.

Maslanka, Halina. 'Women Volunteers at GMHC.' *Women and AIDS: Psychological Perspectives.* Ed. Corinne Squires. London: Sage Publications, 1993. 111–25.

Maynard, Margaret. 'Projections of Melancholy.' *Seeing the First Australians.* Ed. Donaldson and Donaldson. 92–109.

Mazin, Rafael, and Fernando Zacarias. 'Antiretrovirals: Reality or Illusion?' Eye on Latin America and the Caribbean. *Journal of the International Association of Physicians in AIDS Care* (October 1998): 28–9.

Michaels, Eric. *Bad Aboriginal Art: Tradition, Media, and Technological Horizons.* Foreword by Dick Hebdige. Introduction by Marcia Langton. Minneapolis: U of Minnesota P, 1994.

- 'For a Cultural Future: Francis Jupurrulrla Makes TV at Yuendumu.' (1987). In *Bad Aboriginal Art*. 98–124.
- 'If All Anthropologists Are Liars ...' (1987). In *Bad Aboriginal Art*. 127–40.
- 'Para-Ethnography.' (1988). In *Bad Aboriginal Art*. 164–75.
- *Unbecoming*. (1990). Durham: Duke UP, 1994.

Mirzoeff, Nicholas. *An Introduction to Visual Culture*. London: Routledge, 1999.

Mitchell, W.J.T. *Picture Theory: Essays on Visual and Verbal Representation*. Chicago and London: U of Chicago P, 1994.

Mohanram, Radhika. *Black Body: Women, Colonialism, and Space*. Minneapolis and London: U of Minnesota P, 1999.

Monette, Paul. *Borrowed Time: An AIDS Memoir*. San Diego and New York: Harcourt Brace, 1988.

Moon, Michael. 'Memorial Rags.' *Professions of Desire: Lesbian and Gay Studies in Literature*. Ed. George E. Haggerty and Bonnie Zimmerman. New York: Modern Language Association of America, 1995. 233–40.

- Preface. *Unbecoming*. By Eric Michaels. ix–xvi.

Morgan, Stuart. 'Borrowed Time.' *Derek Jarman: A Portrait*. Ed. Roger Wollen. London: Thames and Hudson, 1996. 113–20.

'The Mourner's Kaddish.' *The Complete Art Scroll Sidur*. Trans. Rabbi Nosson Scherman. Co-ed. Rabbi Meir Zlotowitz. Brooklyn: Menorah Publications, 1985. 177.

Nolen, Stephanie. 'The Art of the Positive.' *Globe and Mail* 1 August 2000: R1.

Nunokawa, Jeff. '"All the Sad Young Men": AIDS and the Work of Mourning.' *Inside/Out: Lesbian Theories, Gay Theories*. Ed. Diana Fuss. New York and London: Routledge, 1991. 311–23.

Odets, Walt. Introduction. *In the Shadow of the Epidemic: Being HIV-Negative in the Age of AIDS*. Durham: Duke UP, 1995. 1–10.

O'Quinn, Daniel. 'Gardening, History, and the Escape from Time: Derek Jarman's *Modern Nature*.' *October* 89 (Summer 1999): 113–26.

Patton, Cindy. *Fatal Advice: How Safe Sex Education Went Wrong*. Durham: Duke UP, 1996.

- *Globalizing AIDS*. Minneapolis: U of Minnesota P, 2002.
- '"With Champagne and Roses": Women at Risk from/in AIDS Dis-

course.' *Women and AIDS: Psychological Perspectives.* Ed. Corinne
Squires. London: Sage Publications, 1993. 165–87.

Peake, Tony. *Derek Jarman.* London: Little, Brown and Company, 1999.

Peterson, Nicolas. 'The Popular Image.' *Seeing the First Australians.* Ed.
Donaldson and Donaldson. 164–80.

Philadelphia. Dir. Jonathan Demme. Burbank, California: Tristar,
1994.

Picard, André. 'Treating All Pregnant Women Presents HIV Dilemma.'
Globe and Mail 17 June 2000: A2.

Pratt, Mary Louise. 'Fieldwork in Common Places.' *Writing Culture.* Ed.
Clifford and Marcus. 27–50.

– *Imperial Eyes: Travel Writing and Transculturation.* New York and London: Routledge, 1992.

Rajan, Tilottama. 'Trans-Positions of Difference: Kristeva and Post-Structuralism.' *Ethics, Politics, and Difference in Julia Kristeva's Writing.*
Ed. Kelly Oliver. New York and London: Routledge, 1993. 215–37.

Reinke, Steve. Introduction. *Plague Years: A Life in Underground Movies.* By
Mike Hoolboom. Ed. Reinke. Toronto: YYZ, 1998. 16–17.

Roman, David. *Acts of Intervention: Performance, Gay Culture, and AIDS.*
Bloomington: Indiana UP, 1998.

Ross, Andrew. 'Uses of Camp.' *No Respect: Intellectuals and Popular Culture.*
New York and London: Routledge, 1989. 135–70.

Ruby, Jay. 'In the Belly of the Beast: Eric Michaels and Indigenous
Media.' *Picturing Culture: Explorations of Film and Anthropology.* Chicago:
U of Chicago P, 2000. 221–38.

Rugg, Linda Haverty. *Picturing Ourselves: Photography and Autobiography.*
Chicago: U of Chicago P, 1997.

Sacks, Peter M. *The English Elegy: Studies in the Genre from Spenser to Yeats.*
Baltimore and London: Johns Hopkins UP, 1985.

Salazar, Deborah. 'The Bad News Is that the Bad News Is Still the Same.'
In the Company of My Solitude. Ed. Howe and Klein. 13–17.

Savran, David. 'Ambivalence, Utopia, and a Queer Sort of Materialism:
How *Angels in America* Reconstructs the Nation.' *Approaching the Millennium: Essays on Angels in America.* Ed. Deborah R. Geis and Steven F.
Kruger. Ann Arbor: U of Michigan P, 1997. 13–39.

Schatz, Thomas. 'The Family Melodrama.' *Imitations of Life.* Ed. Landy.
148–67.

Schenck, Celeste. 'Feminism and Deconstruction: Re-Constructing the Elegy.' *Tulsa Studies in Women's Literature* 5.1 (Spring 1986): 13–27.

Schulman, Sarah. *People in Trouble.* New York: E.P. Dutton, 1990.

Sedgwick, Eve Kosofsky. Afterword. *Gary in Your Pocket: Stories and Notebooks of Gary Fisher.* By Gary Fisher. Ed. Sedgwick. 273–91.

– *A Dialogue on Love.* Boston: Beacon, 1999.

– *Epistemology of the Closet.* Berkeley and Los Angeles: U of California P, 1990.

– 'Gender Criticism.' *Redrawing the Boundaries: The Transformation of English and American Literary Studies.* Ed. Stephen Greenblatt and Giles B. Gunn. New York: Modern Language Association of America, 1992. 271–302.

– 'How to Bring Your Kids Up Gay: The War on Effeminate Boys.' In *Tendencies.* 154–66.

– 'Memorial for Craig Owens.' In *Tendencies.* 104–8.

– 'Paranoid Reading and Reparative Reading; or, You're So Paranoid, You Probably Think This Introduction Is About You.' *Novel Gazing: Queer Readings in Fiction.* Durham and London: Duke UP, 1997. 1–37.

– 'Queer and Now.' In *Tendencies.* 1–22.

– 'Tales of the Avunculate: *The Importance of Being Earnest.*' In *Tendencies.* 52–72.

– *Tendencies.* Durham: Duke UP, 1993.

– 'White Glasses.' In *Tendencies.* 252–66.

Senior, Olive. *Gardening in the Tropics.* Toronto: McClelland and Stewart, 1994.

Shilts, Randy. *And the Band Played On: Politics, People, and the AIDS Epidemic.* New York: St Martin's, 1987.

Silverlake Life. Dirs. Tom Joslin and Peter Friedman. Point of View, PBS, 1993.

Simmons, Diane. *Jamaica Kincaid.* Twayne's United States Authors Series No. 646. Toronto: Maxwell Macmillan, 1994.

Singer, Linda. *Erotic Welfare: Sexual Theory and Politics in the Age of Epidemic.* Ed. Judith Butler and Maureen McGrogan. New York and London: Routledge, 1993.

Smith, Julien. *The Constructed Body: AIDS, Reproductive Technology, and Ethics.* Buffalo: SUNY P, 1996.

Smith, Sidonie. *Subjectivity, Identity, and the Body: Women's Autobiographical*

Practices in the Twentieth Century. Bloomington and Indianapolis: Indiana UP, 1993.

Smith, Terry. 'Public Art between Cultures: The *Aboriginal Memorial*, Aboriginality, and Nationality in Australia.' *Critical Inquiry* 27 (Summer 2001): 629–61.

Sontag, Susan. *Illness as Metaphor* (1978) and *AIDS and Its Metaphors* (1988). New York: Anchor Books, 1990.

Sophocles. *Antigone*. In *Sophocles I: Oedipus the King, Oedipus at Colonus, Antigone*. Trans. David Grene. 2nd ed. Chicago and London: U of Chicago P, 1991. 159–212.

Steinberg, Sybil S. Review of *The Gifts of the Body* by Rebecca Brown. *Publisher's Weekly* 241.32 (15 August 1994): 85.

Steps for the Future. <http://www.dayzero.co.za/steps/>.

Stern, Richard. 'Dying with AIDS in Costa Rica.' Access to Care and Treatment. AIDSLink #45. *NCIH* (May/June 1997): 14–15.

Sturken, Marita. *Tangled Memories: The Vietnam War, the AIDS Epidemic and the Cultural Politics of Remembering*. Berkeley: U of California P, 1997.

Taussig, Michael. 'Reification and the Consciousness of the Patient.' *The Nervous System*. New York and London: Routledge, 1992. 83–109.

Taylor, Penny, ed. *After 200 Years: Photographic Essays of Aboriginal and Islander Australia Today*. For the Institute of Aboriginal Studies. Canberra: Aboriginal Studies P, 1988.

'This Piercing Bouquet: An Interview with Eve Kosofsky Sedgwick.' With Eve Kosofsky Sedgwick, Stephen M. Barber, and David L. Clark. *Regarding Sedgwick: Essays on Queer Culture and Critical Theory*. Ed. Barber and Clark. New York and London: Routledge, 2002. 243–62.

Thompson, Mark. Introduction. *Leatherfolk: Radical Sex, People, Politics, and Practice*. Ed. Thompson. Boston: Alyson, 1991. xi–xx.

Tongues Untied. Dir. Marlon Riggs. Point of View, PBS, 1991.

Treichler, Paula A. *How to Have Theory in an Epidemic: Cultural Chronicles of AIDS*. Durham and London: Duke UP, 1999.

'UNAIDS/WHO Global AIDS Statistics.' *AIDS Care* 11.5 (October 1999): 611–22.

Vaid, Urvashi. Foreword. *Hospital Time*. By Amy Hoffman. ix–xv.

Waldby, Catherine. *AIDS and the Body Politic: Biomedicine and Sexual Difference*. London and New York: Routledge, 1996.

– 'AIDS, Death and the Limits of Identity: Reading Eric Michaels's *Unbecoming*.' *Southern Review* 25 (July 1992): 205–12.

Waters, Erika J., and Carrol B. Fleming. '"Replacing the Language of the Center": Botanical Symbols and Metaphors in Caribbean Literature.' *Caribbean Studies* 27.3–4 (1994): 390–401.

Watney, Simon. 'Derek Jarman: 1942–94: A Political Death.' *Artforum* 32.9 (May 1994): 84–5 ff.

– '"Lifelike": Imagining the Bodies of People with AIDS.' *The Masculine Masquerade: Masculinity and Representation*. Ed. Andrew Perchuk and Helaine Posner. Cambridge, MA and London: MIT P, 1995. 63–8.

– 'The Spectacle of AIDS.' (1987). *AIDS: Cultural Analysis/Cultural Activism*. Ed. Douglas Crimp. Cambridge, MA: MIT P, 1989. 71–86.

Watson, Julia, and Sidonie Smith. 'De/Colonization and the Politics of Discourse in Women's Autobiographical Practices.' Introduction. *De/Colonizing the Subject: The Politics of Gender in Women's Autobiography*. Ed. Smith and Watson. Minneapolis: U of Minnesota P, 1992. xiii–xxxi.

White, Edmund. 'Esthetics and Loss.' *Artforum* (January 1987): 68–71.

Williamson, Judith. 'Family, Education, Photography.' *Culture/Power/History*. Ed. N.B. Dirks et al. Princeton: Princeton UP, 1994.

Wollen, Peter. 'The Last New Wave: Modernism in the British Films of the Thatcher Era.' *The British Avant-Garde Film, 1926–1995*. Ed. Michael O'Pray. Luton: U of Luton P, 1996. 239–59.

Wollen, Roger. 'Introduction: Facts of Derek Jarman.' *Derek Jarman: A Portrait*. Ed. Wollen. London: Thames and Hudson, 1996. 15–31.

Wood, Evan, Paula Braitstein, Julio S.B. Montaner, Martin T. Schechter, Mark W. Tyndall, Michael V. O'Shaughnessy, and Robert S. Hogg. 'Extent to which Low-Level Use of Antiretroviral Treatment Could Curb the AIDS Epidemic in Sub-Saharan Africa.' *Lancet* 355.9221 (17 June 2000): 2095–100.

Yingling, Thomas E. 'AIDS in America: Postmodern Governance, Identity, and Experience.' *Inside/Out: Lesbian Theories, Gay Theories*. Ed. Diana Fuss. New York and London: Routledge, 1991. 291–310.

– 'Wittgenstein's Tumor: AIDS and the National Body.' *AIDS and the National Body*. By Thomas E. Yingling. Ed. Robin Wiegman. Durham and London: Duke UP, 1997. 17–36.

Zeiger, Melissa F. *Beyond Consolation: Death, Sexuality, and the Changing Shapes of Elegy.* Ithaca and London: Cornell UP, 1997.

Zero Patience. Dir. John Greyson. Toronto: Zero Patience Productions/ Cineplex Odeon, 1993.

Zivi, Karen. 'Constituting the "Clean and Proper" Body: Convergences between Abjection and AIDS.' *Gendered Epidemic: Representations of Women in the Age of AIDS.* Ed. Nancy L. Roth and Katie Hogan. New York and London: Routledge, 1998. 33–62.

Žižek, Slavoj. 'Melancholy and the Act.' *Critical Inquiry* 26 (2000): 657–81.

Zuger, Abigail. *Strong Shadows: Scenes from an Inner City AIDS Clinic.* New York: Freeman, 1995.

Illustration Credits

Index

Michaels, 127, 129–32, 235n6;
readers of, 130
autothanatographies, 13, 218n12

Baker, Rob, 216n8
Barthes, Roland, 239n21
Baudelaire, Charles, 243n7
Belton, Don, 219–20n18
Benjamin, Walter, 17; and alle-
gory, 23–4, 30–1; and history,
167, 184, 244n13; and melan-
choly, 23–4, 245–6n17; *The Ori-
gin of German Tragic Drama*, 23;
and photography, 156, 163–6,
239n22, 241n28
Beverly, John, 14
Bewell, Alan, 141
Bhabha, Homi K., 177–8
Bibby, Allan, 217n11
Blue (Jarman), 32, 218n12, 221–2n6
body. *See* embodiment
Bottomley, Virginia, 59–60
Boys on the Side, 232n13
Braxton, Joanne, 245n16
Britzman, Deborah, 51, 71, 74,
227n33n37
Brookner, Howard, 32, 39, 41
Brooks, Peter, 234n3
Brother's Keeper, 232–3n16
Brown, Rebecca: *The Gifts of the
Body*, 115–16
Burton, Robert, 30
Butler, Judith, 17, 42, 85; *Anti-
gone's Claim*, 103–4, 106; *Excit-
able Speech*, 223n15; and
homosexual love, 107; and
mourning and melancholia, 22–
3, 135–6, 227n33; *The Psychic Life
of Power*, 22, 42, 104; and societal
norms, 43

Butler, Sandra, 114, 234n20

Cadava, Eduardo, 165
Caravaggio (Jarman), 34, 221n4n5,
224n18, 236n9
caregiving, 18, 115–16, 189–91,
199–200, 233n18; and gender
roles, 101–9, 214–15n5, 231n11
censorship, 60–1, 64–6, 72–3
Chambers, Ross, 10, 20, 80–1, 118,
145–6, 156, 168, 213n4, 217n12,
229–30n5, 235n5, 242n5, 243n7,
246n18; *Facing It*, 11, 20, 235n5
Chatwin, Bruce, 128
Cheng, Anne Anlin, 172–3
Cherniavsky, Eva, 232n14, 234–
5n3
Clifford, James, 235n6, 237n13
Cocteau, Jean, 36
Collins, Keith, 31
Couser, Thomas, 105, 217n12
Covi, Giovanna, 245n16
Crimp, Douglas, 16–20, 96–7,
213n4; 'Mourning and Mili-
tancy,' 16
Croce, Arlene, 219n17
Crosby, Alfred W., 176–7, 185,
243n9

Dancing Ledge (Jarman), 34–5
Dangarembga, Tsitsi, 217n11
Davies, Terence, 70
de Lombard, Jeannine, 231n11
Derrida, Jacques, 13, 17, 44, 53,
110, 246n1; and exorcisms, 25–
6, 47; *Memoires for Paul de Man*,
25, 242n5; mourning and melancholia, 84–5, 135–8, 209,
227n33, 242n5; mourning and
memorialization, 24–7, 88, 173;

Garden, The (Jarman), 60, 76, 207
gardens, 24, 28, 65, 70, 205,
   243n7; and colonialism, 174–83,
   187, 199, 202, 243n8; as pharmacopoeia, 30, 39, 67; at Prospect Cottage, 29–30, 40, 52,
   205–8, 225–6n26, 246n1; as representation of illness, 31, 44
gender roles, 101–7, 188–9, 196, 209,
   214–15n5, 221–2n6, 230–1n9,
   245n16; and *Antigone*, 101–5; and
   grief, 27, 101–5. *See* caregiving
Genet, Jean, 36, 226n32
Gere, David, 7, 15, 17
ghosts: as disturbance, 8, 26, 100,
   112, 197, 230n8; and Jarman,
   41–2, 44, 47, 51, 89; and
   Michaels, 165; and Mike Riegle,
   89, 95. *See* spectres
Gilmore, Leigh, 14, 147–8, 241n2
Ginsberg, Allen, 62, 233–4n20
Goldin, Nan, 164, 217n11
Greyson, John, 229n3
grief, 99–101, 104, 107–9; and
   agency, 15–16; as disenfranchised, 218n14; divergent experiences of, 16–19, 114–15; and
   erotic attachment, 20, 98; and
   gardening, 179; and postcolo-
   nial/racial concerns, 167–74;
   and sexual orientation, 27; and
   social legibility, 42, 53, 234n20;
   and social locatedness, 10; as
   unresolved, 20, 80, 81–2, 84, 87,
   91, 94, 103, 115, 117, 211–12. *See
   also* gender roles, melancholia,
   mourning
Grosz, Elizabeth, 54
Guibert, Hervé, 37

Hacker, Jonathan, 224–5n21
Halperin, David, 209, 228n37
Hannerz, Ulf, 226n31
Haring, Keith, 46, 224n18
Haver, William, 86, 213–14n4; *The
   Body of This Death*, 136
Hawkins, Anne Hunsaker, 8,
   216n9, 217–18n12, 223n13
Hebdige, Dick, 157, 226n32,
   240n23
Hegel, G.W.F.: and *Antigone*, 102–
   3, 231–2n12; *The Phenomenology
   of Spirit*, 102
Hirsch, Marianne, 14, 156
HIV: assumptions surrounding,
   65–6, 140–1, 187–8, 226n27;
   and citizenship/immigration
   procedures, 148; connotations
   of diagnosis, 35–6, 40; and
   death, 184; and health care
   practices, 141–5; representations of, 45–6, 155–66, 240n25;
   as snake, 31–2; spectre of, 32
Hodge, Merle, 244n12
Hoffman, Amy, 10–13, 27–8, 37,
   44, 124, 141, 152, 153, 170, 185,
   191, 232–3n16; and family, 105–
   10, 113; and friendship, 79–84,
   98–9, 100–1, 105–10, 117–18,
   232n13; and gender roles, 101–
   3, 105–7, 230–1n9; and grief,
   91–2, 96, 100; and love, 88, 91,
   95, 98, 100–1, 107–9; and memoir, 80–3, 88–9; and memorialization, 82–3, 88, 91–4, 98–9,
   119–20; and memory, 85, 95–6,
   97–8, 115; and mourning and
   melancholia, 79–84, 85–6, 97–8,
   100–2, 105, 108, 111–14, 134,

CULTURAL SPACES

Cultural Spaces explores the rapidly changing temporal, spatial, and theoretical boundaries of contemporary cultural studies. Culture has long been understood as the force that defines and delimits societies in fixed spaces. The recent intensification of globalizing processes, however, has meant that it is no longer possible – if it ever was – to imagine the world as a collection of autonomous, monadic spaces, whether these are imagined as localities, nations, regions within nations, or cultures demarcated by region or nation. One of the major challenges of studying contemporary culture is to understand the new relationships of culture to space that are produced today. The aim of this series is to publish bold new analyses and theories of the spaces of culture, as well as investigations of the historical construction of those cultural spaces that have influenced the shape of the contemporary world.

Series Editors:
Richard Cavell, University of British Columbia
Imre Szeman, McMaster University

Editorial Advisory Board:
Lauren Berlant, University of Chicago
Homi K. Bhabha, Harvard University
Hazel V. Carby, Yale University
Richard Day, Queen's University
Christopher Gittings, University of Western Ontario
Lawrence Grossberg, University of North Carolina
Mark Kingswell, University of Toronto
Heather Murray, University of Toronto
Elspeth Probyn, University of Sydney
Rinaldo Walcott, OISE/University of Toronto

Books in the Series:
Peter Ives, *Gramsci's Politics of Language: Engaging the Bakhtin Circle and the Frankfurt School*
Sarah Brophy, *Witnessing AIDS: Writing, Testimony, and the Work of Mourning*